art-SITES
SPAIN

contemporary art
+ architecture

sidra stich

san francisco

art-SITES SPAIN
First Edition

PUBLISHED BY
art-SITES, 894 Waller Street, San Francisco, CA 94117
www.art-sites.com

EDITOR
Fronia Simpson
BOOK PRODUCTION
Pete Masterson, Æonix Publishing Group, www.aeonix.com
CARTOGRAPHER
Landis Bennett
PRINTED BY
Hignell Printing Company

Library of Congress Cataloguing-in-Publication Data
Stich, Sidra
    art-sites Spain : contemporary art + architecture handbook / Sidra Stich.
        p.   cm.
    Includes indexes.
    ISBN 0-9667717-4-5
    1. Art museums—Spain—Guidebooks. 2. Art, Spanish—20th century—
    Guidebooks.
    N3410.S78 2001
    708.6—dc21   2001273034
                                                               CIP

Printed in Canada

cover image: Frank O. Gehry, Guggenheim Museum Bilboa

table of contents

9 preface

10 Introduction and Practicalities

16 madrid

18 Atocha—Retiro Park
28 Puerta del Sol
32 Justicia
43 Salamanca
50 Northern Madrid and Periphery

55 excursions from madrid

55 Segovia
55 Valladolid
56 Salamanca
56 Cuenca

58 murcia

59 valencia

59 Calpe
62 Valencia
75 Castelló

78 barcelona

81 El Raval
92 Barri Gòtic and La Ribera
107 Eixample and Gràcia
119 Parc Güell, Parc la Creueta del Coll, Vall d'Hebron
127 Port Vell—La Barceloneta
134 Vila Olímpica
141 Plaça de les Glòries Catalanes
149 Sant Martí
155 Sants
162 Montjuïc
174 Outskirts of Barcelona

table of contents (continued)

177   excursions from barcelona

177   Lleida
177   Girona
178   Figueres
181   Port Lligat (Cadaqués)
181   Púbol

182   país vasco (basque country)

182   San Sebastián (Donastia)
186   Hernani
187   Bilbao
194   Gernika (Guernica)
196   Kortézubi

196   gijón

197   galicia

197   Santiago de Compostela
201   A Coruña
203   Pontevedra

209   extremadura

209   Mérida
211   Malpartida de Cáceres
212   Badajoz

214   sevilla

221   SUBJECT INDEX
228   INDEX
237   PHOTO CREDITS

Spain

PREFACE

art·SITES SPAIN follows the inaugural publication of **art·SITES FRANCE** (1999) and last year's **art·SITES BRITAIN & IRELAND**. Ultimately, the series will include all countries and regions where contemporary art and architecture are flourishing. We aim to identify and discuss sites where you can see works of innovative, intriguing, top-notch creativity from the current era. By providing background, analytic and practical information, we also orient you to a place or project, both in advance and during a visit.

The handbooks are organized geographically so you can easily take walking tours of neighborhoods or excursions beyond urban centers. Sites are keyed by number to detail maps and by icon to subject categories—museums, exhibition and alternative spaces, galleries, architecture, film and media centers, public art, sculpture parks, bookstores. Recent exhibitions and affiliated artists are also named as points of reference.

Each **art·SITES** book is a rich compendium of information on what's happening here and now in a particular location. If you're already familiar with the more famous museums and tourist monuments, these handbooks will help you discover hidden treasures and off-the-beaten-track places. They're invaluable resources whether you have only a few hours or several weeks at your disposal, whether you're an arts professional or neophyte art lover.

art·SITES—Adventure without hiking boots!

ABOUT THE AUTHOR

Sidra Stich is an art historian, museum curator and avid art traveler. She received an master's degree in visual studies from Harvard University and a doctorate in art history from the University of California, Berkeley. She has taught and lectured widely and organized acclaimed exhibitions accompanied by such seminal books as *Yves Klein*, *Rosemarie Trockel*, *Made in USA*, *Anxious Visions—Surrealist Art*. (The Klein and Trockel exhibitions were both shown at the Reina Sofía National Museum in Madrid.) For each **art·SITES** handbook, Stich does extensive research and travel. Relentlessly pursuing leads and delving beneath the surface, she visits cities and remote settings, renowned sites and little-known places. Conversations with people from all sectors and levels of the art world further enhance her investigations.

THANKS

art·SITES thanks the many people who have shared their experiences and provided information or photographs for this book. Special thanks to Fronia Simpson (editor), Landis Bennett (cartographer), Pete Masterson (designer), and most particularly to Phyllis Wattis, our guardian angel.

INTRODUCTION

Although Spain is well represented in early-20th-century art by the likes of Antoni Gaudí, Pablo Picasso, Juan Gris, Joan Miró and Salvador Dalí, the vitality of Spanish culture lay dormant after the Civil War (1936–39) and during the long dictatorial rule of General Franco (1939–75). Avant-garde activity was stymied by censorship, and the bans on freedom of expression virtually eliminated creative growth and international exchange. Contemporary art consisted mainly of staid, derivative variations of conservative, form-based abstraction.

Following the death of Franco, a political and social renaissance, accompanied by explosive energy in the arts sphere, ensued. Despite long lists of national needs, the new government strongly supported the cultural domain. It recognized that a lively art scene would be a boon to tourism and the general economy while simultaneously rekindling a spirit of unbridled creativity and reasserting Spain's presence in the global arts communities.

The development of ARCO (1976), an annual international art fair for contemporary art, and the inauguration of a national modern art center (1986, ultimately named the Reina Sofía National Museum) were seminal in turning the tide. Both these institutions spawned a whirlwind of activity and publicity. Beyond wild expectations, they succeeded in bringing throngs of visitors and exalted press attention to Spain—or at least to Madrid. Maintaining a centrist outlook, the national government focused exclusively on national museums (predominantly located in the capital city), contending that other support was the responsibility of regional and local governments. To their great resentment, artists, museums and cultural organizations in the provinces still do not share allocations from the national budget.

The good news is that various provinces have risen above the situation, creating their own dynamic art centers. Most notable are the Guggenheim Museum Bilbao, Barcelona Museum of Contemporary Art, Valencia Institute of Modern Art, Galego Center of Contemporary Art in Santiago de Compostela, Contemporary Art Space in Castelló, Museum of Art from Extremadura and IberoAmerica in Badajoz. In addition, there are outstanding private centers, such as the Joan Miró Foundation, Picasso Museum, Antoni Tàpies Foundation, CaixaForum, Metronòm in Barcelona and the Wolf Vostell Museum in Malpartida de Cáceres. Not only do their programs and collections tend to be more edgy and diverse, but many of the provincial centers are housed in intriguing buildings designed by such world-class architects as Frank O. Gehry, Richard Meier, Álvaro Siza, Josep Lluís Sert and Araka Isozaki.

The prevalence of governmental support for most Spanish museums and art centers has meant that they are tightly bound to politics, hence subject to party and individual power plays. This has caused havoc on the directorial and curatorial levels, not to mention stagnation and continuous turnabouts in planning, programming and funding. A hotbed of innovative, experimental exhibitions one year becomes a conservative depository of traditional art the next.

Exemplifying the conservatism of the country's contemporary art museums is the lack of, or merely token interest in, the laboratory model, wherein space and exhibitions are devoted to fresh, sometimes controversial ideas and experimental projects by emerging artists. A tradition-bent orientation is also evident in the realm of public art. Except for a spurt associated with the Barcelona Olympics and ubiquitous big sculptures by Eduardo Chillida, support for public art is paltry at best.

Despite or because of all these constraints, you'll find exciting pockets of activity and plenty of artwork that are well worth a trip to Spain—and not just to Madrid! Since a musical-chairs phenomenon prevails and new art sites keep sprouting up in unexpected places, prepare to meander beyond the major museums and galleries and try to explore a few different regions of the country.

A R T I S T S   An overview of Spanish art from the late 20th century reveals a dominant focus on abstraction, often expressionist or reductive in character, and content with a surrealist strain of irrational disorder or enigmatic imagery. These tendencies predominate in art created prior to Franco's death, and their influence can still be felt in the work of artists who achieved international attention in the 1980s and 1990s. Among the leading figures of this generation are Miquel Barceló, José Manuel Broto, Chema Cobo, Pepe Espaliú, Federico Guzmán, Cristina Iglesias, Juan Muñoz, Antonio Muntadas, Perejaume, Jaume Plensa, José María Sicilia, Susana Solano, Francesc Torres, Juan Uslé, Zush.

On one side of these artists, now in their midcareer years, are Antoni Tàpies and Eduardo Chillida, two revered art-stars from the midcentury, modernist tradition. On the other side are emerging artists who are addressing such issues as displacement, consumerism and sexuality using mixed media, photography, installation and video. Included in this group are Antoni Abad, Pep Agut, Ana Laura Alàez, José Ramón Amondarain, Txomin Badiola, José Manuel Ballester, Mira Bernabeu, Daniel Canogar, Victoria Civera, Luis Claramunt, Jordi Colomer, Carles Congost, Pep Durán, Joan Fontcuberta, Carmela García, Dora García, Alberto García-Alix, Susy Gómez, Pep Guerrero, Iñigo Manglano-Ovalle, Pedro Mora, Marina Nuñez, Mabel Palacín, Javier Pérez, MP and MP Rosado Garcés, Francisco Ruiz de Infante, Fernando Sánchez Castillo, Eulàlia Valldosera, Valentin Vallhonrat, Carlos Vidal.

A R C H I T E C T U R E   High-rise apartment blocks, unadorned except for box-balconies (typically strewn with potted plants and laundry) in front of nearly every window, proliferated in most Spanish cities in the mid-20th-century years. Though they filled housing needs, these structures left an indelible mark on the visual and social character of the urban environment. A similarly unappealing, functional aesthetic prevails in office and civic buildings constructed during this period. Not only was there little innovation in architectural design, but new construction was limited to bare-bone essentials, modernization was forestalled and many historical treasures were left to deteriorate without proper conservation or care.

The situation changed radically in the post-Franco era as a new sensitivity to the past became widespread and a rash of public construction projects was undertaken. Impatience for improved conditions and the lack of trained professionals initially produced some disastrous results, but then proper planning was put in place in various cities for the cleaning of facades, rehabilitation of old buildings, urban reform, the development of green spaces and improved transportation systems. Barcelona, in particular, became an internationally acclaimed model, having devised and implemented incredible feats of transformation and growth in tandem with its preparation for the 1992 Olympic Games.

Traveling through Spain today, you'll find that most all the big cities as well as midsize towns are undergoing modernization and have been spruced up to some degree without losing their historic charm. Moreover, the country can pridefully assert its patronage of outstanding contemporary architects of various nationalities—Norman Foster (Britain), Jean Nouvel, Philippe Starck (France), Hans Hollein, Josef Paul Kleihues (Germany), Araka Isozaki (Japan), Álvaro Siza (Portugal), Peter Eisenman, Frank O. Gehry, Philip Johnson & John Burgee, Richard Meier (United States) and its own favorite sons and one daughter, Ricardo Bofill, Santiago Calatrava, Cruz & Ortiz, Enric Miralles, Rafael Moneo, Carme Pinós. Designs by these renowned figures are enhancing the appearance of disparate locales even as they raise Spain's profile as a supporter of avant-garde creativity. In and of itself, Gehry's Bilbao museum, considered by many critics to be the greatest building of the current era, catapulted the nation to a star-studded position in the realm of architecture.

FAIRS & FESTIVALS Festivals are a way of life in Spain, and new contemporary art celebrations and fairs seem to be cropping up everywhere. Though many of these have a national or provincial character, some are red-carpet, international events. The granddaddy of them all is **ARCO** (International Contemporary Art Fair), which had its 25th anniversary in 2001. Indeed, ARCO served as an important catalyst for Spain's revival as a cultural center in the post-Franco years. Early on, it gained the reputation as a lively occasion with lots of after-hour socializing, and this is still true today. The fair takes place in mid-February at Madrid's Parque Ferial Juan Carlos I (91-722-50-00 f: 91-722-57-90. www.arco.ifema.es, arco@ifema.es. Wed, 2–9; Thurs, 12–10; Fri–Mon, 12–9. admission: Wed–Sat, 3500/2000; Sun–Mon, 3000/1500 ptas.) Over 250 galleries (over half are from outside Spain) participate in ARCO, and the displays include a broad range of art in all media. In addition, the fair includes some curated exhibitions (e.g., LA–NY, From Belgium, Crossroads); panel discussions; cutting-edge galleries from a guest country (Britain in 2001; Italy in 2000); project rooms, each featuring a commissioned installation; and a series of lectures and discussions with artists, museum directors, curators, collectors and critics.

Madrid also hosts **PhotoEspaña** or **PHE**, the International Festival of Photography during a four-week period from mid-June to mid-July. Although only begun in 1998, it's already attained a popular following and top ranking within the city's calendar. Nearly all big municipal and private spaces are commandeered for group exhibitions, and virtually every art gallery and museum participates, often by presenting a hot, young starlet or blue-chip artist whose work has not yet been seen in Madrid. Along with the 80-some shows, there are nighttime projections in the open air, studio workshops, lectures, seminars, film programs and other activities. In 2001 the festival theme "From the South" sought to encourage a focus on Africa and South America. (91-360-13-20 f: 360-13-22. www.photoes.com, photoes@photoes.com, organized by La Fábrica, Madrid.)

In 2001 Valencia joins the growing list of cities (e.g., Venice, Lyon, New York, Sydney, São Paolo, Istanbul, Florence, Santa Fe, Liverpool) presenting international biennial exhibitions. **Bienal de Valencia**, which runs from June 13–October 20, focuses on the theme of *The Passions: Human Virtues and Vices.* It comprises several sections to be displayed throughout the city, each organized by different renowned curators. Included among the approximately 150 artists are Nobuyoshi Araki, Massimo Bartolini, John Bock, Cecily Brown, David Byrne, Dinos & Jake Chapman, Clegg & Guttman, Andreas Gursky, Anish Kapoor, Mike Kelley, Los Carpenteros, LOT/EK Architecture, Shirin Neshat, Cai-Guo Quiang, Yehudit Sasportas, Andres Serrano, DJ Spooky, Studio Azzuro, Tunga, Spencer Tunick, Jane & Louise Wilson.

Barcelona has also staked a claim on the art-world calendar with **New Art Barcelona,** a fair held annually in late November. Focusing on cutting-edge, young artists, this event takes place in a hotel with the galleries setting up displays or installations in individual guest rooms. (www.artbarcelona.es/newart.htm.)

FOUNDATIONS Banks (or financial institutions called Caja or Caixa) and corporations play a significant role in Spain's art world through their foundations. These organizations fund exhibitions and special projects, support various art programs, run their own exhibition spaces and purchase art for their own collections. In exchange for giving about 30% of their profits back to society via these foundations, the business entities associated with the foundations don't pay taxes. The arrangement has greatly enhanced the arts and art institutions by providing a private, nongovernmental source of sustenance and patronage.

The prime exemplar of a foundation empathetic to contemporary art and culture is Barcelona's Fundació "la Caixa." It has a notable presence because of its collection and the exhibitions it creates and circulates, some in its own cultural centers located throughout the country. Its strong support of programs (in art as well as in music, education and science) that encourage innovation is also invaluable in lending status to experimentation and avant-garde activities. (Like many foundations, "la Caixa" doesn't only fund things in the cultural sector. It invests heavily in social programs for senior citizens, medical research and assistance to people with Alzheimer's and AIDS.)

CURRENT EXHIBITIONS AND EVENTS Listings in newspapers or in local magazines are the best source of information about what's going on in a particular city or region. The Internet is helpful, though beware that information on most sites is often incomplete and often out of date. The major websites for museum and gallery exhibitions in Spain are: www.arteyparte.com, www.arte10.com, www.bluejoven.com, www.artnewsdigital.com.

MAGAZINES *Lapiz* (1150 ptas) is the most widely circulated magazine dealing with contemporary art in Spain. It tends to be conservative and offers limited coverage of exhibitions, artists and ideas. Far more interesting and informative are the online magazines *artszine* (www.artszin.net) and *Acción Paralela* (www.accpar.org), hosted by the Internet provider www.w3arte.es. The former includes short and long articles, news, commentaries and reviews relating to the contemporary art scene in Spain. The latter began in 1994 and is published once a year, but not every year. It's a magazine of essays, theory and criticism (like *October*), where each issue has a particular theme and focal artist: 1—Deconstruction, Pepe Espaliú; 2—Music and Visual Arts, Jordi Colomer; 3—Documenta X, Queer Art, Basque Art; 4—Art and Politics, Pep Agut; 5—Technical Images, Moving Images, José Maldonado. If you don't read Spanish, these will be of no value since none of the texts are translated.

Exit is a new magazine of images and culture "devoted to the most characteristic visual arts of the XXIst century: photography, video, film." Published four times a year (3000 ptas) with pithy, engaging articles in both Spanish and English, it is a promising venture.

For architecture aficionados, *Arquitectura Viva* (2200 ptas) is a superb magazine with excellent articles and illustrations on worldwide contemporary projects and architects.

Practicalities

We have tried assiduously to present up-to-date and accurate information. Despite our best efforts, you're likely to find different admission prices, hours, new addresses or even that sites no longer exist. We apologize for the inconvenience and hope you will inform us of changes so we can make corrections and update the next edition.

TRANSPORTATION Spain's intracity transportation networks leave a lot to be desired. Only one route (Madrid-Cordoba-Seville-Malaga) offers the new speed train (*Ave*), and other routes are slow with poor connections between cities. If you're using public transportation, it's often faster to take a bus than a regional train. If your time is short, fly.

In contrast, the metros in Madrid and Barcelona are efficient, convenient and economical. Throughout this book, you'll find the nearest metro station included with individual entries both as a suggested means of transportation to a site and as a point of geographic reference. Buses, some trains and a few funiculars are equally good means of transportation but less useful as a reference.

H O L I D A Y   C L O S I N G S   No matter when you travel to Spain, you're likely to encounter a festival or celebration of some type. In addition to national days of observance, there are numerous regional and local holidays. Since there is no consistency within a city or among various cities about holiday closings and hours, it's best to call ahead. Many museums are open for regular, reduced or extended hours on all but a very few holidays, while others close for every local festivity. Some museums offer free admission on holidays.

The standard holidays in most of Spain are: New Year's Day (Jan 1), Epiphany (Jan 6), St. Joseph's Day (Mar 19), Holy Thursday (not celebrated in Catalunya and Valencia), Good Friday, Labor Day (May 1), Corpus Christi (the Thurs after the eighth Sun after Easter), Feast of St. John the Baptist (June 24), Feast of St. James the Apostle (July 25), Feast of the Assumption (Aug 15), National Day (Oct 12), All Saints' Day (Nov 1), Constitution Day (Dec 6), Immaculate Conception (Dec 8), Christmas (Dec 25).

The majority of galleries, some art centers and a few museums close during August or July–August. Since closing dates vary, some running into September, call ahead if you're planning a visit.

T E L E P H O N E   N U M B E R S   In 1998 Spain adopted a nine-digit telephone system. The provincial or city code has two digits followed by seven others, arranged variously and inconsistently in several groupings or as one long number. You need to dial all nine digits regardless of whether you are within or outside the area of a given code. The code for Madrid is 91; Barcelona, 93; Bilboa, 94; Seville, 95; Valencia, 96.

S I T E   I C O N S   The following icons are used to distinguish the sites in this handbook:

🏛 museum		🏛 architecture	
▭ art center or exhibition space		🎨 public art	
🎥 film or media center		🗿 sculpture park	
🗔 art gallery		📖 arts bookstore	

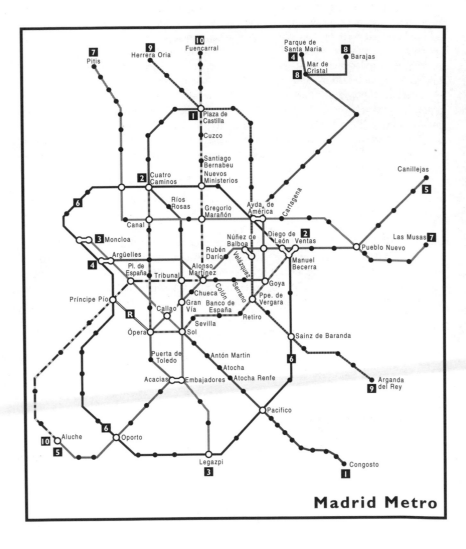

Madrid Metro

MADRID

Spain's capital is a sprawling city crisscrossed by wide avenues that intersect in huge plazas. You feel the urban character far more than in most metropolises, because there is no river or nature-oriented focus, no grand vistas, no eye-catching architecture, no great public monuments and no historic neighborhoods with a particular flavor. However, Madrid does offer lively nightlife and the incredible Prado Museum. On the contemporary art front, the Reina Sofía Museum, exhibition spaces and galleries made a big splash in the late 1980s and early 1990s but have been on a rocky course since then. Most significantly, Madrid, in contrast to Barcelona, lacks a dynamic art community, and this affects all aspects of the art scene, especially its stature as an international center.

CURRENT EXHIBITIONS AND EVENTS
Guía del Ocio is a weekly magazine, sold at most newsstands (150 ptas), and publishes the most complete listing of goings-on in Madrid's cultural and entertainment spheres. Many galleries also publish notices of their exhibitions in the bimonthly *Guía de Exposiciones,* and/or the tri-monthly *ArteMadrid.* Both are fold-up brochures, available for free at gallery reception desks and in some museums. You can also find exhibition listings for Madrid online at www.centrodearte.com and www.artemadrid.net

MUSEUM TICKET If you plan to go to the Reina Sofía, Prado and Thyssen-Bornemisza Museums, you can save money by purchasing a Paseo del Arte for 1275 ptas.

HOLIDAYS Most museums are closed on Mondays or Tuesdays and many galleries are closed on Monday morning or for the whole day on Monday. During the summer months, most galleries are closed on Saturday, or at least on Saturday afternoon, and the majority close completely during August.

Madrid celebrates San Isidro Day in honor of its patron saint on May 15. Nearly everything is closed and festivities and parades occur throughout the city.

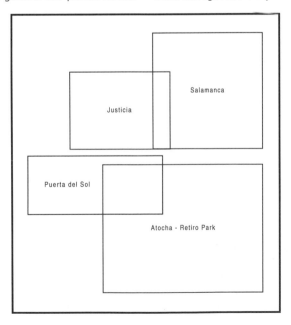

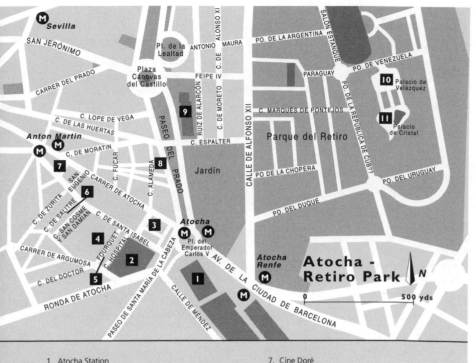

1. Atocha Station
2. Reina Sofía Museum
3. Galería Salvador Díaz
4. Galería Helga de Alvear
5. Galería Espacio Mínimo
6. My Name's Lolita Art
7. Cine Doré
8. PhotoGalería, La Fábrica
9. Prado Museum
10. Palacio de Velázquez
11. Palacio de Cristal

Atocha—Retiro Park

1 Estación de Atocha

architect: Rafael MONEO, 1984–92
Plaça del Emperador Carlos V
metro: Atocha, Atocha Renfe

Atocha is the major station in Madrid for high-speed trains and service on the national and commuter network, so you're likely to pass through here on a visit to Spain. You're also likely to see it on your way to the Reina Sofía Museum, located across the road. What you actually see is the old Atocha Station, a grand 19th-century, iron-and-glass train shed. The new station lies behind. Indeed, it is disorienting to find that the main entrance, barely notable as such, is around the corner.

Moreover, the whole complex is not easily accessible due to high-speed, multilane roadways that virtually detach it from the surrounding areas. Should you cross the new stretch of landscaped roadway in front of the old station, you can take a ramp on the side down into the middle of the concourse. It's confusing, poorly marked and passes alongside a dreary paved plaza whose purpose or use is inexplicable despite its central location.

This said, the new and renovated Atocha Train Station, designed by the Pritzker Prize laureate (the Nobel Prize of architecture) Rafael Moneo, warrants attention. Don't

Rafael Moneo, Atocha Station (courtyard)

expect an expressionist, radical structure, for Moneo is a fundamentalist who adheres to the principles of formal reduction and spatial clarity set forth by such modernists as Mies van der Rohe.

Rather than attempting to expand and update facilities within the old shed, Moneo removed the tracks and transformed the space into a tropical garden (steam jets provide humidity control) lined with offices and fronted by a plazalike setting with café tables. It's a glorious place to wait for a train, though more seating is needed. From here escalators and stairs lead up to the main concourse which in turn leads back to the train tracks and across to the bus station, metro, parking lot and new main entrance. Each element occupies a considerable expanse with interconnections and the various levels adding to the complexity.

Among the features of the architecture is a drum-shaped glass structure surrounded by squared brick columns positioned on an angle and close together like the slats of a window

blind. As elsewhere in the station (and typical of Moneo), the design enables the controlled flow of natural light into the interior. The structure itself serves as an entrance and circulation well for moving passengers from the street level down to the concourse. This is not the main entrance, yet it effectively functions as such despite the lack of a prominent, large doorway and signage.

Rafael Moneo, Atocha Station (roof)

The roof over the long-distance trains reveals the inventive, functionally efficient and simple character of Moneo's creativity. It's a horizontal canopy of ribbed-steel sections delineated by a grid of narrow skylights and supported by tall, slender concrete columns. A glass curtain-wall encloses the area on the east side, beyond which are rental car lots covered by a field of low-lying, aluminum domelike roofs.

2 Museo Nacional Centro de Arte Reina Sofía

Santa Isabel 52, 28012
91-467-50-62 f: 467-31-63
www.museoreinasofia.mcu.es
Mon, Wed–Sat, 10–9; Sun, 10–2:30; closed Tues
admission: 500/250 ptas; free Sat, after 2:30 and Sun
metro: Atocha

Having been shut off from the international art world during Franco's reign, Spain had to jump-start activities to become a participant. One of the first steps was the creation of a exhibition center in the former San Carlos Hospital, a 17th-century, neoclassical building in the Atocha neighborhood. Named for the new queen, Centro de Arte Reina Sofía was inaugurated in 1986. It then closed in February 1989 for renovation and reopened in September 1992. Not only did it have a new appearance, but it also had a new title—Museo Nacional Centro de Arte Reina Sofía (MNCARS). It had become a museum by acquiring the collection (and library) of the Museo Español de Arte Contemporáneo (now defunct). With this modest selection of modern Spanish art as a base, the museum began to purchase objects to expand its holdings. When in July 1992 Picasso's *Guernica* was moved from El Casón del Buen Retiro (a palace adjacent to the Prado) to the Reina Sofía, the new institution was instantly elevated to the upper echelon of world-class museums.

Despite renovations that have created some spacious, light-filled galleries, the building has retained a very bleak, institutional appearance. Long, empty, stone hallways on the inside, barred windows and a barren concrete plaza as the entrance zone on the outside instill an uninviting, cold atmosphere. Not even the two glass elevator shafts on the main facade (designed by the British architect Ian RITCHIE) with their zappy modernist character are enough to transform the harsh image. Perhaps the expansion currently being designed by the cutting-edge French architect Jean NOUVEL will produce a change.

The interior of the museum is organized on four floors as a circuit of interconnecting galleries with an open-air courtyard in the center. It's best to get a brochure with a floor plan (available at the reception desk) so you can keep track of the easily missed corner rooms and galleries running two deep along the front and back sides of the building. If you don't have several hours to spare, you should target the art you most want to see and check the relevant gallery number. There's a lot to see and just walking through a string of galleries takes a long time. Because there are no benches within the galleries (a truly antiart and inhuman gesture), take advantage of the seating in the corridors if you need a break.

Special exhibitions are located on the ground and third floors, and usually there are two or more major shows going on simultaneously. The museum favors retrospectives and thematic projects with a historical bent. These are almost always encyclopedic in scope, encompassing an enormous number of objects. Though embracing contemporary art, the orientation is rather conservative. It was not always this way. During the first years of its existence, Museo Reina Sofía was the talk of the international art world. Its schedule was filled with challenging exhibitions featuring young, adventurous artists and daring projects. As political circumstances shifted, however, staff and ideological directions changed.

Recent exhibitions: *Louise Bourgeois,*

Reina Sofía Museum (Ian Ritchie, facade renovation)

Rafael Canogar, A Century of Photography in Spain, Jean Cocteau in Spain, Ángel Ferrant, Sam Francis, Robert Frank, Gelman Collection (Mexican Modern Masters), German Art (Grothe Collection), Juan Gris, Informelist Revolution (1939–68), Chema Madoz, Roberto Matta, Minimalism, Lucio Muñoz, Painter's Theater, Photography in Print (1919–39), Picasso's Minotaur, Alfonso Ponce de Léon, Rural Moroccan Tapestries, Alberto Sánchez, Signs of the Century, Surrealists in Exile, Antoni Tàpies, Francisco Toledo, Zush.

One place where emerging artists have a voice is in the museum's project room—Espacio Uno. (It's located on the ground floor at the end of the long corridor to the right of the main entrance.) A lively spirit and no-holds-barred mentality are often expressed here in all sorts of mediums, imagery and ideas. Recent exhibitions: *Ana Laura Aláez, Patty Chang, Carles Congost, Carmela García, Ángel Goauche, Maya Goded, Álvaro Machimbarrena, Enrique Marty, Sam Taylor-Wood, Janaina Tschäpel.*

The permanent collection, which largely focuses on Spanish art, is displayed on the second and fourth floors. Included are artists of mainly national reputation who offer a different—sometimes derivative and provincial, at other times intriguing—take on modernity. You can also see major Spanish artists in a degree of depth that is not available elsewhere. Sadly, little or no contextual material or wall texts accompany the art. A strict, chronological arrangement prevails and within this, work by an individual artist of preeminent distinction is shown as a self-contained unit. The museum's practice of hanging paintings far apart and isolating each pedestaled sculpture further conveys an unfortunate impression of the pure, autonomous art object.

The 17 galleries on floor 2 cover the evolution of Spanish art, intermittently complemented by works of non-Spanish artists, from the end of the 19th century to the years following World War II. Room 4 has a strong selection of paintings by Juan Gris, and though the representation of Picasso's early years hardly does justice to his creativity, the section devoted to *Guernica* and related works is a treasure onto itself (room 6). Be sure to see the two sculptures by David Smith in the tiny room 8 (tucked away behind the main galleries) and expect to find crowds in room 10, where the museum's superb collection of paintings *(The Great Masturbator, Invisible Man,* etc.) by Salvador Dalí is installed. A group of very strong, albeit not the best-known work by other surrealists—Yves Tanguy, Max Ernst, Oscar Dominquez, René Magritte and Joseph Cornell—are in room 11, and room 13 includes some terrific objects by such unfamiliar names as Adriano del Valle, Nicolás de Lekuona and Alfonso Ponce de León. If you're not aware of the clever, at times biting humor of Joan Miró, don't miss the fine group of his sculptures in room 16.

The collection display continues on floor 4, where 28 rooms present artists and movements from the late 1940s through the early 1980s. Though Spanish art still predominates, international artists have a significant presence, providing refreshing historical connections. Painting and sculpture, abstract and figurative art are, however, emphasized more than is their due, with only minimal attention paid to the conceptual, installation, multimedia and photographic work that dominated the vanguard ranks during these decades.

In room 22 the sculptures of Jorge Oteiza are venerable examples of Spanish Minimalism, and the monochrome triptych of blue, gold and rose by Yves Klein (room 25) is a significant rarity. Antoni Tàpies, an artist who hasn't received the international attention he deserves, is well represented in rooms 34 and 35, and contemporaneous work by members of the Italian Arte Povera group—Jannis Kounellis, Mario Merz, Pier Paolo Calzolari, Michelangelo Pistoletto—has a good showing in rooms 33 and 36. Among the objects by artists from the United States (rooms 40 and 41), those of Ellsworth Kelly and Bruce Nauman are particularly outstanding. And one of Spain's favorite sons, Eduardo Chillida, can be seen at his best in *Toki-Egin (Homage to San Juan de la Cruz),* a suspended steel sculpture with open and closed forms (room 43).

(There may be variations in the locations and objects named above since the museum modifies the installation to accommodate loans and new acquisitions.)

Sadly, Spain's national museum of modern art has barely any work from the last 20 years on exhibit in its collection galleries. There is therefore little indication of the pervasive explorations with new mediums and the dramatic shifts in imagery and approach—including the deconstruction of subject matter dealing with identity, sexuality, aggression, commonplace settings, commercialism and communication. A good editing job to eliminate the excess and secondary objects now on display would open gallery space for contemporary art.

The museum has a café, restaurant, large book- and gift shop on the ground floor. The selection of monographs and texts on Spanish modern art is among the best you'll

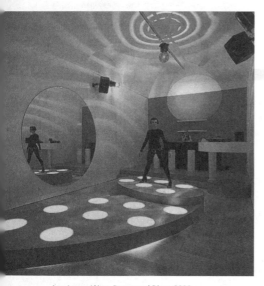

Ana Laura Aláez, *Dance and Disco,* 2000

find in Madrid. Posters and cards of collection objects are also a specialty.

Contemporary music concerts and lectures are part of the museum's ongoing program of events. Information about these can be found in a brochure available at the reception desk.

3 Galería Salvador Díaz

Sánchez Bustillo 7, 28012
91-527-40-00 f: 539-06-10
salvadordiaz@interlink.es
Mon, 5–9; Tues–Fri, 11–2 and 5–9; Sat, 11–2
metro: Atocha

Located across the plaza from the Reina Sofía Museum.

Galería Salvador Díaz presents a range of young artists whose work reflects the latest modes receiving critical attention. More than derivative, the art is often imaginative, offering an individualized take on fashionable themes, issues and creative processes. The vast space of the main room is amenable to large objects and installations, while the balcony area and two side rooms are more intimate.

You might ask to see work by Javier Pérez, an artist whose star is rising though he hasn't yet had much international exposure. Collaging organic materials (horsehair, leather, cow's intestines) with elements made from porcelain or silicone, Pérez explores the interface between the body and the surrounding world of everyday life. Many of his objects take the form of masks or wearable items.

Artists: Josume Amunárriz, José Manuel Ballester, José Manuel Ciria, David Díaz, Gabriel Díaz, Juan Galdeano, Juan Mercado, Antonio Ortega, Javier Pérez, Darío Villalba, María Zárraga.

4 Galería Helga de Alvear

Doctor Fourquet 12, 28012
91-468-05-06 f: 467-51-34
www.artnet.com/dealvear.html
dealvear@w3art.es
Tues–Sat, 11–2 and 5–9; closed Mon
metro: Atocha

Karin Sander exhibition, 2000

The vast, high-ceilinged rooms of Galería Helga de Alvear are a bit overwhelming, so take your time and be sure to walk all the way into and around the exhibition rooms. This is one of the most adventurous galleries in Madrid, and you're likely to see uncompromising work by rising and established artists on display here. Often two artists are featured simultaneously in the main galleries, and the upstairs "studio" presents a site-specific work, special project or objects from the past. The focus is on photography, video, conceptual and minimalist art of the genre that is both mentally and visually arresting. Information sheets are available in Spanish and English to assist with background and context.

If you want to see what's being done by some of the most innovative young Spanish artists, ask to see objects or documentation of work by Pep Agut, Daniel Canogar, José Maldonado and Eulàlia Valldosera. Other artists represented by the gallery include Christine Davis, Roland Fischer, Joan Fontcuberta, John Hilliard, Peter Hutchinson, Axel Hütte, Kazuo Katase, Jürgen Klauke, Jac Leirner, Mitsuo Miura, Tracey Moffatt, Mabel Palacín, Jesús Palomino, Thomas Ruff, Karin Sander, Alexander Timtschenko, Frank Thiel. Exhibitions have also headlined Dan Flavin, Imi Knoebel, Gordon Matta-Clark, Gerhard Merz, Jeff Wall.

5   Galería Espacio Mínimo

Doctor Fourquet 17, 28012
91-467-61-56 f: 467-83-31
www.espaciominimo.com
espaciominimo@logiccontrol.es
Tues–Sat, 11–2 and 5–9; closed Mon

Through its gallery in Murcia, Espacio Mínimo supported young artists and avant-garde activity. When it moved to Madrid in November 2000, the gallery introduced a new group of artists to the capital city. In addition to a strong program of monographic exhibitions, you can count on seeing provocative, thematic shows, like Art & Fashion.

Artists: José Manuel Ballester, Nono Bandera, Rosalía Banet, Bene Bergado, Miguel Ángel Gaüeca, Francesco Impellizzeri, Enrique Marty, Erwin Olaf, Liliana Porter.

6   Galería My Name's Lolita Art

Salitre 7, 28012
tel/fax: 91-530-72-37
lolitart@teleline.es
Tues–Sat, 12–1:30 and 5:30–9; closed Mon
metro: Antón Martí, Atocha

For those who like brash, surreal, funky, kitsch and slick imagery, you'll find variations in this gallery that you've probably not seen before. My Name's Lolita Art represents a wide range of young Spanish artists who work with new modes of figuration. A second space in Valencia promotes the same program with the same energetic spirit.

Artists: Juan Cuéllar, Equipo Límite, Mavi Escamilla, Damián Flores, Ángel Mateo Charris, Joël Mestre, Teresa Moro, Gonzalo

Erwin Olaf, *Royal Blood, Ludwig*, 2000

Sicre, Jorge Tarazona, Santi Tena, Teresa Tomás, Paco de la Torre.

7 Cine Doré

🎦 Santa Isabel 3, 28012
91-369-11-25
metro: Antón Martín
closed Mon

Located up the hill from Reina Sofía just before Plaça Antón Martín.

As the official Filmoteca Nacional, this theater shows historical and art films as well as special series dedicated to movies by a particular director, star, genre or country. Housed in a classic old building, it has lots of charm along with the oddity of being clustered adjacent to the neighborhood market and a sex shop. An expensive café-restaurant and bookshop share the premises.

8 PhotoGalería, La Fábrica

📧 Alameda 9, 28014
91-360-13-20 f: 360-13-22
www.lafabrica.com
lafabrica@lafabrica.com
Tues–Sat, 11–2 and 5–8:30; closed Mon
admission: free
metro: Atocha

La Fábrica is a contemporary cultural center where people, artistic endeavors and ideas come together. It's only a few years old, and unlike most art-culture spaces in Spain, it's a private project. Hence it lies outside the governmental bureaucracy and its tendency to stifle ideas, cut off dialogue or debate and discourage action. Although the visual arts—and most particularly photography—play a significant role in La Fábrica's program, the center embraces literature, theater, architecture, film, music, science and any other domain having a contemporary bias and relating to the world of culture.

PhotoGalería, an exhibition space for Spanish photography, occupies the main physical area of La Fábrica. In addition, a display window facing the street serves as a project zone (La Ventana) devoted to installations. Recent exhibitions: *Luis Baylón, Clemente Bernard, José María Díaz-Maroto, Cristina García Rodero, Pablo Genovés, Cristóbal Hara, Ramón Masats, Isabel Muñoz, Carlos Serrano, Antonio Tabernero.* Recent Windows: *Eugenio Ampudia, García de Cubas, Lupe Estévez, Ciuco Gutiérrez, Fernando Gutiérrez, Matz Mainka, Gervasio Tallo, Silvia Vendramel.*

Every Monday night at 8:30, the center hosts an activity with a creative artist. Inevitably lively, these range from readings by writers or poets, performances by musicians, plays, films, talks by artists or architects and conversations about new ideas or technical issues.

Among its other projects, La Fábrica publishes *Matador,* an annual magazine, and organizes the highly successful International Festival of Photography, PhotoEspaña (see p. 13).

9 Museo del Prado

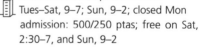

🏛 Paseo del Prado, 28014
91-330-28-00 f: 330-28-56
📖 www.museoprado.mcu.es
museo.nacional@prado.mcu.es
🏛 Tues–Sat, 9–7; Sun, 9–2; closed Mon
admission: 500/250 ptas; free on Sat, 2:30–7, and Sun, 9–2
metro: Banco de España

Even the most committed contemporary art lover doesn't visit Madrid without spending time at the Prado. Topping the encyclopedic collection of art from the 12th–19th centuries are multitudes of major paintings by Velázquez (rooms 12–16), Goya (rooms 32, 34–39, 85–88, 90–94), El Greco (rooms 60A–62A), Rubens (rooms 7–11, 61A) and Hieronymus Bosch (rooms 55A–56A). The newly renovated galleries have more natural light, and now the spellbinding *Las Meninas* (1656) hangs in the midst of other Velázquez masterpieces at the apex of the museum's grand semicircular gallery (room 12).

Although the Prado has been progressively

updating and refurbishing its premises, they have proven inadequate for public and curatorial needs. Thus in 1999 the museum commissioned Rafael MONEO—Spain's esteemed recipient of the Pritzker Prize—to design a new wing. His proposal calls for a simple wedge-shaped steel-and-glass structure to be located behind the main building with connections to it and the 17th-century cloisters of the nearby Jerónimos church. In accordance with his style, the new space will be simple and classy, aimed at showcasing the art. It will include two temporary exhibition galleries, a large reception area, cafeteria, restaurant, bookstore, gift shops, auditorium, library, drawings and prints study rooms, conservation workshops and garden terrace.

10 Palacio de Velázquez

Parque del Retiro
91-573-62-45
winter: Mon, Wed–Sat, 10–6; Sun, 10–4; closed Tues
summer: Mon, Wed–Sat, 11–8; Sun, 11–6; closed Tues
admission: free
metro: Ibiza, Retiro

You may well find yourself walking in circles on your way through Retiro Park to Palacio de Velázquez and Palacio de Cristal since signage within the park is spotty and the routes are circuitous. The sand paths always seem to be muddy and ridden with large puddles even in nice weather, so be prepared.

Palacio de Velázquez (sometimes referred to as Palacio de Exposiciones) is a huge neoclassical, red-brick-and-tile building, originally constructed for a mining exhibition in 1883. It now houses temporary art exhibitions organized by the Reina Sofía. These are typically one-person shows of internationally renowned, midcareer artists. Indeed, the spacious halls with glass-vaulted roofs are well suited to the large objects and installation projects that typify much contemporary art. Since the featured artists tend not to be the same superstars of other retrospectives, the exhibitions are enlightening to even the most conversant art world junky. Contrarily, should you be a novice, they are an excellent way to familiarize yourself with a mode of current creativity.

Recent exhibitions: *The Aesthetic of the Dream, Miguel Ángel Campano, Jiri Georg Dokoupil, Andreas Gursky, Jaume Plensa, Julião Sarmento, Versions of the South (Africa, South America), Franz West.*

Jaume Plensa exhibition, 1999

Kcho exhibition, 2000

11 Palacio de Cristal

Parque del Retiro
91-574-66-14
winter: Mon, Wed–Sat, 10–6; Sun,
10–4, closed Tues
summer: Mon, Wed–Sat, 11–8; Sun,
11–6; closed Tues
admission: free
metro: Ibiza, Retiro

Special exhibitions organized by Reina Sofía also take place in Palacio de Cristal, another royal building in the middle of Retiro Park. It was constructed (1887) as a winter garden for exotic plants and was recently reconditioned. Despite architectural appeal, the tall glass pavilion with a complex, wrought-iron frame painted a greenish taupe color is a challenging, inflexible backdrop for works of art. Trees around the transparent exterior, the pervasiveness of natural light and chirping birds who live within are an unavoidable constant that often is at odds with the art. Large, volumetric or planar sculptures without a dominant content orientation fare best.

If you can block out the romantic, garden atmosphere and the scale discrepancies, you'll see some of the most captivating, uncompromising work from the contemporary era displayed here.

Recent exhibitions: *Vito Acconci, Alexander Calder, The Aesthetic of the Dream, David Hammons, Ilya Kabakov, Kcho, Cildo Meireles, Versions of the South (Africa, South America), Lawrence Weiner.*

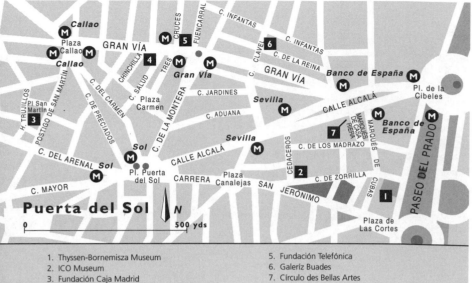

1. Thyssen-Bornemisza Museum
2. ICO Museum
3. Fundación Caja Madrid
4. Casa del Libro
5. Fundación Telefónica
6. Galeríz Buades
7. Círculo des Bellas Artes

Puerta Del Sol

1 Fundación Colección Thyssen-Bornemisza

renovation: Rafael MONEO, 1989–92
Paseo del Prado 8, 28014
91-420-39-44 f: 420-27-80
www.museothyssen.org
mtb@museothyssen.org
Tues–Sun, 10–7; closed Mon
admission: 700/400 ptas; special exhibitions, 500/300 ptas; combination, 900/500 ptas
metro: Banco de España

The Villahermosa Palace, a prime example of Madrid's neoclassical style of architecture (1804), was masterfully renovated by Rafael Moneo to accommodate the Thyssen-Bornemisza Collection. Two generations of this family, whose main residence is in Lugano, Switzerland, had built this amazing collection of 775 paintings tracing the history of European painting from the 13th to the 20th century and American painting from the 19th–20th century. It was Baron Hans Heinrich Thyssen-Bornemisza who signed an agreement in 1988 to lend the collection to Spain. The persuasive voice of his wife, Carmen Cervera, a former Miss Spain, strongly influenced his decision. The country's resolve to house the collection in a grand building near the Prado also proved seminal. Just months after the refurbished palace opened to the public in October 1992, the baron signed a second agreement providing for Spain's permanent acquisition of the Thyssen-Bornemisza Collection.

For the architectural revision, Moneo sought to retain the building's former character but create a modern museum. To achieve this he kept the old facade, lined the walls with Italian stucco, covered the floors with Roman travertine, fabricated doors and elevators from richly grained pine, created striking perspectives even as he added skylight boxes, contrived hidden structures for indirect lighting, expanded the size of the rooms, devised simple circulation paths and installed temperature and security devices. Although Moneo favors a minimalist aesthetic, he pays incredible attention to detail, materials and light.

The collection is arranged chronologically beginning on the second floor with works from the medieval and renaissance periods. The progression continues on the first floor with 17th-century Dutch painting and moves ahead to Impressionism, Post-Impressionism, Fauvism and German Expressionism. A superb selection of American paintings (a rarity in European museums) includes major works by John Singer Sargent, Winslow Homer, William Harnett, John Peto, Frederic Edwin Church, John Sloan and others.

The ground floor is devoted to the 20th century. (In actuality, the collection stops with the styles and ideas developed in the 1960s.) Although many of the expected figures are represented, the survey doesn't follow the usual flow of modernism. Works by lesser-known artists suggest diverse directions, and figurative imagery forms a pervasive thread. Among the highlights are some fine cubist paintings and first-rate works by the surrealists Magritte, Tanguy, Dalí, Delvaux and Giacometti. The strong showing of American modernism includes paintings by Edward Hopper, Raphael Soyer, Georgia O'Keeffe, Ben Shahn, Stuart Davis, Arshile Gorky, Hans Hofmann, Mark Tobey, Joseph Cornell, Willem de Kooning, Jackson Pollock, Mark Rothko, Clyfford Still, Morris Louis, Richard Lindner, Roy Lichtenstein, Robert Rauschenberg, Frank Stella, Richard Estes. The postwar period also includes works by Frank Auerbach, Francis Bacon, Balthus, Lucio Fontana, Lucien Freud, David Hockney, R. B. Kitaj.

Special exhibitions, presented in galleries on the ground and lower levels, are often thematic shows. Though they may include art from the modern era, such work is not a focus. Recent exhibitions: *Meadows Museum Collection, Exploring Eden—American 19th-Century Landscapes, El Greco—Identity and Transformation, Victor Hugo Drawings, Giorgio Morandi, Max Pechstein, Timeless Eye (Krugier-Poniatowski Collection).*

The bookshop on the ground floor stocks only monographs of artists represented in the collection or books specifically dealing with the collection or the special exhibitions. If you want to see a dazzling instance of Moneo's ability to shape space—in this case by using diagonals—check out the café-restaurant on the lower level. And while you're in the area, be sure to look at the cycle of paintings in the lower lobby, *The Blinding Exile* (1966) by the Chilean surrealist Roberto Matta.

2 Museo Colecciones ICO

Zorrilla 3, 28014
91-420-12-42
www.ico.es/frfun
Tues–Sat, 11–8; Sun, 10–2; closed Mon
admission: free
metro: Sevilla, Banco de España

You're likely to pass right by without realizing there is a public exhibition space behind the walls of this uninviting building. The space itself is a makeshift series of unappealing, bland, badly lit galleries rambling across two levels. It's run by the Fundación de Instituto Crédito Oficial. Despite the humdrum ambience, the exhibitions are worth a visit. Don't expect to see anything cutting-edge, just established European art from the modern era.

Temporary exhibitions, on the lower level, have recently included *Alvar Aalto, Luis Buñuel, IVAM Photography Collection, André Kertész, Portuguese Art (1960s–70s).* The upper level, which houses the permanent collection of ICO, features a survey of the leading Spanish sculptors from the 20th century. Each is represented by one object and sometimes a drawing as well. The display is quite modest, comprising only small-scale work. But it's a good overview and an excellent snapshot introduction to many artists unknown outside Spain. You'll see sculptures by Eduardo Arroyo, Miquel Barceló, Eduardo Chillida, Pablo Gargallo, Antoni Gaudí, Julio González, Juan Gris, Eva Lootz, Joan Miró, Juan Muñoz, Jorge Oteiza, Pablo Picasso, Jaume Plensa, Susana Solano, Antoni Tàpies.

Contemporary Spanish painting forms a complementary (albeit less significant) section of the ICO collection. The focus is on work from the 1980s and is largely of an abstract expressionist character. Artists represented include Federic Amat, José Manuel Broto, Ferrán García Sevilla, José María Sicilia, Darío Villalba.

A separate staircase at the entrance leads to a room devoted to the display of Picasso's *Vollard Suite,* a series of 100 engravings from 1930–37. If you're not familiar with this revered group of images, this is a rare opportunity to see them all together.

3 Fundación Caja Madrid

⌁ Plaça de San Martín 1, 28013
91-379-24-61 f: 379-20-20
Tues–Sat, 11–8, Sun, 11–2; closed Mon
metro: Sol, Opéra

Located off Calle del Arenal in a newly landscaped pocket of the center city.

The marble staircase and frescoed ceiling of the entrance area are only hors d'oeuvres for the main, three-story-high, balconied exhibition space—Sala de las Ahajas (Jewel Room). Granted, it's not the best setting for art and may indeed be transformed by renovation work that will close this venue until 2002.

Exhibitions organized by Fundación Caja Madrid are a mixed bag. Many are juried competitions of little note, but occasionally there's one like *The Avant-Garde in Spanish Wood Sculpture (2000).* It presented a wonderful selection of imaginative work challenging the tradition of carving as the way to create sculpture in wood. Included were artists not often seen internationally, such as Ángel Ferrant, Alberto Sánchez, Adolfo Schlosser.

Other notable exhibitions presented here during the past decade were *Max Ernst, Sam Francis, Sol LeWitt, Vincent van Gogh.*

4 Casa del Libro

Gran Vía 29, 28013
▦ 91-521-21-13
Mon–Sat, 10–9
metro: Grand Vía

This superstore has a large selection of art and architecture books on the second floor. Most are monographs by major Spanish publishers. It's a nice place for browsing and you can actually find a few books on contemporary art not found elsewhere in Madrid. Unfortunately, there are no museum catalogues and few texts in English.

5 Fundación Telefónica

⌁ Calle de Fuencarral 3, 28013
91-522-66-45 f: 531-71-06
www.telefonica.es/fat
fat@telefonica.es
Tues–Fri, 10–2 and 5–8; Sat–Sun, 10–2; closed Mon
admission: free
metro: Gran Vía

Located on the corner of Grand Vía.

Like various corporate giants in Spain, Telefónica has developed a multidimensional art program within its foundation. One aspect is a permanent collection with objects by leading 20th-century Spanish artists like Picasso, Gris, Miró, Tàpies, Chillida. Beginning in 1997 this was supplemented by a "new art collection" emphasizing trends leading to a renewal in Spanish figurative painting, especially those connected to the Schools of Paris and Madrid. A permanent display of this collection is installed in one of the foundation's exhibition halls. It's largely a mix of interesting, not great modernism and retrograde, academic painting.

A second hall contains the foundation's technological collection. Two other halls present temporary art exhibitions. One of these features painting, sculpture and prints and tends to be more historical and conservative. Recent shows here include *Luis Fernández, 25 Years Later—A Graphic Memory of the Transition, Hernando Viñes.*

The other gallery has an adventurous, contemporary art program. It shows a diverse range of trailblazing work, especially by artists who are using telecommunications and informational technologies in their creative processes or as the art medium itself. Some projects are commissioned and some are virtual exhibitions on the Fundación Telefóónica website. (The site—www.telefonica.es/fat/futura/007.htm— has an excellent selection of work by Spanish artists.) Most of the shows evince a sophisticated link between art and technology. They're not flamboyant displays of highfalutin gadgetry pretending to be art.

You may not recognize the artists by name but this space is usually worth visiting. Recent exhibitions: *Marcel-lí Antúnez, Gabriel Corchero, Marisa González, Ignacio Iturria, Yasumasa Morimura, Antonio Muntadas, 7 x 7 x 7, Francesc Torres.*

6 Galería Buades

Gran Vía 16, 3rd flr-C, 28013
91-522-25-62 f: 522-31-12
buadesgal@eresmas.com
Tues–Sat, 11–2 and 5–9; closed Mon
metro: Gran Vía, Sevilla

Galería Buades has been presenting exhibitions of contemporary art longer than any other gallery in Spain. Since opening in 1973, it has shown work by international art stars and neophyte talents working in a broad diversity of orientations. Over the years it has shown neofiguration, minimalist painting and sculpture, conceptual art, architectural projects and photography. Constantly seeking to present new tendencies, the gallery has played a significant role in supporting vanguard expression in Madrid. Notably, many of the most adventurous Spanish artists received early recognition through exhibitions at Buades. This is still the case today.

Artists: Ricardo Cadenas, Ana Carceller & Helena Cabello, Gennaro Castellano, Macu Díaz, Alonso Gil, Jaime Lorente, Herminio Molero, June Papineau.

7 Círculo des Bellas Artes

Marqués de Casa Riera 2, 28014
91-360-5400 f: 523-2812
www.circulobellasartes.com
areas@c-bellasartes.com
exhibitions: Tues–Fri, 5–9; Sat, 11–2 and 5–9; Sun, 11–2; closed Mon
admission: 100 ptas
metro: Banco de España, Sevilla

This is an amazing, old-style cultural center and meeting place for people associated with the arts and letters. It dates back to 1880 and occupies a grand building at the confluence of Calle de Alcalá and Grand Vía. All sorts of activities go on here—conferences, lectures, author readings, concerts, plays, performances, seminars, workshops, courses. There's a grand café off the lobby (on the right) where you can sit and read a book or just absorb the atmosphere and people-watch for hours without interruption. Ernest Hemingway used to stay in the hotel next door and hang out at Círculo des Bellas Artes. Since the furnishings look as if they've been around for at least a century, you might even sit on the same couch he did!

There are four exhibition spaces. The main one, located to the left of the atrium lobby, serves as a venue for retrospectives and exhibitions covering a wide range of cultural topics (*e.g., Architecture of Today in Portugal, Classics of Swedish Design, James Nachtweg, New York Digital Salon, Sebastião Salgado, Time for Radio, 1924–99*).

The building also contains studios, meeting rooms, game rooms, a library, theater, concert hall and auditorium. Cine Estudio (the center's cinema) has its own entrance a bit farther along the street. Functioning as a *filmoteca*, it presents thematic cycles, series featuring a particular director, star or country, shorts, documentaries and first-run films. Special projects like a 48-hour film marathon (which captured a Guinness record) form another part of the program.

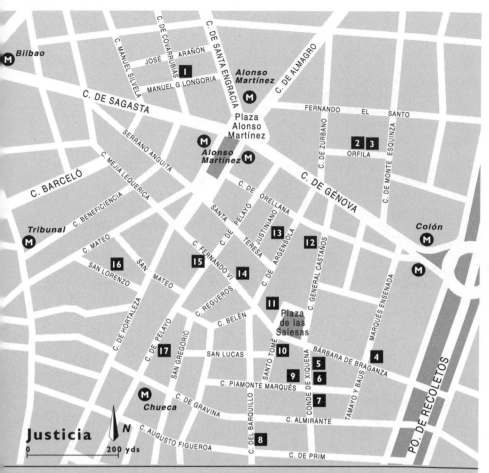

1. Galería Javier López
2. Galería Marlborough
3. Galería Soledad Lorenzo
4. Galería Metta
5. Galería Arnés & Röpke
6. Galería Fúcares
7. Galería Antonio Machón
8. Galería Juana de Aizpuru
9. Fundación COAM
10. Galería Max Estrella
11. Galería Marta Cervera
12. Galería Elvira González
13. Librería Gaudí
14. La Caja Negra
15. Sociedad General de Autores y Editores
16. Galería Elba Benítez
    Galería Heinrich Ehrhardt
18. Galería María Martín

Justicia

The area around Palacio de Justicia embracing the artsy-bohemian Chueca neighborhood and the upscale zone just north of Calle de Génova is where the preponderance of the city's best contemporary art galleries are located.

1 Galería Javier López

Manuel González Longoria 7 (2a, right),
28010
91-593-21-84 f: 591-26-48
www.galeriajavierlopez.com
gjl@galeriajavierlopez.com
Tues–Sat, 11–2 and 5–9
metro: Alonso Martínez

Located just northwest of Plaça Alonso Martínez on the corner of Calle de Covarrubias.

Galería Javier López opened in London in 1995 and moved to Madrid a year later. Its location on the second floor of an upscale apartment building with carved ceilings, stained-glass windows and a decidedly domestic appearance is deceptive since the artworks shown here are anything but staid, interior-design accouterments. That's not to say they're outrageous, irreverent statements, just objects of solid, innovative creativity. Indeed, the exhibition program, which features postconceptual and minimalist art by cream-of-the-crop, international artists not otherwise represented or seen in Spain, has added a significant dimension to the city's and country's art scene.

Be sure to put this gallery on your art tour! Artists: Greg Bogin, Liam Gillick, Andreas Gursky, Peter Halley, Donald Judd, Alex Katz, Jana Leo, Matthew McCaslin, Igor Mischiyev, Tatsuo Miyajima, Elena del Rivero & Tere Recarens, Thomas Ruff, Edward Ruscha, Jane Simpson, Lorna Simpson, Hiroshi Sugimoto, Katrin Thomas, Xavier Veilhan, Jeff Wall.

Peter Halley exhibition

Miguel Navarro exhibition, 2000

2 Galería Marlborough

architect: Richard GLUCKMAN
Orfila 5, 28010
91-319-14-14 f: 308-43-45
Mon–Sat, 11–2 and 5–9
metro: Colón, Alonso Martínez

For its Spanish headquarters, Marlborough hired Richard Gluckman—the architect who has designed many of the chic, minimalist galleries and boutiques in Soho, Chelsea (New York), Beverly Hills and Santa Monica. Here, too, he has created a handsome, utterly reductive, wide-open setting.

Orfila is a quiet little street and the gallery has a modest frontage. Inside, however, the space stretches way back with expansive white walls, high ceilings and a raised rear area with natural light streaming in from above. It's a perfect setting for the large paintings and sculptures that Marlborough often shows. There is also a small side gallery for drawings or smaller works.

In line with the program of other Marlborough Galleries, this one represents blue-chip artists whose work is more traditional (abstract, figurative) than vanguard, more modern than contemporary. Many of the artists are major names on the national level and their exhibitions here usually give access to their latest or strongest work. You can also peruse the well-illustrated gallery catalogues at the front desk to get a good overview of the artists.

Artists: Juan José Aquerreta, Martín Chirino, Juan Genovés, Francisco Leiro, Antonio López, Javier Mascaró, Lucio Muñoz, Miquel Navarro, Pelayo Ortega, Daniel Quintero, Joaquín Ramo, Antonio Saura, Manolo Valdés.

3 Galería Soledad Lorenzo

Orfila 5, 28010
91-308-28-87 f: 308-68-30
www.soledadlorenzo.com
galeria@soledadlorenzo.com
Mon, 5–9; Tues–Sat, 11–2 and 5–9
metro: Colón, Alonso Martínez

From the street the gallery may seem smallish, but it actually comprises a sequence of sizeable spaces with wide stairs nicely separating some of them. A lower level, accessed from the front, is also used for display.

Not only is this one of the foremost galleries in Spain (begun in 1986), but Soledad Lorenzo is a charming, vibrant woman who has her fingers on the pulse of what's happening nationally and internationally. She has nurtured the careers of would-be stars, supported little-known young artists and given acclaimed artists their first shows in Madrid. Since the gallery represents some of the major midcareer and established Spanish artists, this is a good place to see what the country has to offer. Look through the gallery catalogues (produced for most exhibitions) to get an overview.

Though the schedule is dominated by one-person shows, occasional thematic projects broaden the base of choice objects and new directions. Recent examples include *Bad Habits (Young British Artists), Cruising L.A. and Speaking through Photography.*

Artists: Txomin Badiola, Miquel Barceló, José Manuel Broto, Victoria Civera, Jorge Galindo, Susy Gómez, Pello Irazu, Pedro Mora, Pablo Palazuelo, Soledad Sevilla, José María Sicilia, Antoni Tàpies, Juan Ugalde, Juan Uslé, Guillermo Pérez Villalta.

Recent one-person exhibitions by non-gallery artists feature painting and sculpture as well as video, photography and new media installations. Artists include Richard Billingham, Ross Bleckner, Louise Bourgeois, Mat Collishaw, George Condo, Eric Fischl, Ceal Floyer, Joan Hernández Pijuán, Martin Kersels, Jonathan Lasker, Iñigo Manglano-Ovalle, Manuel Ocampo, Catherine Opie, Tony Oursler, Lari Pitman, David Salle, Julian Schnabel, Georgina Starr, Sam Taylor-Wood, Adriana Varejao, Jane & Louise Wilson.

4 Galería Metta

architect: Rafael MONEO, 1975
Marqués de la Ensenada 2, 28004
91-319-02-30 f: 319-59-64
metta@afinsart.com
Tues–Fri, 11–2 and 5–9; Sat, 11–2; closed Mon
metro: Colón

Located on the corner of Calle de Doña Barbara de Braganza.

Rafael Moneo originally designed the

Pedro Mora, *4>11*, 2000

elegant but simple space of this gallery in 1975 for Galería Theo (now defunct). The organization of horizontal planes, glass surfaces, lines and volumes is fine-tuned to produce a visual flow and sense of openness in very limited square footage. By including a balcony in the layout, the gallery not only gains additional display space but also has an intimate viewing area for small objects and works on paper.

Since 1997 Galería Metta has occupied the space. Its program mixes Spanish and international artists, big names and newcomers. As suggested by its solo exhibitions of Edward Ruscha and Kiki Smith, its group shows including the likes of Anselm Kiefer, Richard Long, Sigmar Polke and Cy Twombly, and its participation in art fairs, this is a high-energy, ambitious gallery.

Artists: Andreu Alfaro, Eduardo Arroyo, Adolfo Barnatán, Luis Canelo, Nacho Criado,

Jonathan Hammer, *Pretty, Pretty,* 2000

Juan Giralt, Philippe Halsman, M. P. Herrero, Dennis Hopper, Antón Lamazares, Amanda Mean, Antonio Murado, Kenneth Noland, Jules Olitski, Larry Poons, Albert Ráfols-Casamada, Edward Ruscha, Kiki Smith, Eduardo Úrculo, André Villers.

5 Galería Arnés + Röpke

Conde de Xiquena 14, 28004
91-702-14-92 f: 702-16-39
arnesyropke@wanadoo.es
Mon, 5–9; Tues–Fri, 11–2 and 5–9; Sat, 11–2
metro: Colón

Thanks to its connection with Galerie Stefan Röpke in Cologne, interchanges between Germany and Spain are promoted. The program in Madrid is eclectic, including a fair amount of landscape and figurative painting as well as abstract sculpture and photography. Shows by artists not represented by the gallery are the most notable. These have included *Georg Baselitz, Thomas Joshua Cooper, German Abstraction since 1950, Oliver Jordon, Robert Mapplethorpe, A. R. Penck.*

Artists: Adochi, Enrique Asensi, Cveto Marsic, Zoran Music, Max Neumann, Apostolos Palavrakis, Max Uhlig.

6 Galería Fúcares

Conde de Xiquena 12 (1, left) 28004
91-319-74-02 f: 308-01-91
galefucares@wanadoo.es
Tues–Sat, 11-2 and 5–9; closed Mon
metro: Colón

Having developed a name for promoting young artists via its location in Almagro (near Ciudad Real), Galería Fúcares decided to open a second space in Madrid. True to form, the exhibitions call attention to innovative work (Spanish, European and some American) often using spunky or disquieting imagery and unorthodox mediums, for example, the manipulated archival photographs of unknown exiles or famous writers by Ana Teresa Ortega. Within the sprawl of three modest rooms (a converted apartment), there is enough on display to give a good indication of an artist's approach, proficiency and breadth.

Artists: Jordi Alcaraz, Eduardo Alvarez, Ángel Bados, Javier Baldeón, Maggie Cardelús, Anne Deleporte, Concha García, Thomas Grünfeld, José María Guijarro, Jonathan Hammer, Candida Höfer, Sara Huete, Sofía Jack, Abraham Lacalle, Philippe Laleu, Alvaro Machimbarrena, Xisco Mensua, Angela Nordenstedt, Ana Teresa Ortega, José Luis Pastor, Alberto Peral, Pedro Proença, Simeón Sáiz Ruiz, Carlos Schwartz, Ignacio Tovar, José Manuel Vela, Oriol Vilapuig.

7   Galería Antonio Machón

☐ Conde de Xiquena 8, 28004
91-532-40-93 f: 531-21-40
www.antonio.machon.net
antonio@machon.net
Tues–Sat, 11–2 and 5:30–9:30; closed Mon
metro: Colón

Located just off the corner of Calle de Piamonte.

This spacious gallery with three separate rooms specializes in Spanish painting—mainly lush, abstract compositions. Abstraction and large oil paintings are strongly embedded within the country's contemporary art scene, and Antonio Machóon has been at the forefront of supporting such creativity since 1973. The gallery also shows graphic art and publishes finely illustrated books by the artists it represents.

Artists: Juan Barjola, Bonifacio, Félix de la Concha, Luis Gordillo, Alejandro Garmendia, María Gómez, Josep Guinovart, Pilar Insertis, Jesus Lazkano, Alberto Reguera, Antonio Rojas, Angeles San José, Juan Carlos Savater, Luis Vigil.

In addition to these artists, one-person exhibitions have featured work by such well-known figures as Eduardo Chillida, Chema Cobo, José Guerrero, Antonio Saura, Antoni Tàpies, Jordi Teixidor.

Luis Gordillo, *Head with Bands,* 1964

8   Galería Juana de Aizpuru

☐ Barquillo 44, 28004
91-310-55-61 f: 319-52-86
aizpuru@navegalia.com
Tues–Sat, 10–2 and 5–9; closed Mon
metro: Chueca

Located on the first floor.

The art experience here begins in the entrance corridor, where you are greeted by animals painted on the walls. The gallery itself has a front room and a long, extended space perpendicular to this.

Juana de Aizpuru, who also has a thriving gallery in Sevilla, is one of the dynamos of the Spanish art world. She's been actively involved with ARCO and has played a significant role in bringing work by first-rate contemporary artists (virtually all mediums) to Spain while simultaneously developing the careers of Spanish artists both at home and abroad.

In addition to presenting notable exhibitions, the gallery produces good catalogues. Be sure to look at these if you want to learn more about local art activity and contemporary art.

Artists: Rafael Agredano, Ana Laura Aláez, Pilar Albarracín, Art & Language, Juan Navarro Baldeweg, Miroslaw Balka, Sigfrido Martin

Begue, Pedro Cabrita Reis, Miguel Ángel Campano, Nuria Carrasco, Rui Chafes, Eduardo Chillida, Luis Claramunt, Jordi Colomer, José Pedro Croft, Jiri Dokoupil, Alberto García-Alix, Carmela García, Dora García, Ferrán García-Sevilla, Pierre Gonnord, Federico Guzman, Georg Herrold, Juan Hidalgo, Mike Kelley, Martin Kippenberger, Joseph Kosuth, Aitor Lara, José María Larrondo, Sol LeWitt, Rogelio Lopez Cuenca, Ingeborg Lüscher, Albert Oehlen, Markus Oehlen, Andres Serrano, Xesús Vazquez, William Wegman, Franz West.

With a list like this, you wouldn't expect the gallery to feature Cindy Sherman's latest photographs in a solo show, but this was indeed the case in December 2000.

9 Fundación COAM

Piamonte 23, 28004
91-319-16-83 f: 319-88-90
www.fucoam.es
fucoam04@coam.es

Mon–Fri, 9–1 and 4–7; closed Sat
admission: free
metro: Colón

This is the location of Colegio Oficial de Arquitectos de Madrid (COAM), an architectural association that offers lectures, exhibitions, conferences and classes. The exhibitions, presented in the split-level lobby, are modest in scale and nature. They deal with historic and contemporary topics of varying interest to the general public. The lecture schedule is impressive, featuring esteemed architects like Juan Navarro Baldeweg, Carlos Rubio Carvajal, Eleuterio Población Knappe, Rafael Moneo.

10 Galería Max Estrella

Santo Tomé 6 (patio), 28004
91-319-55-17 f: 310-31-27
www.3art.es/galerias.html
maxestrella@w3art.es
Mon–Fri, 10–2 and 5–9; Sat, 11–2

Carmela Garcia, Untitled, 2000

Loris Cecchini, *No Casting*, 2000

and 6–9

metro: Colón, Alonso Martínez

Located at the rear of the ground floor in a renovated space within a patio area.

If you like a touch of zaniness or want to see unmannered work that is refreshing, this is the gallery to visit. The focus is on young artists, many of whom are on upwardly mobile trajectories due to their inclusion in high-profile shows. For example, there's Fernando Sinaga who represented Spain at the São Paulo Biennial and had some of his colorful, minimalist sculpture in Expo Hannover 2000. Or Loris Cecchini, who has shown his common objects (radiators, ladders, bicycles, etc.) fabricated from idiosyncratic materials and his digital photographs of them as a special project at ARCO and in the Contemporary Art Museum in Santiago de Compostella.

The character and quality of the art shown here vary considerably but it's rarely boring or predictable. Be sure to look at the display of small objects by various gallery artists in the reception office. You might also ask to see some of the catalogues and brochures that have accompanied past exhibitions.

Artists: Sergi Aguilar, Javier Arce, Fernando Bellver, Pedro Castrortega, Loris Cecchini, Florentino Díaz, Jorge Fin, Chus García-Fraile, Arancha Goiyeneche, Javier de Juan, Agustín de Llanos, Aitor Ortíz, Bernardi Roig, Fernando Sánchez Castillo, Manuel Saro, Fernando Sinaga, Eduardo Vega de Seoane, Curro Ulzurrun, Daniel Verbis, Carlos Vidal.

11 Galería Marta Cervera

Plaça de las Salesas 2, 28004
91-308-13-32 f: 308-39-63
galmcervera@jazzfree.com
Tues–Fri, 11–2 and 5–9; Sat, 11–2; closed Mon
metro: Colón, Alonso Martínez

Occupying an inconspicuous storefront in the corner of Salesas Square, Galería Marta Cervera shows a range of artists, many of whom may not be name-brand stars though they have attained strong followings and respect from the art world cognoscenti. Unfortunately, the gallery space has only two small rooms for display so exhibitions don't include a lot of work.

Artists: Lara Almárcegui, Pedro Álvarez,

Isidro Blasco, Rebecca Bournigault, Peter Fend, Victoria Gil, Antonio Muntadas, Luca Pancrazzi, Jorge Pardo, José Álvaro Perdices.

12 Galería Elvira González

General Castaños 9, 28004
91-319-59-00 f: 319-61-24
galeriaeg@entorno.es
Mon–Fri, 10:30–2 and 5–9; Sat, 11–2
and 6–9
metro: Colón, Alonso Martínez
Galería Elvira González shows a wide range of work by big-name modern masters, leading minimalist sculptors and abstract painters, established and young Spanish artists. It tends to be blue-chip art that once had a radical edge but is now in the history books as an accepted mode of creativity. Alternatively, the work shown here might best be called conservative modernism because it is strongly formalist, typically with a figurative or purely abstract base.

The gallery space is modest, a few rooms in a converted apartment, so exhibitions feature a few, very select objects. If you're not familiar with the contemporary monochromes of Günter Umberg or the letter-based compositions of Elena del Rivero (these are decidedly not formalist), take the opportunity to check these out.

Artists: Josef Albers, Alfredo Alcain, Juan Asensio, Elena Asins, Jaime Burguillos, Alexander Calder, J. M. Caneja, Eduardo Chillida, Dan Flavin, Gonzalo Fonseca, Lucio Fontana, Pablo Gargallo, Ramón Gaya, Julio González, Adolph Gottlieb, Donald Judd, Joan Miró, Perico Pastor, Pablo Picasso, Elena del Rivero, Mark Rothko, Adolfo Schlosser, Richard Serra, Günter Umberg, Esteban Vicente.

13 Libreria Gaudí

Argensola 13, 28004
tel/fax: 91-308-18-29
Mon–Fri, 9:30–1:30 and 5–8; Sat, 9:30–2
metro: Alonso Martínez
This tightly packed, overflowing bookstore is a great resource for Spanish and foreign books on art and architecture. It's an old-style storefront operation that's a great place for browsing. If you don't have a lot of time, just ask the well-informed, helpful staff to find specific titles or point you in the direction of the topics that interest you.

14 La Caja Negra

Fernando VI 17, 28004
91-310-43-60 f: 308-72-38
lacajanegra@teleline.es
Mon–Sat, 10–2 and 5–9
metro: Alonso Martínez
Located on the 2nd floor, left side.

This gallery specializes in graphic work (etchings, lithographs, silkscreens, digital stamping) and has a large stock of prints by diverse artists on hand. Exhibitions of leading figures, mainly Spanish, feature a particular series or a broad range. Some shows also present limited-edition, illustrated books. If you ask questions, the gallery staff is likely to show you work by artists you may not know and significant objects from bygone years.

Artists: Alfredo Alcain, Antonio Alcaraz, Darío Basso, Miguel Ángel Blanco, Marta Cárdenas, Miguel Catalá, Alejandro Corujeira, José María Diaz-Maroto, Ángel Ferrant, Alfonso Fraile, Ferran García Sevilla, Gonzalo González, Jan Hendrix, Joan Hernández Pijuan, Antón Lamazares, Juan M. Moro, Robert Motherwell, Blanca Muñoz, Fumiko Negishi, Javier Pagola, Perejaume, Pablo Picasso, Bernandí Roig, Unai San Martín, Richard Serra, Santiago Serrano, Susana Solano, Manuel Sonseca, Jordi Teixidor, Curro Ulzurrun.

15 Sociedad General de Autores y Editores

Fernando VI 4, 28004
corner of Calle de Pelayo
metro: Alonso Martínez

Madrid's version of modernista architecture (c. 1900) is very visible in the Justicia area, and the building housing the General Society of Writers and Publishers is a prime example. From the outside, the stark white facade and simple curvature of the wrought-iron lamps and railings seem mild compared with designs in Barcelona. But take a peek inside. You enter a small reception area opening onto a grand, sensuously bowed staircase theatrically framed by a circular shaping of the surrounding wall and lined by a balustrade decorated with sinuous, delicate stems and flowers (wrought iron and glass). The balustrade also encloses the balconies surrounding the atrium, which in turn is capped by an exquisite, finely crafted, stained-glass dome whose center is a golden sunburst.

Although you can't walk all around the interior unless you're a member, the atrium and carved wooden doors of nearby offices indicate the scope and artistry of the all-embracing design.

16 Galería Elba Benítez

San Lorenzo 11 (patio), 28004
91-308-04-68 f: 319-01-69
www.artnet.com/ebenitez.html
elbab@retemail.es
Tues–Sat, 11–2 and 5–9; closed Mon
metro: Tribunal

Located on the left side of the middle courtyard. You won't see a big sign or grand entry, just an inconspicuous door.

Though looking a bit like an artist's studio and having a low-key ambience, this is a well-established gallery where you're likely to see high-powered art. That's not to say it's audacious, trendy work, but rather well-conceived, engaging, unconventional creativity enriched by a grasp of contemporary ideas, theories and subject matter. Some exhibitions feature installation, photography and video art and others showcase the

José Antonio Hernández-Díez, *Marx*, and *Kant*, 2000

serene beauty of spare compositions. If you're not familiar with the imaginary, sound environments of Francisco Ruiz de Infante or the fabric constructions of Fernanda Fragateiro, take the opportunity to get acquainted with these artists.

The gallery program also includes projects like *Collaborations: Architects and Artists* (1999) with Kiessler/Dan Flavin, Gomes da Silva/Fernanda Fragateiro, Barcelona Architectural Service/Francesc Torres, Herzog & De Meuron/Thomas Ruff and Robbrecht, Daem, van Hee/Cristina Iglesias.

Artists: Ignasi Aballí, Juan Cruz, Fernanda Fragateiro, José Antonio Hernández-Díez, Cristina Iglesias, Beatriz Milhazes, Juan Luis Moraza, Vik Muniz, Ernesto Neto, Francisco Ruiz de Infante, Montserrat Soto, Dario Urzay, Valentin Vallhonrat.

16 Galería Heinrich Ehrhardt

San Lorenzo 11 (patio), 28004
91-319-44-15 f: 310-28-45
www.artnet.com/nehrhardt.html
gehrhardt@retemail.es
Tues–Sat, 11–2 and 5–9; closed Mon
metro: Tribunal

This gallery has a dual existence in Madrid and Frankfurt. (In Frankfurt it goes under the name Galerie Grässlin-Ehrhardt.) German connections are used effectively to bring artists with a decidedly northern, conceptual character to Spain. For the most part, exhibitions feature current or past work in solo or triad shows. Since each year's program presents different artists (most of whom aren't officially represented by the gallery), a range of art not otherwise visible in Madrid is on view.

Recent exhibitions: Herbert Brandl, Thomas Joshua Cooper, Ángel Borrego Cubero, Helmut Dorner, Olafur Eliasson, Günther Förg, Claus Goedicke, Asta Gröting, Bendix Harms, Thilo Heinzmann & Thomas Zip, Stefan Hirsig, Axel Hütte, Stephan Jung, Hubert Kiecol, Imi Knoebel, Christopher Muller, Roberto Ruiz Ortega, Guillermo Paneque, Tobias Rehberger, Roberto Ruiz, Ulrich Rückriem.

17 Galería María Martín

Pelayo 52, 28004
91-319-68-73 f: 310-44-39
mariama@santandersupernet.com
Tues–Sat, 11–2 and 5–9; closed Mon
metro: Chueca

In its compact, two-level space, Galería María Martín presents exhibitions of sculpture or photography related to nature. Considering that a concern with nature or a "return to nature" have become issues with regard to food, lifestyle, health, fabrics and many other realms of existence and production, perhaps a focus on nature in art was inevitable. But don't expect sylvan landscapes or flower paintings. Indeed, the gallery takes a very loose and broad approach to nature as subject, theme, medium and concept. In the mixed-media installations of Alberto Carneiro, for example, the underlying theme is the relationship between man and nature, natural and artificial. And in the digital photographs of Daniel Blaufuks, attention is directed toward haunting oddities that upset a semblance of the natural.

Artwork shown here tends to have visual appeal and conceptual complexity. The artists are independent-minded, emerging talents of various nationalities whose work is gaining recognition across Europe.

Artists: Miguel Ángel Blanco, Daniel Blaufuks, Alberto Carneiro, Denmark, Javier Garcerá, Michel Haas, Ana Malagrida, Blanca Muñoz, Pamen Pereira, Gabriel Perezzan, Mayte Vieta, Xawery Wolski.

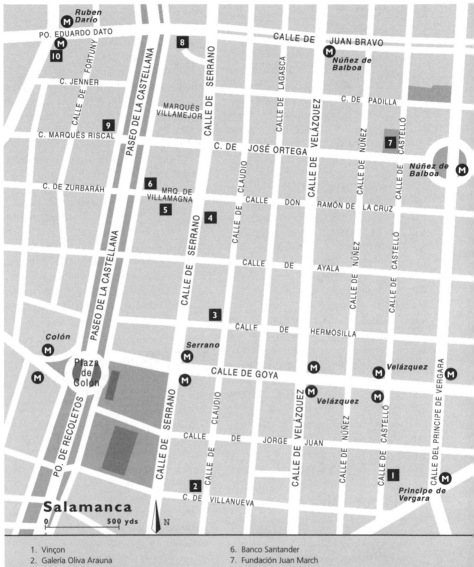

1. Vinçon
2. Galería Oliva Arauna
3. Teatriz
4. Fundación "la Caixa"
5. Fundación Santander Central Hispano
6. Banco Santander
7. Fundación Juan March
8. Museo de Escultural Aire Libre
9. Bankinter
10. Galería Estiarte

Salamanca

1 Vinçon

Castelló 18, 28001
91-578-05-20 f: 431-16-11
vinconmad@globalcom.es
Mon, 5–8:30; Tues–Sat, 10–2 and
5–8:30
metro: Principe de Vergara, Velázquez

The entrance is down a passage between #18 and #20 on Calle Castelló. The building does not front the street, so look carefully for the inconspicuously marked sidewalk leading back from Calle Castelló.

Surrounded by fashionable apartment houses, Vinçon is located in a 1920s, two-story structure built as a silversmith workshop and then used by the city's electric company. Now the open-space interior serves as a chic environment for one of Spain's most prestigious design firms. Founded in 1941, Vinçon is devoted to all sorts of products for the home, things for cooking, dining, office work, children, the bath, garden, etc. The objects are distinctive for merging creative design with innovative technical prowess. Like the flagship Vinçon store in Barcelona (and like many trendy superstores), products are displayed on shelves or platforms for easy visibility and access. This is a great place to shop for gifts or just to explore for fun so you can be in-the-know about the inventive new gadgets devised to replace all the familiar little gizmos you take for granted.

2 Galería Oliva Arauna

Claudio Coello 19, 28001
91-435-18-08 f: 576-87-19
oarauna@hotmail.com
Tues–Sat, 11–2 and 5–9; closed Mon
metro: Retiro

Located on the corner of Calle de Villanueva.

Galería Oliva Arauna has a high-class address in a posh neighborhood and a prime storefront location, so you might expect grandeur inside. On the contrary, the display area is a smallish, very compact white-walled room with sectional dividers. Depending on the exhibition, space limitations affect what can be shown and how it appears. Nevertheless, this stalwart gallery manages to feature sizeable objects and multipartite installations. It represents a range of notable artists, favoring those who have carved out their own realm of expression within the minimalist and conceptual genres. Included are the photo-based creations of Alvargonzález, Jaar, Moura and Rio Branco with their highly particularized, edgy subject matter and engaging modes of presentation.

Artists: Antoni Abad, Chema Alvargonzález, Cristina Arias, Per Barclay, Christophe Boutin, Rosa Brun, Sally Gutiérrez, José Herrera, Alfredo Jaar, Alicia Martín, Leonel Moura, Zwelethu Mthethwa, Christian Philipp Müller, Tomi Osuna, Concha Prada, Miguel Rio Branco, Juan Carlos Robles, Alfredo Romano, Susana Solano, Mitchell Syrop, Marion Thieme, Laura Torrado.

3 Teatriz

architect: Philippe STARCK
Hermosilla 15, 28001
91-577-53-79
daily, 11:30 pm–3 am
metro: Serrano

Located on the corner of Claudio Coello.

The inimitable Philippe Starck created another of his ultra-chic, eccentric social settings here by appropriating a theater (the Infanta Beatriz Theater) for a restaurant. Even if you don't want to indulge in a costly late-evening meal, you can absorb the ambience and watch the people-watchers by ordering something simple in the café-bar just inside the entrance. No matter where you eat or drink, be sure to visit the men's or ladies' room with a detour that allows you to meander through all the dining areas.

Following his reductive, architectonic proclivities, Starck has clad the interior of Teatriz in dark veneered or painted walls and designed style-conscious furnishings for each of the spaces. On the one hand the decor is decidedly trim and austere. But checker-patterned floors, emphatically shaped cut outs as doorways or ceiling apertures and freestanding curvy walls used to reshape corridors wreak havoc with what at first seems a minimalist aesthetic. Instead it is De Chiricoesque with dramatic dead-ends, elongated perspectives, intense light and dark shadows.

The main space, formerly the theater's auditorium, retains the configuration of circular orchestra and low-hanging balconies extending far out from the periphery. The sense of a lurking presence or impending event is heightened by the velvet curtains hanging from the extremely high ceiling and the surreal spareness of the setting. Dining occurs on the ground and balcony levels as well as on stage and backstage, where barrenness is exaggerated by the old, raw brick walls and hollow tower. A big, box-shaped, backlit onyx bar surrounded by aluminum stools is the focal element, situated dead center on stage. For dramatic enhancement, Starck has hung a mirror on the wall and tilted it to reflect the scene in a side space.

A corridor between the front café-bar and the main restaurant also has dining tables. The area is noisy and congested, not great for an intimate tryst but perfect for being seen and surveying everything and everyone. Adding to the ongoing entertainment here are waiters scurrying past with trays held high and huge black-and-white photo blowups in light boxes leaning against the wall. The one depicting a diver in midair, closeup, is especially captivating, albeit an idiosyncratic oddity in a denaturalized, dark interior.

Downstairs the setting is more plush, highlighted by a cozy, upholstered-furniture bar and a small, leather-padded room for dancing.

Starck's bathrooms are always curios and Teatriz doesn't disappoint. On the main floor they are bare to an extreme, featuring a single basin placed atop a table with a drinking fountain–like faucet extending from the wall

above. The design here is mild compared to the lower level, where marble tables with water-pipe legs, blue lighting and etched-glass toilet enclosures create an eye-popping experience.

4 Fundación "la Caixa"

Serrano 60, 28001
91-426-02-02 f: 426-02-44
www.fundacio.lacaixa.es
info.fundacio@lacaixa.es
Mon, Wed–Sat, 11–8; Sun, 11–2:30; closed Tues
admission: free
metro: Serrano

This is one of the main exhibition outposts of the "la Caixa" Foundation, which is headquartered in Barcelona (see p. 173). Widely known for its prowess in creating museum-quality projects and supporting contemporary art, "la Caixa" plays a prominent role in Madrid. Unfortunately, the space it has to work with here is a fragmented layout of oddly shaped rooms spread across several levels. It's interestingly renovated but not very flexible and not well scaled for sizeable, complex shows.

The exhibition program takes a broad approach to art, embracing non-Western and Western cultures alike, hot young artists and venerated figures from the early and mid-20th century, new media and conventional modes of creativity. Often the shows call attention to overlooked or forgotten realms and artists who are working against the grain of what is easy, comfortable art. For each exhibition, "la Caixa" produces a brochure and catalogue, but there are no wall texts within the galleries.

Recent exhibitions: *African Art from Nigeria, Harry Callahan, Collection of Fundació "la Caixa," Arshile Gorky, Latin American Art, Monasteries and Lamas of Tibet, Russian Symbolism, Sean Scully, Ettore Spalletti, Spirits of Water—Alaskan and British Columbian Art, Hiroshi Sugimoto, Gillian Wearing.*

Tony Cragg, "la Caixa" collection

5 Fundación Santander Central Hispano

📠 Marqués de Villamagna 3, 28014
91-337-74-33
www.fundacion.bsch.es
fundacion@fundacion.bsch.es
Tues–Sat, 11–2 and 5–9; Sun, 11–2:30;
closed Mon
admission: free
metro: Serrano

Located around the corner from "la Caixa,"
on the lower level of Torre Serrano, an office
tower fronting Calle de Serrano.

In its spacious galleries, Fundación
Santander Central Hispano presents museum-
quality, historical exhibitions. Many shows
deal with 20th-century art but focus on early
or prime elements of the modern tradition
rather than the contemporary period.
Recent exhibitions: *Catalan Modernismo,*
*Corot to Barceló, Lucio Muñoz, Rare and
Precious, Rodchenko, Spanish Abstract Art.*

6 Banco Santander

🏛 renovation: Hans HOLLEIN, 1993
Paseo de la Castellana 24, 28046
metro: Serrano

Located on the corner of Calle de Jose Ortega
y Gasset.

Though often referred to as Banco
Santander, the official name since a merger
in 1999 is Banco Santander Central Hispano
(BSCH). Don't think you're at the wrong
address based on the classical style (19th
century) of the building, articulated on all five
stories by an alignment of the same French
windows, white shutters and ironwork grills.
Indeed, nothing about the exterior suggests
that this is a stunning exemplar of innovative
architecture by the Austrian Pritzker laureate

Hans Hollein. As with Moneo's Bankinter (located just across Paseo de la Castellana), city regulations required that new construction not change the character of the facade of old mansions on the grand boulevard.

To see Hollein's radical design, you must pass through the revolving glass doors into the reception hall, where you can see the atrium of the bank's headquarters. Visitors can't pass beyond this point, but since Hollein was not responsible for renovating the offices and space beyond, this viewpoint is excellent. (If for some reason you can't enter here, go around the corner to the bank's branch, where it's also possible to peer inside.) All remnants of the classical exterior immediately disappear just inside the lobby doors. Marble floors and unembellished planar walls, also stone, convey the cold but august, rock-solid impression of an indestructible institution. However, the reception desk, placed beside a bridge crossing into the atrium, puts you on notice of the architectural panache lying ahead. Composed of a plate of glass set atop a steel beam that extends from a stone block, the desk epitomizes Hollein's mode of heightening form and drama by combining different materials and creating asymmetrical modes of balance. In actuality, the desk tends to fall by the wayside since the wondrous spectacle of the atrium comes into view when you stand at the desk. The narrow bridge, spanning a cut to the lower level, is a nice touch, accentuating the passage into the core of the building. Down below, an unpretentious fountain adds decor and the sound of a gurgling stream to the setting.

The curvature of the atrium reverberates in the circular skylight and in various curvilinear shapes and spaces. More emphatic, however, is the sharpness of straight edges, the eccentric positioning of key elements and the use of disparate materials. There are dark columns surrounding the base three-quarters of the way around; a grand staircase of to one side of the entrance level; silvery stainless-steel surfaces, cream marble and peach-toned walls; isolated windowlike

Hans Hollein, Banco Santander

apertures marking each floor; a private balcony at the top level; overlapping and layered sequences throughout; projecting panels in the shape of sliced disks; bronze-colored mesh screens rimming the upper three floors with long vertical delineations; and square screens arranged as zigzags around the bottom of the cupola. All together the architecture is a captivating harmony of contrapuntal rhythms and autonomous zones precisely situated.

7 Fundación Juan March

[==] Castelló 77, 28006
91-435-42-40 f: 576-34-20
www.march.es
webmast@mail.march.es
Mon–Sat, 10–2 and 5:30–9; Sun, 10–2
admission: free
metro: Nuñez de Balboa

Commanding the corner of Calles de Castelló and Padilla in a plush section of Salamanca is the Juan March Foundation. The seven-story building of marble and glass (1975) and the two large sculptures astride the entrance pathway—*Lugar de Encuentios* by Eduardo Chillida (1975) and *Organo* by Eusebio Sempere (1977)—are refined, archetypal examples of Spanish modernity. They also suggest the foundation's penchant for historical works from or akin to the modern era rather than radical contemporary statements.

Fundación Juan March, established in 1955 by the wealthy financier Don Juan March Ordinas, is one of the largest philanthropic institutions in Europe and a venerated patron of the arts in Spain. Indeed, this headquarter's building was conceived as a cultural center. It contains a large exhibition space, two auditoria, libraries, conference rooms and an outdoor sculpture garden (normally inaccessible to the public). In addition to organizing numerous cultural activities (exhibitions, concerts, plays, lectures, classes, etc.) in Madrid and elsewhere, the foundation has a notable publication program and awards grants to artists and scholars. It also maintains a collection, parts of which are displayed in museums in Cuenca (see p. 59) and Palma de Mallorca.

Art exhibitions here are always high-quality. The focus is on art from the early 20th century, prints, photographs and contemporary Spanish art. Free brochures, substantive catalogues and lectures accompany each project. Recent exhibitions: *Abstract Expressionism—Works on Paper, Barceló Ceramics, Chagall, Lovis Corinth, Paul Delvaux, From Caspar David Friedrich to Picasso, Goya Graphics, Karl Schmidt-Rottluff, Kurt Schwitters, Victor Vasarely.*

8 Museo de Escultura al Aire Libre

[血] Paseo de la Castellana 41, 28046
daily, 24 hrs
[Δ] admission: free
metro: Rubén Darío, Núñez de Balboa

Located under and alongside the elevated highway linking Paseo Eduardo Dato and Calle de Juan Bravo. A short flight of steps leads down to the area from Calle de Serrano just north of Calle de Martínez de la Rosa.

When the roadway crossing Paseo de la Castellana was constructed, the engineers and the sculptor Eusebio Sempere had the idea of transforming the bleak, concrete zone underneath into an Outdoor Sculpture Museum. The museum, begun in 1979, now comprises 17 objects all situated on the east side (Salamanca) of Castellana with a lone work by Paolo Serrano set below the overpass on the west side. A waterfall and pool were added to enhance the setting, but the dark, cavernous ambience of the inner space remains.

The collection, a sampling of Spanish sculpture from the 1950s and 1960s, includes work by Andres Alfaro, Eduardo Chillida, Martin Chirino, Amadeo Gabino, Julio Gonzalez, Rafael Leoz, Marcel Martí, Joan Miró, Pablo Palazuelo, Manuel Rivera, Gerardo Rueda, Alberto Sanchez, Eusebio Sempere, Francisco Sobrino, José Maria Subirachs, Gustavo Torner. The objects, in stone, steel and bronze, are mainly abstract and smallish except for Chillida's six-ton concrete form *(Stranded Siren)* suspended in the air by four industrial cables. The sculptures were all donated by the artists and most are middling in quality.

The museum could use some clean-up and some of the objects need restoration, but for an outdoor public space it's not bad. Be forewarned that the highway noise can be excruciating. You can lessen the problem by visiting on a Sunday when traffic is at a minimum.

Outdoor Sculpture Museum

9 Bankinter

architect: Rafael MONEO, 1972–77
Paseo de la Castellana 29 (Calle Marqués de Riscal 13), 28046
metro: Ruben Darío

This early project by Rafael Moneo indicates a masterful sensitivity to scale and context. The building, Bankinter's headquarters, sits on a narrow plot of land between an 18-story, mid-20th-century apartment house on a quiet residential street and a late-19th-century villa (renovated for additional bank offices) fronting Paseo de la Castellana, Madrid's most prominent avenue. Barely visible from the grand boulevard and having only a discreet presence on the side road where its entrance is located, the structure is a compact aggregate of forms with each facade oriented differently. The core has a vertical wall that serves as a backdrop for the villa in front. But in back the center volume is shaped like a wedge whose diagonal opens up space and light for the adjacent dwelling.

A low unit with a patio as its roof and a curved side cushions the area between the villa, its gardens and the high elevation of the new building. Characteristically, Moneo has kept the surfaces of the brick exterior utterly simple using an emphatic geometry of recessed windows alone to articulate the facades.

10 Galería Estiarte

Almagro 44, 28010
91-308-15-69 f: 319-07-30
www.estiarte.com
galeria@estiarte.com
Mon–Sat, 10:30–2 and 5–9
metro: Rubén Darío

If you like graphic art, this is the place for you. The gallery specializes in prints and has an abundant stock of work by both 20th-century masters and contemporary artists. Its exhibitions often highlight big names from the present and past. The publication of its own prints by Spanish artists (e.g., Juan Navarro Baldeweg, Victoria Civera, Soledad Sevilla, Jordi Teixidor, Juan Uslé) is also part of the gallery program.

Recent exhibitions: Pierre Alechinsky, David de Almeida, José Manuel Ballester, Georg Basilitz, José Manuel Broto, Rafael Canogar, José Manuel Ciria, Jannis Kounellis, Sol LeWitt, Henri Matisse, Pablo Picasso, José María Sicilia, Gustavo Torner, Manolo Valdés, Pepe Yagües.

Northern Madrid and the Periphery

Sala del Canal de Isabel II

⌑ Santa Engracia 125, 28003
91-545-10-00 f: 545-14-38
Tues–Sat, 11–2 and 5–9; Sun, 11–2; closed Mon
metro: Ríos Rosas (exit Bretón de los Herreros)

When you visit this exhibition space you also see a stellar example of industrial architecture. In fact, the building with steel stairs connecting its four floors is a restored water tower from 1907–11 which still belongs to the Water Company of Madrid.

Sala del Canal de Isabel II is a center for contemporary photography, and its exhibitions are worthy of the unique setting. The program includes top-notch, imaginative shows, many of which are thematic, featuring artists from all over the world.

There are also projects like *Photographic Action,* wherein 32 artists, selected on a first-come first-served basis for a block of time, had the use of a space in the galleries.

Recent exhibitions: *Rafael Agregano, Aztlán Today, British Photography, Diverse Worlds, Games and Simulacra, Susy Gómez, Purges & Exhortations.*

Fernando Botero

⚘ *Left Hand,* 1992
⌑ Plaza de San Juan de la Cruz
metro: Gregorio Marañon

As you continue down Paseo de la Castellano, the grand old mansions give way to high-rise office towers and shopping malls. This bronze sculpture by Fernando Botero, a Colombian artist with a popular, worldwide following, is set like a marker as you move out of the center city into the expanded zone beyond.

The sculpture commands attention from its location at a major intersection on the main axial road going north. More specifically, it is positioned front and center on the lawn of a giant traffic circle with a water-jet fountain as a backdrop. True, it's just a pudgy hand turned upward with the palm facing forward, but characteristically, Botero represents it as a swollen form to increase the sensuality quotient. He views art as the deformation of nature and has focused mainly on deformations of the human body through volumetric enlargement. Though the gesture and image of this hand with its

Botero, *Left Hand*

elongated center finger may be seen in terms of Botero's interest in Eastern art and religion, his creativity often has a comic, erotic side that may well suggest alternative interpretations.

Fundación Banco de Bilbao y Vizcaya

architect: Francisco Javier SÁENZ DE OIZA, 1971–81
Paseo de la Castellana 81, 28046
91-374-69-88 f: 374-42-31
metro: Nuevos Ministerios

Intermittently, the Fundación Banco de Bilbao y Vizcaya presents art exhibitions in a gallery space at the base of the BBV tower. The exhibition program is not continuous, but there are usually a few, quite notable shows in any given year. Recent exhibitions: *Dubuffet's Dubuffets, From Goya to Zuloaga, Sagasta and Spanish Liberalism.*

The 29-story tower itself is a landmark in the city's skyline. Faced in glass and Cor-ten steel, its squarish form with rounded corners has a nonindustrial elegance. Architecturally, its silhouette and stack structure, with floor slabs spreading out from a central trunk, bears a likeness to Frank Lloyd Wright's Johnson Laboratory Tower (Racine, Wisconsin, 1950).

Joan Miró

mural, Palacio de Congresos y Exposiciones
Plaça Joan Miró
metro: Santiago Bernabéu

The building is on the corner of Paseo de la Castellana at Plaça de Lima. The mural is over the main entrance facing Avenida de General Perón.

Miró's murals are timeless. They are among the most delightful, successful works of public art, invariably enlivening the environments in which they are situated. Though made of small, square tiles arranged in a grid, there is nothing constrained or regularized about the

imagery. As in his paintings, the composition is a fantasy narrative composed of wayward, curvilinear figures—human, animal, bird, extraterrestrial, galactic—boldly colored red, yellow, blue, green and black.

Fundación Cultural Mapfre Vida

Avenida de General Perón 40, 28020
91-581-15-96 f: 581-16-29
Mon–Sat, 10–9; Sun, 12–8
admission: free
metro: Santiago Bernabéu

Located on the lower level of the shopping center (Centro Comercial Moda Shopping) across the street from the Miró mural.

This is another of the city's museum-like spaces created by a corporate foundation for art exhibitions. The program here is mainly retrospectives and group shows of Spanish art from the late 19th and early 20th centuries. Presentations are high-class and grand-scale, highlighting major objects and featuring impressive catalogues. Since the exhibitions tend to showcase seminal figures in Spanish art history from the modern period, though they may not be universally known, they offer a great opportunity to see something different and distinctive. Unfortunately, if you don't read Spanish you won't have access to the superb content of the object labels, and there are no informational brochures in English or other languages.

Recent exhibitions: *French Symbolist Painting, Gardens of Spain, Xavier Gosé, Nonell, At the Seashore (The Sea as a Theme in Modern Spanish Painting), Joaquim Sunyer, The Twentieth-Century Circle, Daniel Vázquez Díaz.*

P. Johnson and J. Burgee, Puerta de Europa

crisscrossed by aluminum strips and a red grid pattern, exude a kitschy rather than a monumental aura.

The setting that surrounds the gateway is a site onto itself. Several metro entrances, a water tower, civic edifices, a curious memorial (comprising a sharply angled, tall marble structure and statue devoid of identifying inscriptions), a bus station and endless streams of sidewalks flank, extend from or lie in the midst of the ultrawide axial roadway, Paseo de la Castellana. Though some lanes of the boulevard go underground, others pass between the towers and become part of its unappealing centerpiece—a mammoth traffic circle with a bland lawn and geyser-spurting fountain.

Torres Blancas

architect: Francisco Javier SÁENZ DE OIZA, 1962–69
Calle del Corazón de María 2 (Avenida América 37), 28002
metro: Cartagena

F. Javier Sáenz de Oíza, Torres Blancas

Puerta de Europa

architects: Philip JOHNSON, John BURGEE, 1990–98
Plaça de Castilla
metro: Plaça de Castilla
Located near the end of Paseo de la Castellana.

Called the "Door of Europe" or KIO Towers (the Kuwaiti Investment Office commissioned the original project), these twin 24-story buildings are positioned and styled as a gateway into Madrid from the north. Leaning toward one another at a 15% slant, their simple shapes bear witness to territorial markers of yore even as their boxy forms clad in black reflective glass, outlined and

If you arrived in Madrid by air, you may have noticed this striking building on your way into the center city along Avenida de América. Its unusual form, looking like a clump of long, ribbed tubes, attracts attention even today, four decades after it was created. Considered to be the most important work of architecture in Madrid from the 1960s, Torres Blancas (White Towers) reveals an embrace of radical ideas from Le Corbusier even as it conveys the originality of Sáenz de Oíza.

Designed as a high-end office and housing structure, it has 23 floors each divided into four sections and serviced by two elevators. Curves, sculpted from cast concrete, dominate the interior, where they shape circular rooms and flowing surfaces, and the exterior, where they define the facade as a ring of towers. Glazed walls—glass bricks around bathrooms and windows covered with shutters—are also a feature element of the design. For good measure, add a terrace and swimming pool on the roof, underground parking, a garden expanse at the base and a metro stop one block away!

Tesauro Video Production

architect: Javier BELLOSILLO, 1989–93
Bócangel 23
metro: Ventas

On exiting the metro at the main gate of Madrid's monumental bullring, cross Calle de Alcalá and go west (right); turn left at the second street, Calle Bócangel, and continue around the curve passing through a residential area interspersed with office and industrial buildings.

Should you indulge an urge to attend a bullfight, take a slight detour from the main bullfight arena to see one of the few blatantly postmodern buildings in Madrid. Commissioned as an office-studio complex for Tesauro Video Production, the structure features an idiosyncratic facade that is unabashedly conspicuous. An almost rectangular wall of cast concrete with cutouts signifying windows and doorways stands in front of a second concrete wall with a giant void, defined by a circular-angled shape, glazed surface and black steel framing partitions, as its centerpiece. On the side, a tower and eccentric steel configuration with balconies complement the street-side design.

This was actually a remodeling project in which Bellosillo created a glass-and-steel passageway and staircase between the refurbished front office structure and studios housed in a renovated, two-story building in back. Tesauro vacated the building in 1999 (for unknown reasons), from which time it has lain empty.

Javier Bellosillo, Tesauro

Biblioteca Pedro Salinas

architect: Juan Navarro BALDEWEG, 1990–94

Glorieta Puerta de Toledo 1, 28005
Mon–Fri, 8–2:45; Sat, 9–1:45
metro: Puerta de Toledo

Located on the northeast side of Glorieta Puerta de Toledo, just above the metro and below Calle de Toledo.

Seemingly every foreigner and half the residents of Madrid go to the flea market (El Rastro) on Sunday morning. Tables are filled with mostly new products, easily described as schlock merchandise. Should you be inclined to join the masses, you'll end up near the monumental arch in Puerta de Toledo and can easily walk to the new library by Juan Navarro Baldeweg, an architect who has taught at various American universities.

Set on the edge of a plaza bustling with activity during the week because of the adjacent market, this small public library is a humble but notable presence. Walled off from the street, its cylindrical form sits atop a granite base with a curving staircase going up to a terrace. What looks to be a grand entrance is in fact only a fire-escape exit! The real doorway, looking more like a service entrance, opens directly onto the pavement in front. It is shaded by a scant overhang and attains a degree of prominence from a glazed pitched roof just behind. The cylinder itself, wrapped in limestone and sparsely punctuated by windows, occupies the center. Surprisingly, the clarity of this core volume remains intact despite a collage of add-ons, including an extension encircling the rear half of the core structure.

Inside, Baldeweg also designed realms to obscure, reinforce and counterbalance the preeminent, cylindrical space. Indeed, he created a multipartite, sunlit, unusual building well suited to the functions of a neighborhood library.

J. Navarro Baldeweg, Pedro Salinas Library

EXCURSIONS FROM MADRID

Segovia

Famous for its Roman aqueduct (1st century a. d.), Gothic cathedral and fairy-tale Alcázar castle, this charming city, 55 mi (88 km) from Madrid, makes a great day-trip despite being lean on contemporary art. Train from Madrid (Chamartín), 1 3/4 hr.

🏛 Museo de Arte Contemporáneo Esteban Vicente

Plazuela de las Bellas Artes, 40001
921-46-20-10 f: 46-22-77
Tues–Sat, 11–2 and 4–7; Sun, 11–2; closed Mon

Although called a Museum of Contemporary Art, the term "contemporary" is used very loosely to characterize a program focused on the 20th century and most particularly the early and middle years. But this might well change since the museum is quite young, having opened only in 1998.

The core of the museum lies in a gift of 142 works from the artist Esteban Vicente (1903—2001) that now occupies a major part of the building, a renovated palace of Enrique IV. Born in the Segovia region, Vicente moved to New York in 1936 and became an early devotee of abstract expressionist painting. His seemingly simple compositions are formed by luminous color that floats gently on the surface and in space.

In addition to the collection of Vicente's art, the museum presents a mixed bag of temporary exhibitions. Though the titles suggest big-name modernists, the shows tend to feature lesser-known works, some of which are hidden gems and others that qualify as curios. But you can't go wrong with exhibitions like Morandi, which gathered a stellar group of watercolors and prints that enriched an appreciation of the artist's paintings even as they exuded their own distinctive power.

Recent exhibitions: The Avant-Garde and Wood, From Picasso to Bacon (Works from the Collection of Museo de Bellas Artes de Bilbao), Morandi, Picasso in Spanish Collections.

Valladolid

Train from Madrid (Chamartín), 2 hr.

Museo de Arte Contemporáneo Español de Valladolid

🚃 Patio Herreriano, Monasterio de San Benito
San Benito 1, 47080

In the summer of 2001, the Museo de Arte Contemporáneo Español de Valladolid will open its doors to the public. Housed in renovated rooms in the Patio Herreriano of the San Benito Monastery, a 16th-century building, with additional space in a new annex, the museum will present the evolution and history of avant-garde art in Spain from 1918 to the present. The objects on display are part of the extraordinary Colección Arte Contemporáneo (CAC) formed by a conglomerate of corporations since 1988. Comprising more than 800 paintings, sculptures and works on paper, the collection, which will be ceded to the city in 2006, represents a significant aspect of Spanish heritage and a unique slice of 20th-century art.

Among the 150 artists included in the collection are Eduardo Arroyo, Miquel Barceló, Joan Brossa, Eduardo Chillida, Equipo Crónica, Angel Ferrant, Pablo Gargallo, Julio González, Cristina Iglesias, Lucio Muñoz, Pablo Palazuelo, Benjamin Palencia, Antonio Saura, José María Sicilia, Antoni Tàpies, Joaquin Torres Garcia, Daniel Vázquez Díaz, Pérez Villalta.

Salamanca

The oldest university in Spain, founded 1218, vitalizes this city. The environment is also rich in historic architecture of Roman, Romanesque, Gothic, Renaissance, baroque and Moorish persuasion. Just walking through the campus and around the town is an eyeful and cultural activities of all varieties abound. During 2002 Salamanca will be especially lively; it's been designated that year's Cultural Capital of Europe. Train from Madrid (Chamartín), 2 1/2 hr; from Valladolid, 2 hr.

Palacio de Abrantes

Calle de San Pablo 54, 37008
923-294-400
Mon–Sat, 12–2 and 6–9; Sun, 12–2
admission: free

This remodeled 15th-century mansion now serves as a cultural center belonging to the university. All sorts of events and activities take place here, including exhibitions of contemporary art. These range from venturesome projects by young artists, to curated shows from elsewhere, to presentations of foreign figures with established careers. The ambience is carefree and high-energy both, and you're bound to see work that will capture your imagination or at least make you think. Recent exhibitions: *Pierre Alechinsky, Aztlán Today, Per Barclay, State of Suspension—Elisa Sighicelli, Xawery Wolski.*

Sala de Exposiciones

Patio de Escuelas Menores, 37008
923-294-480 f: 923-263-006
Mon–Sat, 12–2 and 6–9; Sun, 12–2
admission: free

Across the street (Calle de los Libreros) from the main courtyard of the university with its breathtaking 16th-century facade is Patio de Escuelas Menores. Various exhibition spaces are located around this arcaded cloister, among them (on the right side of the entrance) one devoted exclusively to photography. In this seemingly out-of-the-way place not known for its support of cutting-edge art, you'll find engaging work by up-and-coming artists, some of whom haven't yet been shown in Madrid or Barcelona.

Recent exhibitions: *British Fashion and Photography, Lynne Cohen, Paul Seawright, Valentín Vallhonrat.*

Museo Art Nouveau y Art Decó

Calle de Gilbralta 14, 37008
423-121-425
www.museocasalis.org
summer: Tues–Fri, 11–2 and 5–9; Sat–Sun, 11–9; closed Mon
winter: Tues–Fri, 11–2 and 4–7; Sat–Sun, 11–8; closed Mon
admission: 300/200 ptas; free on Thurs, 11–2

Located south of the two cathedrals.

The modernist Casa Lis, built in 1905, provides an appropriate setting for the museum's collection. Stained-glass windows cover walls and ceilings, and displayed throughout are all sorts of decorative-arts objects designed with flowing, romanticized images of flowers, vines and women or fine-lined, geometric elegance. The collection, mainly French and German, includes Fabergé jewels, glassware by Gallé and Lalique, dolls, silver, furnishings and some paintings and posters. It's not a comprehensive, outstanding representation, though choice treasures lurk within.

Cuenca

The old part of Cuenca is one of those irresistible, picturesque hill towns that make travel in Europe such a delight. Big-city hustle and time pressures disappear as you leisurely meander through an arcaded plaza, climb up and down stone steps and walk along winding, narrow streets between houses and back gardens. Train from Madrid (Atocha), 2 1/2 hr.

Museo de Arte Abstracto Español

🏛 Casas Colgadas, 16001
96-921-29-83 f: 921-22-85
museocuenca@expo.march.es
Tues–Fri, 11–2 and 4–6; Sat, 11–2 and
4–8; Sun, 11–2:30; closed Mon
admission: 500/250 ptas

A visit here is as much to enjoy the site as it is to see the art. Set atop the hill constituting the old town, the museum is installed in one of Cuenca's historic "hanging houses." These unique examples of local medieval architecture are characterized by multistoried, wood balconies precariously suspended over a high cliff that drops straight down to a river ravine. Originally built in the 14th century, they were abandoned in the late 18th century. Some are still empty and others have been, or are in the process of being, rehabilitated.

The house occupied by the Museum of Abstract Spanish Art was restored in 1927 and 1950 and completely refurbished in 1978. Inside there are numerous levels with one or two rooms on each level. The old coffered ceilings of raw timber are still in place, and some of the original carvings in wall and ceiling beams have been preserved. Windows on the cliff side also remain intact providing spectacular views of the nearby hillside, the riverbeds and sweeping stretches of the valleys beyond.

The museum was opened in 1966 by the artist Fernando Zóbel (1924–1984) to house the collection he had developed to celebrate and document abstract Spanish art. Fundación Juan March subsequently purchased the collection (1980) and expanded the display space by enlarging the number of galleries (1985) and adding a new temporary exhibition section (1994).

The permanent exhibition includes 110 abstract paintings and sculptures by the 1950s–60s generation. Some are familiar names but most are largely unknown outside Spain. The list includes Rafael Canogar, Luis Feito, Antonio Lorenzo, Manolo Millares, Manuel Mompó, Jorge Oteiza, Pablo Palazuelo, Gerardo

Museum of Abstract Spanish Art (hanging houses)

Rueda, Antonio Saura, Eusebio Sempere, Antoni Tàpies, Gustav Torner.

Many of the paintings are not oil on canvas but compositions using raw fabrics (burlap, sackcloth, etc.), wood, metal, wire screen and other materials. Clearly, there's no evidence of a group style or Spanish aesthetic, only pure abstraction as a common ground. Indeed, an overriding consciousness about form, structure, texture, color and spatial dynamics is apparent. Though correspondences with gestural expressionism, Arte Povera, color field, assemblage and minimalist art come to mind, the similarities are generally superficial. Far more significant are the differences in concept, method and emotive tone and the individuality of the artists.

The permanent collection galleries encompass a limited selection of work by younger artists from the 1980s–90s generation, and the new annex is devoted to monographic shows of works on paper. Recent exhibitions: *Lucio Muñoz, Nolde Watercolors, Zóbel Graphic Work.*

MURCIA

Train from Madrid, 4 hr; from Valencia, 2 hr; from Calpe (change to "trenet" in Alicante), 2 3/4 hr. There are no direct trains from Cuenca; bus service is possible.

Ayuntamiento

architect: Rafael MONEO, 1995–98
Plaza del Cardinal Belluga

If you're enamored with contemporary architecture and appreciate excellence in finely tuned, manipulated simplicity in design, then take a major detour to Murcia to see Rafael Moneo's City Hall. It's situated on the main square of the historic city center, sque7zed in by narrow streets on both sides, facing a baroque palace on the right and a very decorative 18th-century cathedral across the plaza. Hence, it was a premier location

rife with visual, physical and contextual complexities.

Moneo's response was to create a very compact structure filling the site from corner to corner, playing with compositional aspects of the neighboring buildings yet presenting it as a decidedly modern, inventively irregular and intriguing component of the setting. Using sandstone with a rose-beige tone, his stately design derives inspiration from the clearly defined windows and open balconies on the palace and the tall, thin columns on the church. Indeed, these features, dramatically transformed into a new vocabulary, become the essence of a four-story, colonnaded plane, asymmetrically divided into openings behind which are porches, glazed walls and the exterior surface of the volumetric core of the building. The bottom two levels provide extreme contrast in the form of a solid, flat expanse of stone pierced by a few deep, dark voids. Despite the utter reductive, geometric character of the facade, it is imbued with a rhythmic, somewhat whimsical flavor.

Skewing the notion and image of a staid block structure even further, Moneo sets the main entrance—a large, cutout opening leading back diagonally to the door—around the corner on Calle de Freneria. Actually, you can enter the City Hall directly from the plaza if you take the stairs on either side of the low, curving wall at the base of the facade. Interestingly, these lead down to a café—a nice touch for the main municipal building.

Rafael Moneo, Murcia City Hall

VALENCIA

This region, known as the "garden of Spain," includes some of the country's most beautiful beaches and coastal landscape. Historically, Valencia has ties to Catalonia, though the fervor to revive Catalan customs and language is not as intense as it is within the province of Catalunya proper. Many signs and public names are increasingly appearing in Catalan, although there is no consistency. Don't be surprised to find maps, brochures and official designations using one or the other language or a combination of both. In an attempt to provide the current reference terms for streets, neighborhoods, museums and the like, the following discussions shift between Castilian and Catalan. Regrettably, this may add to your confusion, especially since more changes will undoubtedly occur by the time of your visit.

Calpe

This seaside resort town along the Costa Blanca has special distinction due to Penyal de Ifach, the striking limestone rock jutting out from the shoreline. Having a physical presence akin to Gibraltar, this immense promontory is now a nature park. Like most all coastal villages on this stretch of the Mediterranean, Calpe is undergoing expansion and urbanization. Though not as overrun with high-rises and paved terrains as its infamous neighbor Benidorm, the evidence of ongoing construction does not bode well.

Train from Murcia (change to "trenet" at Alicante) 2 3/4 hr. Bus (UBESA) from Alicante, 1 1/2 hr, from Valencia, 2 1/2 hr.

Ricardo Bofill's renown as an imaginative postmodern architect of multiunit housing blossomed with the buildings he designed in Calpe. The three residential complexes sit high on cliffs facing the rock of Ifach from the south. Although each is an isolated realm onto itself, Bofill originally conceived them as part of an enclosed Garden of Eden with sports facilities and other amenities. If you have any curiosity about innovative ideas for the organizational structure and design of housing, you'll enjoy an excursion to Calpe.

The three complexes are clustered together in the neighborhood of La Manzanera, located on the hillside adjacent to the old town center. It's not too far to walk from the village (or the UBESA bus stop) if you don't mind a mildly sloping terrain. Head toward Avenida Masnou, the main artery at the southern edge of the old town; at Casa de Cultura (Masnou 1) turn the corner onto Avenida Mare de Deu del Carme; turn right at the end and continue on a set of short curves going around and down. You should see directional signs for the Bofill buildings, or just head for the sprawl of elongated, reddish structures and the olive green chateaulike edifice facing the sea.

Xanadu

architect: Ricardo BOFILL, 1966–68
La Manzanera 2

Using a scale model, Bofill created an experimental prototype for a garden city in space and then constructed it as the building named *Xanadu*—the mythic village of idyllic beauty. The image of a castle lies within but the shape derives from the flat-topped contour of the rock of Ifach. Unlike the solid mass of the rock, however, Bofill's structure is a composite of unaligned cubes stacked, projecting and interconnected around a supporting circulation spine. Windows and patios are positioned to give the best light, ventilation and privacy, and tiled roofs form downward-curving Vs to provide better views.

Many of the 18 apartments are duplexes and all are laid out with an exceedingly compact use of space. Each room (none is very large) is a different cube angled off or atop another with shaded balconies and terraces created by the voids in between.

Ricardo Bofill, *Xanadu*

Unfortunately, the exterior surface of the building has not been well cared for, and the deterioration looks worse than it really is because the original dark olive color has faded to a sickly yellowish tone. The appearance of scaffolds being readied for installation in the spring of 2000 suggests that repair and repainting were finally going to happen.

Bofill had built a private pool for Xanadu, setting it within the sea extending from the beachfront down below. But the government disallowed construction on the shoreline so the pool had to be removed. Now a sandy white beach curves around the bay.

La Muralla Roja

architect: Ricardo BOFILL, 1968–72
La Manzanera 3

The Red Wall is one of Bofill's fantasy designs, so playful and absurd that it's hard to believe people really live in it. Even from a distance the apartment complex stands out and appears decidedly unlike typical housing developments. The red tones emphasize a

Ricardo Bofill, *La Muralla Roja*

Ricardo Bofill, *Anfiteatro*

contrast with the landscape while articulating the attenuated, blocklike towers that constitute the eccentric ensemble. Stairs and some balcony walkways are painted in blue tones, however, to suggest a relationship to the sky. (Though the colors were initially bright, the strong sun has softened them considerably.)

Walking around and through the complex is like entering a labyrinthian set from *Alice in Wonderland*. Winding paths lead to courtyards with disproportionately tall doorways and zigzagging staircases, which in turn lead to patios, apartment entrances, narrow passageways, terraces with spectacular views of the coastline and dead ends. No clear separation between private and public space exists and the various sections are entangled in an all-encompassing web of connections.

As in his source of inspiration—the Mediterranean tradition of the Casbah, where alleys meander through fortresslike aggregates of interlocking units—Bofill has made circulation and spatial relationships the key organizational factors in his housing community. Borrowing a premise from Le Corbusier, he also developed the roof as a terrace. Rather than wasted territory, it becomes a communal area with swimming pool, sauna and solaria.

Anfiteatro

architect: Ricardo BOFILL, 1983–85
La Manzanera 1

Located above the other two Bofill complexes with a gated enclosure ensuring privacy, especially in the back, where the facade is close to the street. If you can't gain entrance via the gate or parking area off to the side, try the path bordered by stone walls leading up from Xanadu.

For the third complex, sited majestically on a promontory over a cliff with prime views of Penyal de Ifach, Bofill borrowed freely from classical architecture, a styling mode he would subsequently adopt for his signature postmodern housing developments in France. *Anfiteatro* is the pinnacle of refined, pristine, upscale vacation living. Twenty-seven luxury duplex apartments, all with a front face to the sea and back face to the street, are arranged in three buildings shaped like a Greek amphitheater around a pool positioned as the stage. The two side units are rectangular, and the third, a semicircular structure, forms a secluded central space, configured as an inclined brick plane with tier seating at the bottom adjoining the pool.

Taking superb advantage of the setting, Bofill opens up interior and exterior spaces to views of the landscape. He also creates dramatic viewpoints by having narrowing passageways, super-tall doorways and steep staircases end abruptly with a framed perspective of the natural surrounds. Minimalized pediments, pilasters and other architectural elements of the classical heritage embellish the white surfaces of the facades, and rich green vegetation adds touches of color and cultivated, natural beauty to the ambience.

Not only is every element conspicuously defined by its material and form, but every inch of space is utilized. Thus, the roofs are sun decks and the area underneath the inclined wall houses shower facilities, locker rooms, storerooms, and a community lounge.

For all its architectural whimsy and obsessive design control, Anfiteatro, like most of Bofill's housing projects, presents a strong challenge to conventional practices regarding multiunit dwellings. If you haven't seen any of his buildings, the three in Calpe offer a good opportunity.

Valencia

Spain's third-largest city ought to be placed high on a list of must-see culture centers. With its quintessentially Mediterranean flair and cosmopolitan character, it is one of the country's hidden secrets. The art scene, in particular, is quite lively, enhanced by many young artists living in the area and students from the university and art schools in the region.

A majority of the important art venues are located in the historic center, roughly bounded by Carrer de Guillem de Castro, Carrer de Colom and the Túria River Gardens. You can easily visit them in a walking circuit that will also take you through the maze of picturesque streets in the old city. For those sites on the periphery or just beyond the center, bus and metro transportation are available and convenient. You can get a list of current exhibitions at the information office in the train station or in the various museums and galleries. Alternatively, check www.turisvalencia.com/paseo/galeria.htm.

If you're not familiar with the extraordinary designs of the engineer-architect-artist Santiago de Calatrava, a Valencian native, here's your chance. Don't miss seeing his buildings in the new City of Arts and Sciences and take a look at Calatrava Bridge. Both are part of urban planning efforts geared to put Valencia on the map as a 21st-century city.

Train from Madrid (Atocha), 3 1/2 hr; from Murcia, 2 hr; from Cuenca, 3 1/4 hr; from Barcelona, 3 hr. Bus from Calpe (UBESA), 2 1/2 hr.

Jardí del Túria

⚰ architect: Ricardo BOFILL, 1981–85

As a means of coming to terms with a chronic problem of flooding, in 1957, after a disaster that caused numerous deaths and widespread destruction, Valencia decided to divert the Túria River away from the city center. In a wise move, the empty riverbed was transformed into a park rather than a superhighway. Forming a long loop all around the northern edge of the old sector and leading to the sea, Túria River Gardens create a leisure-oriented public space within the urban environment. Don't expect lush greenery as you might find in an English garden. You can find a rich garden zone under the Calatrava Bridge and verdant lawns around Palau de la Música, but for the most part, Ricardo Bofill used indigenous trees and native vegetation—pines, cypresses, orange, palm, and olive trees with sand as the ground cover.

The park is actually a sequence of gardens structured in harmony with the riverbed. A pine forest differentiates the zones, which are either nature-based with a particular focus, like the orange grove, or designed for sports, recreation and communal activities, like the soccer and rugby fields, plazas and Gulliver, an amusement park for children. Promenades, jogging and bicycle paths and water motifs (a lake, ponds, streams) further define and diversify the space.

Julio Gonzáles Center

Institut Valencià d'Art Modern, Centre Julio González

🏛 Guillem de Castro 118, 46003
96-386-30-00 f: 392-10-94

📖 www.ivam.es
ivam@ivam.es

Tues–Sun, 10–7, closed Mon
admission: 350/175 ptas; free on Sun

IVAM, as it usually is called, has two components, each located at a separate address. The main building is Centre Julio González, and a few blocks away is Centre del Carme, a space devoted to exhibitions of recent art. Although IVAM is relatively young, having only opened its doors in 1989, it has a formidable exhibition history and firm standing as a respected museum of modern art.

From the outside, Centre Julio González is an imposing, four-story structure with a boxy, modernist appearance. Inside, the austere, icy, empty entrance lobby of dehumanizing proportions does little to welcome or orient you. Off to the right are a bookstore and café. On the left are two of the major exhibition galleries, each with high ceilings and structured as a succession of five rooms with a passage down the central axis. Two more major galleries laid out in the same manner are on the first floor,

which also contains a smaller gallery, library and assembly room. A gallery for drawings lies to the right side of the mezzanine level, and Sala de la Muralla, a long, low, narrow gallery revealing the remains of the medieval wall surrounding Valencia, occupies the basement and has its own entrance around the corner to the right.

The museum's name pays homage to a Catalan artist whose abstract, linear-styled iron sculpture, developed during the 1920s–30s, holds a significant place in the history of modern art. During the late 19th century, González lived in Barcelona and was part of El Quatre Gats, a group of young artists that included Picasso. (See p. 99.) Years later (1928–30), when both were living in Paris, he assisted and collaborated with his famous friend on a group of welded metal sculptures. IVAM owns some 360 sculptures, drawings and paintings by González and devotes the large back gallery on the first floor to him. Unfortunately, the display is pretty monotonous, with objects set atop bland, box pedestals in a harsh, white space with an empty, shabby feel about it. Each sculpture is isolated and there are no informational labels, photographs or comparative and contextual materials. Surely a brochure (or even a video) is warranted for a permanent installation of art by the museum's namesake!

Selections from the rest of IVAM's collection are usually on display in other galleries except when special exhibitions take over all available space. Indeed, the space crunch has become so critical that the museum will soon be adding an annex with galleries specifically for the collection.

No matter how inviting the featured shows may be, be sure to save time to see the collection. It has particular emphases that offer an unorthodox perspective on the history of art from the 1930s to the present. It also includes many top-notch objects. Abstraction, especially modes with constructivist and *informel* (free, spontaneous expression developed in postwar European art) tendencies, and Dada, especially photomontage, are focal aspects of the modernist years. Pop art also has a strong presence, as well as a notable mixture of both European and American artists (e.g., Öyvind Fahlström, Roy Lichtenstein, Claes Oldenburg, Sigmar Polke, Martial Raysse, Gerhard Richter, James Rosenquist, Andy Warhol). This mix continues for objects from the last decades. These include seminal works by John Baldesarri, Georg Baselitz, Christian Boltanski, José Manuel Broto, Tony Cragg, Peter Fischli & David Weiss, Robert Gober, Peter Halley, Georg Herrold, Gary Hill, Cristina Iglesias, Juan Muñoz, Bruce Nauman, Richard Prince, Cindy Sherman, Rosemarie Trockel, Juan Uslé, Gilberto Zorio and many others.

Photography is another central concentration within the collection, and holdings span the entire history of the medium up to the present. Pioneering figures are well represented with choice prints by Berenice Abbott, Eugène Atget, Brassaï, Robert Capa, Walker Evans, Robert Frank, André Kertész, Lisette Model, Irving Penn.

Its collection notwithstanding, IVAM is perhaps best known for its special exhibitions and scholarly catalogues. Whether retrospectives or thematic shows, they look beneath the surface to clarify or shed new light on significant moments in the development of modern art. Sometimes projects deal with mainstream artists; sometimes the names are relatively obscure and unfamiliar. Not only do these exhibitions tend to be very large and comprehensive (a bit more editing would be nice), but typically two or three presented simultaneously. Just walking through all the galleries in IVAM will take a fair amount of time, so plan accordingly. (This is not a sleepy, provincial outpost!)

Recent exhibitions: *Magdalena Abakanowicz, Pierre Alechinsky, Antonio Ballester, Berlin in the 20th Century, Brasil (1920–50), Luis Buñuel, Enric Crous Vidal, Ramón Gaya, Alex Harris, Roy Lichtenstein, Richard Lindner, Lucebert, Manolo Millares, Pierre Molinier, Giorgio Morandi, Filippo de Pisis, Frank Lloyd Wright, José María Yturralde, George Zimbel.*

Complementing the exhibition program are conferences, film series, lectures, concerts and educational workshops. If you have time to browse in the bookshop, you won't be disappointed, since it is nicely stocked with books on modern, contemporary and Spanish art and culture.

Centre del Carme

▨ Museu 2, 46003
96-386-30-00
Tues–Sun, 11–2:30 and 4:30–7; closed Mon
closed during the summer (variable, July–Sept)
admission: free

From IVAM, walk down Carrer Na Jordana (left side of the museum) for three blocks until it ends; turn left and then immediately right into Carrer del Museu. Though it doesn't look like the correct address and lacks prominent signage, the large structure on the corner with a church facade is where you want to be. On entering, walk back and around the cloistered courtyard to the exit on the right

Michael Craig-Martin, installation, 2000

leading into the exhibition space.

This neighborhood, El Carme, is considered to be the most typical of old Valencia. Still showing signs of its bohemian heritage (now ranging from grungy to artsy chic), it is especially lively at night, when music abounds and café tables spill from cubbyhole bars and restaurants into the open air. The cobblestoned streets are narrow with tightly packed dwellings, many of which are dilapidated or in the process of rehabilitation, lining the maze of passageways.

Centre del Carme has a long history within the area, dating back to the 13th century, when it was built as a Carmelite convent. It subsequently acquired a classical Renaissance courtyard and underwent various architectural modifications. Its vast interior spaces, cleared of accouterments but still possessing mammoth sculpted columns, stained-glass windows, high ceilings, side chapel rooms and old stone floors, now serve as IVAM's contemporary art space. It's a friendly, whitewashed, bare, shabby-chic environment quite amenable to large-scale contemporary art, including video, site-specific work and multimedia installations.

Exhibitions here feature known international and emerging local artists in monographic shows. Usually two different artists have exhibitions at the same time. The space is such that you'll pass through a grand hall with many adjacent rooms in the first section and then enter a totally separate section, an equally immense area also containing numerous rooms. The good part is, there's lots of space for artists to play with if they want to develop or show big, multipartite objects. The bad part is, there's too much space for most young, emerging artists who'd be better off in a modest-size gallery exhibiting a choice selection of their best work. All things considered, Carme is a prime setting for contemporary art, and IVAM has used it to great advantage.

Recent exhibitions: *Marco Bagnoli, Juan Navarro Baldeweg, Michael Craig-Martin, Ángel Mateo Charris, Nacho Criado, Günther Förg, Susy Gómez, Francisco Leiro, Manuel Sáez, Philip Taaffe, Terry Winters.*

Sala Parpalló

📠 Centre Cultural La Beneficència
Corona 36, 46003
96-388-35-69 f: 388-35-72
summer: Tues–Sat, 10–2:30 and 5–8;
Sun, 10–8; closed Mon
winter: Tues–Sat, 10–2:30 and 4–8; Sun,
10–8; closed Mon
admission: free

Located on the mezzanine level of the three-story, salmon-colored building running along Carrer de Guillem de Castro adjacent to IVAM. (The entrance is around the corner on Carrer de la Corona.)

Originally constructed as a convent (1538), then used as an almshouse (after 1841), this massive building opened in 1995 as a multidisciplinary cultural center. Aiming to be flexible, it contains various permanent institutions (like the Museums of Ethnology and Prehistory) and accommodates a multitude of concerts, theater productions, conferences and one-night events.

The municipal exhibition space known as Sala Parpalló is one of the established residents in the building. (Parpalló was the name of a group of abstract Valencian painters.) Occupying four large rooms, it shows contemporary art from home and abroad with special attention paid to notable work by young Valencian artists.

Although the institutional character of the setting might suggest a dull, staid program, it is surprisingly receptive to experimental, topical and controversial artwork. It was here, in fact, that a *Robert Mapplethorpe* exhibition, comprising portraits, still lifes and the highly erotic X and Z portfolios, was held in 2000.

Recent exhibitions: *Olga Adelantado, Javia Chapa, Ciber@rt, Equipo Límite, Experimental Cycle of Photography (1992–97), Generation 2000, Leonardo Gómez, Angela Grauerholz, Blasco Ibáñez, Vance Kirkland, Mediterranean Crossroads, Enric Mestre, Photography from the Cuban War, Phototropy, Susana Rodriguez, Christa Sommerer, José Vento.*

Filmoteca de la Generalitat Valenciana

📹 Plaça de l'Ajuntament 17, 46002
🎬 96-351-91-30
daily, shows at 6, 8, 10:30

Located on the northeast side of the city's main plaza, site of the grand 18th-century city hall.

Housed in one of the oldest cinemas in the city, the Filmoteca has a top-notch program of classic films, shorts and documentaries organized in series featuring actors, directors, themes and genres.

La Gallera

📠 Aluders 7, 46001
96-352-14-37
admission: free

Located in the district of El Mercat, just west of the large intersection in the middle of Carrer de Sant Vincent Màrtir (one of the major arteries through the old quarter), where you should turn into Carrer la Llanterna and then turn right at the second street (Aluders).

This is a good place to start a walking tour to the art venues located in the center area of the old city. La Gallera is an exhibition space run by a consortium of museums in the city. It's worth visiting just to see the looks of a building designed in the 19th century for cockfights. As you will discover, the interior is a tall, modest space with two balconies surrounding it at high elevations and brick arches providing a passageway around the center on the ground floor.

Exhibitions in La Gallera are generally site-specific installations. Artists typically take full advantage of the space and develop wondrous, thematic shows with lots of pizzazz.

Recent exhibitions: *Marina Abramovic, Ana Laura Aláez, Helena Cabello, Eugenio Cano, Ana Carceller, Teresa Cebrián, Ricardo Cotanda, José Maldonado, Carmen Michavila, Pedro Ortuño.*

Espai Lucas

Jofrens 6, 46001
tel/fax: 96-391-56-55
Mon–Sat, 10–2 and 5–9

From La Gallera turn left (north) on Carrer de Sant Vicent Màrtir; after the large intersection turn left at the fourth street and make an immediate right into Carrer Jofrens. The gallery is on the left side near the end of this narrow street. Should you end up in Plaça de la Reina, you missed the turn but can enter Carrer Jofrens from its north end, which abuts Plaça Santa Caterina, an extension of the southwest corner of Plaça de la Reina. You may also end up in the circular Plaça Redonda, where stalls selling local products will surely catch your attention. This plaza is just west of Carrer Jofrens, so you can again easily retrace your steps. You're bound to get lost among all the tiny streets (many are pedestrianized), since many are unmarked and all seem to fork off one another and converge in little plazas. Meandering about is half the fun, and ultimately you'll either find your way or discover something completely unexpected.

This compact, split-level space shows video, photography and new media by both young and midcareer artists of varied nationalities and diverse artistic proclivities. In November 1999, for example, Espai Lucas presented *Invocations*, the riveting series of photoserigraphs by the celebrated Australian artist Tracy Moffatt.

Artists: Daniele Buetti, Andrea Fogli, Chelo Matesanz, José Antonio Orts, Günther Selicher.

Galería Visor

Corretgeria 26, 46001
tel/fax: 96-392-23-99
Tues–Sat, 5–9; closed Mon

Walk the length of Plaça de la Reina on the left (west) side and turn left into Carrer Corretgeria just after you pass the dominant garden section of the square.

Begun in 1982, Galería Visor specializes in photography, including large-scale con-temporary photos, mixed media and video projections. Each year the gallery selects a theme as the unifying thread for all its exhibitions. In 1998–99 it was *South American Photography* and in 1999–2000, *Space*. The level of talent is quite high among the gallery artists, so you'll typically see rigorous, imaginative work on display. Bernabeu's eccentric nudes, Valldosera's penetrating photomontage projections concerning sexual identity and Vallhonrat's disturbing, closeup portraits are but a few examples. Exhibitions by photographers not represented by the gallery (e.g., Lynne Cohen, Joan Fontcuberta, Candida Höfer, Vic Muniz) are also a significant part of the annual schedule.

The physical space of Visor is small, but if you're interested, ask to see works by other artists, many of which are stored in the archival files near the front. In addition to functioning as an exhibition space, the gallery teaches courses in a darkroom upstairs. The darkroom walls are used as a second exhibition space for neophyte artists, but it's accessible only on Saturdays when there are no classes in session.

Artists: Margarita Andreu, Gabriele Basilico, Mira Bernabeu, María Bleda & José M. Rosa, Luis Contreras, Mario Cravo Neto, Angustias Garcia & Isaias Griñolo, Flor Garduño, Luis González Palma, Ángel Marcos, Ana Teresa Ortega, Iñigo Royo, Eulàlia Valldosera, Valentin Vallhonrat, Mayte Vieta.

Galería My Name's Lolita Art

Plaça Correu Vell 3, 46001
96-391-98-48 f: 391-13-72
Mon–Sat, 5:30–9

Continue west on Carrer Corretgeria until it intersects with Carrer Calatrava; turn right and then left on Carrer Valencians, which leads into Plaça Correu Vell. The gallery is in the northwest corner of the plaza.

Inaugurated in 1998 as a collective of young Spanish artists, Galería My Name's Lolita Art has continued to show and promote

Mira Bernabeu, *Stories from a Sinister Home,* 2000

the feisty work of artists from Valencia, with splashes from elsewhere. The ambitious zeal of the enterprise led to the opening of a second space in Madrid, and a national presence as a result. The orientation is largely painting, albeit not the abstract variety that's so popular in Spain. Instead, funky and surreal imagery is preponderant.

Artists: Juan Cuéllar, Equipo Límite, Mavi Escamilla, Damián Flores, Ángel Mateo Charris, Joël Mestre, Teresa Moro, Gonzalo Sicre, Jorge Tarazona, Santi Tena, Teresa Tomás, Paco de la Torre.

Almudí

🚉 Plaça Sant Lluis Beltrán 3, 46003
   96-352-54-78, ext. 4521
   Tues–Sat, 9:30–2 and 5:30–9; Sun,
   9:30–2; closed Mon
   admission: free
Located behind the cathedral within a cluster of splendiferous plazas marked by a rich assortment of architectural memorabilia.

From Galería Lolita My Name's Art, head east on Carrer Cavallers; cross Plaça de la Verge and pick up Carrer Almudí on the far side of the square in front of the basilica. The Almudí (Almudín) building is just ahead on the left with its entrance around the corner.

Constructed in the 16th century as a granary to store the city's wheat, this fine old structure was recently renovated for use as an exhibition hall. Since opening in 1996, it has housed a diversity of art exhibitions, including *Constructed Spaces,* a thematic project featuring signature works by Miquel Barceló, Andreas Gursky, Richard Long, Miquel Navarro, Soledad Sevilla and others. Although few shows are on a par with this one, don't overlook this venue as a possible place to see high-powered contemporary art.

You might want to look inside to see the newly restored wall paintings surrounding the main space. They depict scenes of daily life in 16th-century Valencia.

Galería Tomás March

Aparisi i Guijarro 7, 46003
96-392-20-95 f: 391-52-84
www.tomasmarch.com
gtm@wanadoo.es
Tues–Sat, 11–2 and 6–9; closed Mon
Located in La Xerea neighborhood, a short walk (southeast) from Almudí by crossing Plaça Sant Lluis Beltrán and Plaça Sant Esteve, going down Carrer Baro Petrés and then skirting the top of Plaça Nàpols i Sicília, exiting off to the left into Aparisi i Guijarro.

Galería Tomás March occupies an industrial workshop on the ground floor of a 17th–18th century building in an attractive residential area. Now that the space has been superbly renovated, there's a roomy display area in front extending back to an expansive area in back covered by a pitched-roof skylight. It's a stunning setting for art, and the installations, paintings and photographs shown in it seem all the more impressive.

The gallery program focuses on venturesome young artists and painters from the 1980s–90s generation. Most all are Spanish, though exhibitions of foreign artists occur periodically. This is not to say that the gallery is insular. Tomás March, who energetically supports and takes pride in his artists, is a well-respected figure and major player in the international art scene. He and his staff are also very receptive and informed about local and national things art-wise, so should you have questions, this is the place to get answers.

If you want to expand your horizons and don't know the names Federico Guzmán and Mabel Palacín, ask to see catalogues or examples of their compelling work.

Artists represented by the gallery: Rafael Agredano, Antonio Doménech, Yamandú Canosa, Ricardo Cotanda, José Gallego, Curro González, Federico Guzmán, Also Iacobelli, Xisco Mensua, Mau Monleón, Begoña Montalbán, Alberto Peral, Concha Prada, Pedro G. Romero, Gerardo Sigler, Tanja Smit, Ian Wallace. Artists exhibiting regularly: Javier Baldeón, Patricio Cabrera,

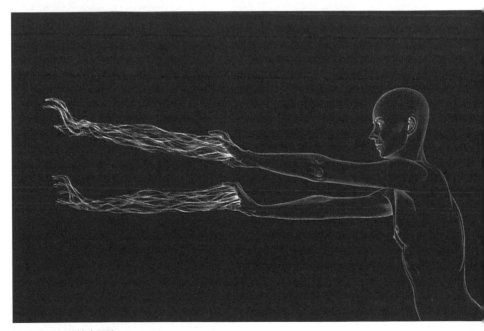

Marina Nuñez, Untitled, 2000

Miquel Ángel Campano, Luis Claramunt, Rogelio López Cuenca, Abraham Lacalle, Mireya Masó, Marina Nuñez, Mabel Palacín, Simeón Saiz Ruiz, José María Sicilia, Juan Ugalde.

Galería Ray Gun

🖵 Bretón de les Herreros 4, 46003
tel/fax: 96-352-32-93
www.galeriaraygun.com
correo@galeriaraygun.com
Mon–Sat, 10:30–1 and 6–9
From Galería Tómas March, turn left on Aparisi i Guijarro and right at the first corner onto Carrer Vell Governador; continue until it ends at Carrer de la Mar; turn left for one block and you'll be at Bretón de les Herreros; turn right and the gallery will be immediately on the left side of the street.

Begun in 1989 as a gallery intent on promoting emerging artists, Ray Gun is still presenting tough, at times zany, or at least unorthodox art. Nothing is sacred here and virtually any and all mediums, subject matter and conceptual approaches are free game for creative expression. Current trends are well represented, often in derivative variants but occasionally in trailblazing directions. The provocative disco installation of Ana Laura Aláez at Reina Sofía (2000) was the talk of the Spanish art world, so you might want to look at the gallery's documentation of her work and perhaps see some objects that might be on hand.

Artists: Ana Laura Aláez, Lara Almarcegui, Rodolphe Auté, Juan Pablo Ballester, Anne Deguelle, Jean Fléaca, Patricia Gadea, Alfonso Gortázar, Catherine Howe, Jarbas Lopes, Enrique Marty, Carmen Morales, Joana Pimentel.

Juan Pablo Ballester, *Nowhere*, 1999

Galería Luis Adelantado

🖵 Bonaire 6, 46003
96-351-01-79 f: 353-20-09
www.galerialuisadelantado.com
mail@galerialuisadelantado.com
Mon–Sat, 10–2 and 5–9
Located just down the street from Galería Ray Gun. The street name changes to Carrer Bonaire after you cross Carrer de la Pau; the gallery is just ahead on the right side.

With its Madison Avenue–chic architec-

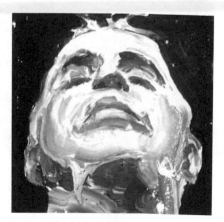

Santiago Ydáñez, Untitled, 2000

ture—five floors of exhibition space around a central atrium—and its high-profile program, this is a gallery you won't want to miss. Spanish painters are a mainstay, but the gallery also shows young upstarts working with body and identity transformation issues in photography and performance-based art. These artists (e.g., Calvo, Codesal, Congost, Francés, Pérez Bravo, Soto, Sourrouille, de la Torre, Ydáñez) may not be widely known yet, but their work is engaging and well worth seeing.

After viewing the main exhibition, be sure to visit the top floor, where you'll see a display of various gallery artists. Here as on the other floors, the sequence of intimate spaces with one painting or object per wall enables the luxury of directed concentration.

Artists: Emilia Azcárate, Sergio Barrera, Pedro Calapez, Sophie Calle, Carmen Calvo, Javier Codesal, Carles Congost, Álex Francés, Juan González, Eva Lootz, Miguel Mont, Juan Navarro Baldeweg, José Noguero, Marta Pérez Bravo, Gabriel Perezzan, Charo Pradas, Montserrat Soto, Eduardo Sourrouille, Milagros de la Torre, Dario Villalba, Santiago Ydáñez, Gilberto Zorio.

In addition to the regular fare of single-artist exhibitions, the gallery organizes some group shows, like the recent *Five Visions of the Body* and *The Other Side*. Catalogues accompany each exhibit, and original works of limited edition produced by the gallery are also available.

Pont de Calatrava

architect: Santiago CALATRAVA, 1991–95

Return to Carrer de la Pau and turn right (east); continue as the road curves around to the right in front of Palau de Justícia; go halfway around the traffic circle, to Plaça Porta de la Mar; just ahead is the Túria River Gardens and Calatrava Bridge.

This bridge is variously referred to as Pont

Carles Congost, *The Story of Grains,* 2000

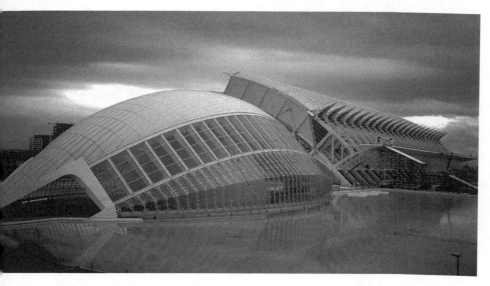

Santiago Calatrava, Hemisféric

Alameda, Pont de Calatrava and Pont de l'Exposició and commonly called "La Peineta" because the bridge's image resembles the Spanish ornamental comb (*peineta*). It connects the old city with the university quarter, crossing the riverbed with a striking, white steel structure. Unlike the traditional stone bridges in the city or classic suspension spans, the engineer-architect Santiago Calatrava created an inclined arch bridge whose asymmetrical design is both graceful and distinctive. Here, as in his other projects, he has used modern technology as a means to invent new forms and alternative support systems.

Cuitat de les Artes y les Ciències

architect: Santiago CALATRAVA, 1991–
Avinguda del Saler, 46013
96-352-55-07 f: 352-60-23
www.cac.es
bus 13, 14, 15
Located at the south end of the Túria River Gardens.
If for no other reason, go to Valencia to see

the mind-boggling, breathtaking buildings designed by Santiago Calatrava for the new City of Arts and Sciences (CAC). Like Frank Gehry's Guggenheim Museum in Bilbao, the surging, imaginative forms and wondrously engineered structures, which are as much sculpture as architecture, capture your attention from first glance to last. Indeed, the more you walk around and get different perspectives, the more incredible they seem. What's more, each building is individually distinctive yet all fit harmoniously together.

CAC radically transformed what was formerly an abandoned, peripheral sector of the city into a prideful, urban centerpiece. With one fell swoop, moreover, it catapulted Valencia into the 21st century. Not only is the 90-acre complex featuring four major activity centers (three of which are by Calatrava) visually intriguing, but its combination of urban recreation park, education and entertainment center is conceptually advanced.

L'Hemisfèric

architect: Santiago CALATRAVA, 1998
Avinguda del Saler, 46013
90-210-00-31
www.cac.es
Mon–Thurs, 10:30–8; Fri, 10:30 am– 11 pm; Sat, 12–11; Sun, 12–8
admission: 1100/800 ptas
bus 13, 14, 15

L'Hemisfèric (Planetarium) opened in 1998, inaugurating the CAC and revealing the ingenious nature of Calatrava's architecture. Shaped like an arched pod with a semispherical dome housed inside, its white concrete and transparent glass form is seductive and futuristic. The image resembles a giant eye, a metaphor Calatrava reinforced by engineering the glazed wall along the base as a gate that slowly folds, hence opening and closing like an eyelid; by positioning a row of long, vertical mullions above the eyelid-gate to suggest lashes; and by surrounding the whole structure with a shallow pool so that the reflection completes the contours of a full pupil and eye.

Equipped with state-of-the-art audiovisual systems, the dome serves as a planetarium, IMAX theater for films and laserium for light shows.

Museu de les Ciències Príncipe Felipe

architect: Santiago CALATRAVA, 2000
Avinguda del Saler, 46013
96-316-24-40 f: 316-24-56
www.cac.es
Mon–Fri, 10–8; Sat–Sun, 10–9
admission: 1000/700 ptas
bus 13, 14, 15

This is one of the new breed of science museums that have interactive, experiential displays geared toward arousing curiosity and enabling the discovery of ideas. Technology has star billing on a par with science, and special focus is given to hot topics like the human genome, prediction of natural phenomena and structure of the universe.

The spacious, hangarlike interior has an array of platforms suspended from a

Santiago Calatrava, Prince Filipe Museum of Sciences

structural system conceived by Calatrava as large concrete trees whose branches support the roof. An inclined facade of glass runs along the north side, shielding a public zone called Carrer Major (Main Street). Joined to it on the opposite side is a sloped aluminum roof bordered at both ends by projecting fins. Following his signature style Calatrava has whitened the reinforced concrete and steel but added no decorative elements to the surfaces. Spatial and structural dynamics in and of themselves produce a majestic, sensorial ambience even as they creatively accommodate functional requirements.

Palau de les Artes

architect: Santiago CALATRAVA
Avinguda del Saler, 46013
www.cac.es
bus 13, 14, 15

The building located at the northwest end of CAC is a center for music and the performing arts. Shaped like a multidecked ocean liner

set inside a volumetric, quadruple boomerang frame, which is in turn capped by a fish-spine arch, this edifice is yet another of Calatrava's unbelievably spectacular designs. Though often referred to as the Opera House, it in fact contains three auditoria of varying sizes meant to accommodate all sorts of music, dance and theater events.

If all goes according to schedule, the building will open in 2003.

L'Oceanogràfic

architect: Félix CANDELA, 2000–
Camí de les Moreres, 46013
www.cac.es
bus 13, 14, 15

Oceanographic Park covers a vast area at the eastern end of CAC. The setting includes a large lake, lagoons, play areas and an underwater city comprising re-creations of the most noteworthy marine ecosystems in the world—the Atlantic Ocean, Arctic Ocean, Tropical and Temperate Seas, Dolphinium. These aquaria are visible

Norman Foster, Convention Center

from underwater towers interconnected above ground by floating footbridges and landscaped walkways and below ground by glass-enclosed corridors and ramps. A main reception tower and restaurant, the two key architectural structures within the park, feature the trademark hyperbolic paraboloid ("hypar") roofs developed by Félix Candela. Most dramatic is the floating rosette of eight thin-walled lobes rising up in the center of the lake. It's actually the entrance to the underwater restaurant whose glazed walls give direct visual access to the various fish habitats.

Pont de Montolivet

architect: Santiago CALATRAVA, 1986–89

This combination road bridge and pedestrian walkway runs through CAC between the Palace of the Arts and Planetarium, crossing over a proposed lake and park. The flat spans are vertically defined by alignments of lampposts down the center and by winglike forms set atop cone-shaped columns at the ends of the bridge.

Palau de Congressos

architect: Norman FOSTER, 1998
Avinguda de les Corts Valencianes 60, 46015
96-317-94-00 f: 317-94-01
metro: Palau de Congressos

Located in the northwest outskirts of the city, Valencia's Convention Center was the focal point of urban development for the area. A smattering of new buildings, a park and transportation routes were added, but the landscape is still pretty desolate, fringed with patches of dilapidated houses and dirt roads.

Isolated and quite distinctive from its surroundings is Norman Foster's sleek, 1990s architecture defined by two long, curving facades and a floating aluminum roof that rises up and extends in front like a peaked visor on a baseball cap. The gigantic entrance canopy also accentuates the shape of the building, described as a shimmering fish.

Housing three technologically advanced auditoria of varying sizes (1,463, 468 and 250 seats), nine conference rooms, an exhibition hall, banquet facilities and a café, Valencia's Convention Center has become one of the most popular sites in Europe for business meetings and trade shows. The main foyer, which runs the length of the east facade, adds great appeal to the building. Its outer wall, sheathed in glass but sun-protected, bathes the interior in natural light and opens onto an open-air terrace. Shallow pools, water-jet fountains, trees and ground-cover plants, which make up the well-tended landscape around the exterior, suggest the Mediterranean setting even as they differentiate this plot of land from its neighborhood.

Castelló

The Catalan name Castelló is becoming more common than the Castilian name Castellon, and often the full name Castelló (Castellon) de la Plana is used. Train from Valencia, 45 min; from Barcelona, 2 1/4 hr.

Espai d'Art Contemporani de Castelló

Carrer Prim, 12003
96-472-35-40 f: 426-07-71
eacc@culturalcas.com
Tues–Sun, 11–8; closed Mon
admission: free

There's good reason to plan a stop in Castelló if you're on Spain's Mediterranean coast: the new Contemporary Art Space of Castelló (EACC). This exhibition center has been relatively overlooked by the international press, though it warrants front-page attention. In contrast to a program of monographic, "star-artist" shows, the reigning fare in virtually all museums and exhibition spaces, EACC presents thematic exhibitions that set top-notch exemplars of recent art within a compelling context. These are not megaprojects, just reasonably sized, well-crafted gems.

Aesthetic issues are seen as part of the cultural, social and ideological questioning of the current era, and different artistic approaches are linked rather than categorized separately by style, medium or ostensible subject matter. Works by well-known and less-familiar names, international and local artists converge on the same playing field, revealing a provocative relatedness to the theme at hand. Indeed, the thematic context and intermix of the objects often challenge existing ideas about a particular work or artist even as they suggest totally new, unexpected responses to broader issues. All this without placing art in the service of an imposed curatorial idea or simplistic interpretation!

If this seems too good to be true, just consider, even abstractly, the following makeup of two recent exhibitions: *The Eternal Instant* (winter 2001)—Marina Abramovic & Ulay, Joseph Beuys, James Lee Byars, Walter de Maria, Mona Hatoum, Wolfgang Laib, Ana Mendieta, Gina Pane, Antoni Tàpies, Bill Viola; and *Zone F: An Approach to the Spaces Inhabited by Feminist Discourses in Contemporary Art* (spring 2000)—Eija-Liisa Ahtila, Nicole Eisenman, Alicia Framis, Jim Hodges, Jac Leirner, Sarah Lucas, Yasumasa Morimura, Marina Nuñez, Jane & Louise Wilson.

Other recent exhibitions: *Against Architecture, Apparent Movement—The Cinematic Experience, Hypertronix—Fictionalizations in Youth (Sub)Culture, The Power of Narration, Images of Violence in Contemporary Art, Places of Memory, Suspended Time.*

A large, wide-open, double-height hall serves as the main gallery at EACC. Running down the middle, an island with an upper-level balcony provides a more intimate setting for photographs, small objects, videos and a reading area.

In line with its multidisciplinary approach, the center has an impressive cultural and educational program of films, performances, concerts, lectures, conferences and special events. It also publishes excellent catalogues, typically containing two essays presenting different points of view on the same subject. (Texts are in Catalan, Castilian and English.)

Txomin Badiola, *LM&SP (A Man of Few Morals and Some Persuasion)*, 1998, in *Hypertronix* exhibition, 1999

Espai d'Art Contemporani de Castelló

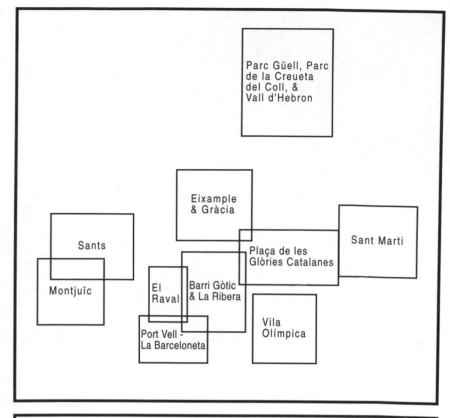

Parc Güell, Parc de la Creueta del Coll, & Vall d'Hebron

Eixample & Gràcia

Sant Marti

Sants

Plaça de les Glòries Catalanes

Montjuïc

El Raval

Barri Gòtic & La Ribera

Vila Olímpica

Port Vell - La Barceloneta

Barcelona Metro

BARCELONA

This is one of the world's most charming, lively cities. Echos of Paris abound, in the prevalence of croissants, baguettes, sidewalk cafés, tree-lined avenues and cultural flair. But here people are outgoing and hospitable, and pets are more likely to be Great Danes and English sheepdogs rather than miniature poodles. Don't be surprised to find throngs of people, both locals and foreigners, at the popular sites, in shops and on the boulevards, no matter what time of day or night, no matter what day of the year.

Despite the crowds, the city is very livable and tourist-friendly with informational signage and telephones everywhere you turn. Metro and bus systems are efficient and extensive, though pedestrianized zones and esplanades with public benches make walking a delight. Just pay extra attention to the traffic lights because cars won't stop if you cross when they have the right of way.

Now that almost all the old buildings in the city have been cleaned of a century's worth of soot and grime, the city looks dazzling. Stone facades no longer are shades of charcoal but rose, orange and yellow tones. And those charming wrought-iron balconies so prominently depicted in paintings by Goya are again visible. It seems everyone has gotten into the act of giving the city a facelift, for even old car repair and service garages are ultra-tidy with shiny tile floors.

URBAN PLANNING Since the mid-1980s ambitious urban planning and regeneration efforts have dramatically transformed the city. So successful have they been that the results, now known as the "Barcelona model," have won numerous awards and are widely emulated. By incorporating economic, cultural, social and environmental factors into the design projects, the plans attacked many fronts at once and produced integrated solutions. The key directives were: opening the city to the sea and recovering the waterfront; restoring and pedestrianizing the historical city center; constructing countless public spaces; paying careful and coherent attention to the development of urban furniture, micro-architecture and other subsidiary elements.

After the death of Franco, Barcelona, like other cities, engaged in a rash of construction and rehabilitation projects lacking a schema of real reform. The situation changed when the 1992 Olympic Games triggered a major building campaign and a succession of comprehensive, strategic master plans. Under the direction of Oriol BOHIGAS, the city began developing infrastructure systems and civic edifices designed by some of the most innovative, prestigious architects in the world. Instead of clustering the new cultural and public buildings in the center-city area, they were dispersed around as a means of upgrading the most derelict areas and giving outer districts a point of distinction and identity. Functioning as magnets, these buildings were to draw people together and improve the quality of life. New parks, pedestrian boulevards, plazas and public art served similar ends while also adding leisure and green zones, especially in high-density housing and office areas.

Significantly, all the construction done specifically for the Olympic Games was geared to broader city needs and a long-lasting revitalization. Not only did the surge of activity yield an amazing change in Barcelona's appearance and outlook, but it laid the groundwork for ongoing public initiatives and a commitment to high-quality design in the post-Olympic years.

PUBLIC ART As part of the urban development spearheaded by the Olympic Games, Barcelona commissioned numerous works of public art for plazas and parks. Here, too, these were placed in various neighborhoods throughout the city. Big-name artists were chosen and a stream of high-profile projects resulted. Unfortunately, the initial burst of energy (and money) dissipated after the Olympics. Few works have been added in the past decade, and the caliber of art has shifted to a lower level. Although the city budget includes funds for maintenance, many objects are in need of conservation work, and most would profit by having a label identifying the artist's name, title and date.

A R T I C K E T This pass provides half-price admission to six of Barcelona's major museums and art centers: Museu Nacional d'Art de Catalunya, Fundació Miró, Fundació Antoni Tàpies, Centre de Cultura Contemporània de Barcelona, Centre Cultural Caixa Catalunya, Museu d'Art Contemporani de Barcelona. You can order it in advance or buy it at the museums or branches of the Caixa Catalunya bank. 93-479-99-22, www.telentrada.com. It's a great deal!

C U R R E N T A R T L I S T I N G S Guia del Ocio (125 ptas) is an inexpensive weekly (sold at the news kiosks) listing most of the ongoing exhibitions and special events. In addition, various small brochures and calendars are available for free in museums, exhibition spaces and galleries. A good place to find these is at the reception desk in Palau de la Virreina. For on-line reference, see www.artbarcelona.es and www.bcn.es.

Barcelona Metròpolis Mediterrània (B.MM) is a bimonthly, glossy magazine (450 ptas) with excellent coverage of contemporary culture. Each issue is devoted to a specific theme, and articles and topics focus on history, design, architecture, music, art, literature, photography, social science, theater, dance, urbanism and cinema.

The best Internet information about current art exhibitions is at www.bcn.es, www.artbarcelona.es and www.estrelladigital.es/Cartelera/paginas/arte_barcelona.htm.

A R T F A I R S Barcelona is a big festival city. In additional to specific art-related gatherings, citywide theme events, which take place throughout the year, often have an arts component.

New Art Barcelona, an annual art fair held during a weekend in late November, has been building momentum since its inauguration in 1996. Some 50 galleries are represented and the focus is on young artists. Like the Grammercy Park Fair that began the hotel-fair idea, this one takes place in Hotel Barceló Sants (above Sants railroad station) with each gallery situated in a different guest room. Most of the galleries are from Spain, though a few from Holland, Canada and other countries also participate. (See www.artbarcelona.es/newart.htm.)

La Primavera Fotogràfica has taken place in Barcelona every other spring since 1982. Nearly all galleries, museums and art centers present photography exhibitions during the designated period, and all sorts of events and activities occur. Artists from all over the world, young and established, are given shows, often making their first appearance in Spain. You can check specifics at www.artplus.es/primaverafotografica.

The International Design Festival of Barcelona is a biennial spring event (in odd-numbered years) promoting the city's status as a world-class design center. See www.bcndesign.org.

Sònar, the International Festival of Avant-Garde Music and Multimedia Art, has become an annual Barcelona event since 1994. Organized as a power-packed affair lasting three days and three nights (usually in mid-June), it comprises over 250 activities, 50 concerts and lots more.

S P E C I A L C E L E B R A T I O N The year 2002 has been declared "The Year of Gaudí" in honor of the 150th anniversary of his birth. The celebration will focus on the achievements and creations of this renowned, Catalan artist-architect and on Modernisme, the style with which he is identified. This style, the Spanish version of Art Nouveau, flourished in Barcelona during a period of prosperity in the late 19th and early

20th centuries when middle-class patrons commissioned numerous building projects.

CATALAN   Within Barcelona and the province of Catalunya, the preferred and nearly omnipresent language is Catalan. You'll see it used exclusively in many public signs and written materials, and you'll commonly hear it spoken on the streets and in official realms. The language shares similarities with both Castilian Spanish and French. Most art centers and museums have signage and brochures in Catalan and Castilian. A few have English translations of labels and informational texts, but they may not be readily available. It's always best to ask at the reception desk.

Airport Terminal

architect: Ricardo BOFILL, 1992
El Prat de Llobregat

If you haven't arrived in Barcelona by air and want to see Bofill's design, it's only a short distance (6 mi) from the city with a direct train (RENFE) connection.

For the Olympics, the existing terminal, built in 1968 and decorated with a ceramic mural by Joan MIRÓ, was remodeled and expanded with the addition of two massive buildings. Bofill unified the old with the new by aligning the three buildings and connecting them with a long, glazed esplanade.

On the exterior, Bofill's terminal appears to be an utterly modern building, a steel frame sheathed with a smooth skin of dark glass. This ambience recurs on the interior, where all the shops, restaurants, kiosks and other services occupy freestanding structures clad in glass or white stone. True to his character, Bofill combines his techno-modern design with oversize classical columns and other decorative features from the past. There are also tall, precisely shaped palm trees positioned to emphasize the square configuration of spaces.

Ciutat Vella

The Old City stretches from the Barcelona's main square, Plaça de Catalunya, down to the ports. Cutting through the center of this area is the popular attraction, La Rambla—actually a mile-long sequence of five individually named *ramblas,* or boulevards. Lined with historic buildings, hotels, shops and restaurants and enhanced by a tree-lined median strip punctuated by talented mimes, lively musicians, newsstands, flower and bird vendors, it's invariably crowded day and night, weekday and weekend.

Ciutat Vella is an irregular labyrinth of narrow, winding streets, back alleys, occasional open spaces and a few large plazas. In this historically rich, incredibly diverse and unbelievably compact district, aristocratic residences mix with bourgeois and working class housing; modern merchants and traditional craftspeople occupy neighboring storefronts; and bohemian, government, office and cultural sectors abut squalid slums. In the late 19th and 20th centuries, many artists lived in this part of Barcelona. Urban renewal efforts, particularly the major transformation of the old shipyards and industrial ports into a leisure and shopping complex, displaced them to Poblenou and other low-rent areas on the outskirts of downtown.

Within the Old City, the zone to the west of La Rambla is called El Raval; the zone between La Rambla and Via Laetana is Barri Gòtic; and the easternmost zone from Via Laietana to Parc Ciutadella is La Ribera.

El Raval

Large pockets of El Raval are still in need of major renewal work. Especially the section known as Barri Xinès (Chinese Quarter, named by a local journalist owing to its resemblance to San Francisco's Chinatown as seen in a 1920s film) is still a seedy district, where congested streets are filled with dingy bars, low-grade shops of indeterminate nature,

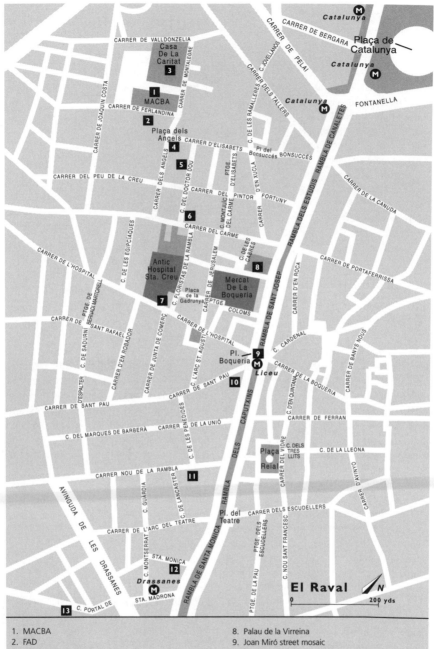

El Raval

0   200 yds

1. MACBA
2. FAD
3. CCCB
4. Galería Ferrán Cano
5. Galería Cotthem
6. La Xina Art
7. La Capella

8. Palau de la Virreina
9. Joan Miró street mosaic
10. El Liceu
11. Palau Güell
12. Centre d'Art Santa Mònica
13. Fernando Boteró sculpture

drug dealers, delinquents and prostitutes standing in doorways. Don't write off El Raval or Barri Xinès (the neighborhood below Carrer de Sant Pau), however. If you do, you'll miss some important art sites, not to mention La Boqueria—a classic farmer's market—or the multitude of cabarets offering some of the best music reviews and comedy entertainment in the city.

1 Museu d'Art Contemporani (MACBA)

architect: Richard MEIER, 1990–95
Plaça dels Àngels 1, 08001
93-412-08-10 f: 412-46-02
www.macba.es
macba@macba.es
Mon, Wed–Fri, 11–7:30; Sat, 10–8; Sun, 10–3; closed Tues
summer: Mon, Wed, Fri, 11–8; Thurs, 11–9:30; Sat, 10–8; Sun, 10–3; closed Tues

admission: 800/400 ptas; Wed, 400 ptas
metro: Catalunya, Universitat
From Plaça de Catalunya go down Rambla Canaletes and turn right (west) onto Carrer Bonsuccés, whose name changes to Plaça Bonsuccés and then Carrer d'Elisabets. The street ends in a small square, Plaça dels Àngels, that hooks around to the right and opens into a paved field in front of a long, white building. A 5-min walk.

This area was formerly dominated by a cluster of run-down institutional buildings occupied by convents, orphanages, hospitals and schools. Slum dwellings and poverty were (and to a somewhat lesser extent still are) also everywhere to be seen. A comprehensive renovation plan for the northern sector of the Raval district centered on the creation of Plaça dels Àngels. It was conceived as the nucleus of a new cultural hub, with Museu d'Art Contemporani, known as MACBA, as the crown jewel. The demolition of a section

Richard Meier, MACBA, 1990–95

of an old monastic enclave, Casa de la Caritat, freed up the necessary plot of land in the midst of the densely packed neighborhood.

The contrast between new and old could not be more stark. According to the critic Peter Buchanan, the utter detachment of the museum from its environs is disastrous: "The new plaza is treated as a void from which to view the haughty new building, which is uncontaminated by context, or good urban manners—a startling departure in a setting so heavy with history." But others view the classical museum as "a beacon of white perfection," praising it for bringing order and light to a dark, congested area.

Richard Meier, the world-renowned American architect, officially began the project in 1988. Since there was no museum director, collection or exhibition program in place throughout much of the planning and construction phases, he had to proceed on an "as if" basis. The building's design was oriented to a contemporary museum but premised on a hypothetical institution whose specific nature and activities were yet to be defined and the subject of considerable debate. (As a consortium of three entities—the City Council, Regional Council and MACBA Foundation, composed of corporations and businesspeople—the museum responds to political, financial and cultural interests not always in unison.)

A ramp runs parallel to the facade leading to the public entrance positioned off-center on the left. The main doorway is not extremely obvious, but a foregrounded, hovering large wall, punctuated by cutouts and a projecting balcony, denotes its location. As a counterbalance, a curvilinear, windowless tower raised off the ground adds an eccentric, volumetric form to the right front of the building. In the middle, an open grid of horizontal sun screens emphasizes the long, sweeping expanse of the museum. The dazzling whiteness of the whole, the enameled aluminum panels that sheath most of the exterior and the complex articulation of surfaces and voids are hallmarks of Meier's architecture.

To the left of the entrance, a curved passage connects the plaza with a delightful rear garden, which in turn merges with the back patio of MACBA's neighbor, the contemporary culture center known as CCCB (see below). The museum's office wing, with a gift-bookshop and café-restaurant on the ground floor, is located on the far side of the passage.

Before going inside, take notice of the black-and-white tile painting by Eduardo CHILLIDA (*Barcelona*, 1998) on the wall facing the museum at the west end of the plaza. It's a classic example of this artist's work, showing his proclivity for bold, flat, rectangular shapes, a few rhythmically positioned void spaces and a contrasting circular detail. The austerity of the abstraction is especially dramatic due to its utter contrast with the variegated clutter in the street and the buildings just behind.

Like Chillida, Jorge OTEIZA, whose sculpture *La Ola* (*Wave*, 1998) is located on

MACBA (atrium)

the platform in front of the museum, is one of the country's foremost artists. Revered for having kept modernism alive during the Franco years, his work influenced several generations. This object typifies his creation of complex geometric shapes by cutting away corners of a simple cube. The resemblance to crystalline rock formations is perhaps not so surprising since Oteiza comes from the Basque region, where high, amazingly faceted cliffs are common.

Having whetted your appetite with the exterior displays of art and architecture, it's time to go inside. From the entrance door you weave through a curving corridor to a cylindrical reception area with a glazed wall looking onto the back garden. You then double back toward the front to arrive at the atrium lobby. Meier aimed to simulate the labyrinthian pathways of Ciutat Vella by this entrance route. He reinforced the association by designing a crisscrossing ramp as the dominant feature in the long, narrow, three-story-high lobby. Complementing this on the opposite side of the atrium are balcony-like walkways with glass-brick floors. Like the exterior, the interior is dazzling white. Here, too, cutout and planar components accentuate the surfaces even as they produce spatial complexity.

The windowed south facade behind the ramp floods the space with natural light, another hallmark of Meier's architecture. Since intense, direct sunlight is a conservation nightmare for most artwork, the atrium is an architectural showpiece and circulation area rather than a display space. This is the case in some of the most interesting museums built in the past few decades. Such bravado in the design of lobbies has become acceptable, if not desirable, as a lure to the public. The situation becomes problematic, however, when architecture has primacy over art in the galleries. This is not the case in MACBA, where Meier has walled off the main galleries from the sunlit lobby, constructing them as ample, flexible, nearly windowless spaces. They are hardly a boring sequence of boxy

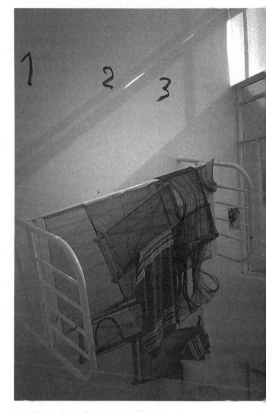

Antoni Tàpies, *Rinzen* (installation detail), 1903

rooms, however. Double-height ceilings, interspersed light wells, room dividers, enclosed areas and wide-open spaces vary the layout.

Utter divergence from the museum's basic form as a rectangular block also occurs thanks to an eccentric two-story-high gallery inside the curvy tower in the southeast corner (conducive to site-specific projects and video projections) and a spacious cylindrical gallery on the middle and top floors.

The ground-floor galleries usually contain selections from the permanent collection and the two upper floors are generally used for temporary exhibitions. A more intimate exhibition space at the west end of the atrium on the middle floor is particularly suited to works on paper or small objects. Don't overlook the nearby staircase tower

Beat Streuli, *Plaça dels Angels*, 1977–88

where a zany assemblage by Antoni TÀPIES (1993) is installed. *Rinzen*—the Japanese word for "sudden awakening, enlightenment"—sprawls across a lobby-to-roof wall with a detour outside to an adjoining terrace.

Collection exhibitions change several times a year with extensive displays occurring during the summer months. As one might expect for a collection developed at the tail end of the 20th century in a country isolated until recently from vanguard developments until recently, the museum's holdings are modest. They include some excellent works from the 1980s and 1990s by such high-profile international artists as Vito Acconci, Jean-Michel Basquiat, Joseph Beuys, Christian Boltanski, Marcel Broodthaers, James Lee Byars, Francesco Clemente, William Kentridge, Anselm Kiefer, Richard Long, Mario Merz, Bruce Nauman, Tony Oursler, Michelangelo Pistoletto, Sigmar Polke, Robert Rausch-enberg, Dieter Roth, David Salle, Jana Serbak, Rosemarie Trockel, Jeff Wall, Gilberto Zorio. Representation of established and young Spanish artists, the dominant thrust of the

collection, is also strong with quality works by Pep Agut, Miquel Barceló, José Manuel Broto, Jordi Colomer, Pepe Espalíu, Luis Gordillo, Perejaume, Joan Hernández Pijuan, Juan Muñoz, José María Sicilia, Susana Solano, Juan Uslé, Zush. The mix between traditional mediums, installation and video is appealing, and the inclusion of midcentury Catalan precedents—particularly the objects from Dau al Set, a post-surrealist, Barcelona group—adds a nice touch of historical context to the collection.

Special exhibitions at MACBA range from *El Lissitzky*, a retrospective of an important, influential modernist, to *Artificial: Contemporary Figurations*, a group show featuring works by Maurizio Cattelan, Thomas Demand, Damien Hirst, Charles Ray, Thomas Ruff and other daring trendsetters. Typically there are three temporary exhibitions going on simultaneously in addition to displays in the collection galleries. They tend to be major projects comprising a multitude of well-chosen objects. They are accompanied by praiseworthy catalogues, free pamphlets or gallery cards (available in Catalan, Castilian and English), an education room with related books and materials, conferences, lectures, films and music events.

Clearly MACBA is still a work in progress, not yet certain of its character and direction. A more vanguard orientation, including the presentation of emerging artists, may emerge (as rumored) once the programs of the new director (appointed in late 1999) take hold.

Recent exhibitions: *Dau al Set, Tacita Dean, Rineke Dijkstra, Fischli & Weiss, Luis Gordillo, Raymond Hains, Gary Hill, Thomas Hirschhorn, William Kentridge, Perejaume, Pere Portabella, The Prinzhorn Collection, Albert Ràfols-Casamada, Gerhard Richter, Martha Rosler, Dieter Roth, Susana Solano, Philippe Thomas, The Un-Private House, Zush.*

2 FAD

▱ Plaça dels Àngels, 5–6, 08001
   93-443-75-20
   Mon–Thurs, 9:30–8; Fri, 9:30–1:30;
   closed Sat
   admission: free
   metro: Catalunya, Universitat
Located across the plaza from MACBA

FAD (Fomento de les Artes Decorativas) is a conglomerate of professional associations dating back to 1903 and dedicated to debate and reflection about, activity related to, and the promotion of design. The term "design" is used in its most comprehensive sense. It embraces fashion, graphic, interior, industrial and audiovisual design as well as the realms of architecture, advertising, illustration, photography, furniture, cuisine, craft, theater and jewelry.

Located in the restored and modernized Convent dels Àngels, FAD presents a diverse range of exhibitions and public activities in the open space on the ground floor and in the auditorium. The upper floors contain offices and meeting rooms. Discussions about converting half of the ground floor into a restaurant and expanding the exhibition space were prevalent in 1999–2000, so

don't be surprised if the layout is different when you visit.

Exhibitions often include models and sketches for chic, experimental, eccentric, wildly imaginative and futuristic objects and ideas. The contents fall anywhere within the full gamut of design possibilities. Though shows may be extremely informal, if not utterly haphazard, with displays lying on the ground or pinned to any available surfaces, the individual designs are so mind-boggling that it doesn't much matter. Indeed, because FAD lacks a museum mentality, you might not find explanatory texts or labels identifying the works and designers. The setup instead tends to have the aura of a peer review or press showing, where late-breaking initiatives and the most adventurous new creations are being presented publicly for the first time. In keeping with this, exhibitions at FAD aren't included in published listings or announced on posters. It's best just to drop in and see what's going on.

In addition to its exhibition program, FAD organizes conferences, lectures and debates, publishes a magazine and bestows prestigious awards in architecture and various other realms of design.

3 Centre de Cultura Contemporània de Barcelona

▱ renovation: Helio PIÑÓN, Albert VIA-
📖 PLANA, 1993
   Carrer de Montalegre 3–5, 08001
▯ 93-306-41-00 f: 306-41-01
   www.cccb.org
☖ eposicionsweb@cccb.org
🎥 Tues, Thurs, Fri, 11–2 and 4–8; Wed, Sat,
   11–8; Sun, 11–7; closed Mon
   summer: Tues–Sat, 11–8; Sun, 11–7
   admission: 600/400 ptas; reduced on
   Wed
   metro: Catalunya, Universitat
CCCB—Contemporary Culture Center of Barcelona—occupies the former hospice and

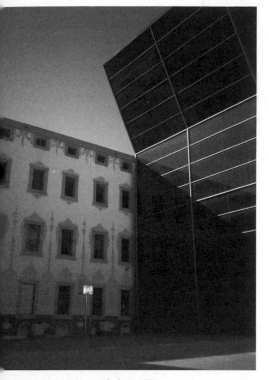

H. Piñón & A. Viaplana, CCCB

floors have been converted into vast, flexible U-shaped spaces amenable for exhibitions. The new wing serves as the circulation nucleus with escalators, elevators and lobbies filling each level except for the two-story Sala Mirador on top. Crowning the building with its boldly slanted, gazed wall, this space, which functions as a reception-conference room, offers spectacular views of the city.

From the courtyard you can also go down a side ramp (south wing) to the lower level, where you'll find an information desk, huge foyer (variously used for social gatherings, special events, concerts, projections, performances, installations), auditorium (used to present experimental music, dance, video, film, lectures) and meeting rooms. Alternatively, you can cross the courtyard and pass through the west wing to the gift-bookshop. **Llibreria Laie—CCCB** (tel/fax: 93-481-38-86; laiecccb@laie.es) is a great place to browse. It has an extensive, unusual selection of books on contemporary art, architecture, urban planning, film, mass media and various realms of the humanities.

Behind the bookstore is a café-restaurant (Metròpoli), situated within a quiet, terraced patio. It's so serene and isolated here that you totally lose sight of the fact that you're in the midst of a bustling, crowded city. Peripheral exits lead to surrounding streets and to MACBA.

The point of departure for all activities at CCCB is the theme of the city. The thematic core is hardly a constraint, however, since the subject is viewed broadly, approached from a multitude of disciplines and interpreted in diverse and unexpected ways. Variety is also expressed in the program since several projects with very different orientations occur simultaneously.

Though many exhibitions don't focus explicitly on art, often work by both major and unfamiliar artists is included. These are not your classic didactic shows with lots of text and esoteric documentary material. More typically, ideas are transmitted via engaging image projections, multimedia installations

monastic enclave called Casa de la Caritat (Charity House). Somewhat modeled after the Centre Pompidou in Paris, it is a large, multipurpose building with a conglomerate program and flexible spaces.

From the street, the center has the appearance of a proper, 18th-century institutional building. However, when you walk through the archway into the inner courtyard, you encounter the new north wing—a reflective, two-tone glass-walled structure that dramatically signifies a radical shift in time and spirit. The courtyard itself (officially named Pati de les Dones—Women's Courtyard) is an unencumbered, open area faced by three historic wings with elegant tile and fresco designs (precisely refurbished) around the rows of windows. The ground floor of these wings contains offices, workshops and seminar rooms; the second and third and photographs, which are actually works of art.

Recent exhibitions: *Architecture without Shadow (Balthasar Burkhard, Günter Forg, Andreas Gursky, Thomas Ruff, Jeff Wall), Art & Time, Barcelona—Madrid: Harmony and Distance, Body and City, The City of K (Kafka and Prague), Cosmos: From Romanticism to the Avant-Garde (1801–2001), Gisèle Freund, Ferrán García-Sevilla, Memory of a Mirage, Muted (Live Art), Radio Days, Sónar—Festival of Advanced Music and Multimedia Art, TV World, Voices of Africa.*

Zhang Huan exhibition, 2000

If you have time, you might enjoy attending an evening lecture, seminar, workshop or weekend conference. Apart from having the opportunity to hear or talk with a person of international renown, you'll also meet interesting Barcelona natives and catch up on current thinking on a particular subject.

4 Galería Ferrán Cano

Plaça dels Àngels 4, 08003
tel/fax: 93-301-15-48
Tues–Sat, 5–8; closed Mon
metro: Catalunya, Universitat

In addition to the huge open space between MACBA and FAD, Plaça dels Àngels encompasses the little side area that confusingly seems to be the beginning of Carrer d'Elisabets. This is where you'll find #4, next to the corner bakery.

Galería Ferran Cano is one of Barcelona's well-established galleries (it's been around since 1973), representing mainly Spanish artists and having no proclivity to a particular art orientation. The gallery has developed an international presence through its participation in art fairs and its second space on Palma de Mallorca.

Artists: Biel Capllonch, Luis Cruz Hernández, Joan Font, Pep Guerrero, Bárbara Juan, Biel March, Ana Marin, Mateo Maté, Pedro Oliver, M. A. Pascual, Eloi Puig, Idros Sanigne, Joan Sastre, Joan Trobat, Trosales & Compañía, Aaron Vidal.

5 Galería Cotthem

Carrer de Dr. Dou 15, 08001
93-270-16-69 f: 270-12-25
cotthem@teleline.es
Wed–Sat, 11–2 and 4–7:30; closed Mon–Tues
metro: Catalunya

Cotthem began in Belgium, where it still operates a gallery. Both locations show international artists, mainly those at the midcareer level. Not only does the gallery bring to Barcelona the work of celebrated foreign artists, but its ample exhibition space enables the display of a large, varied selection of each.

Artists: Michael Ray Charles, Yook Keun-Byung, Robert Longo, Jean Pierre Raynaud, Keith Sonnier, Michel Verjux, Yukinori Yanagi, Zhan Wang, Zhang Huan.

6 La Xina Art

Dr. Dou 4, 08001
tel/fax: 93-301-67-03
Tues–Fri, 5:30–8:30; Sat, 11–2 and
5:30–8:30; closed Mon
metro: Catalunya, Liceu

The narrow space of this gallery is the home of an art collective founded in 1997 with the aim of bringing work by young artists from elsewhere to Barcelona. It's a very professional operation, showing a diverse selection of objects and producing catalogues for many of its shows. Though you probably won't see high-end vanguard art, a visit here provides a good perspective on current tendencies favored by Spanish artists.

Artists: Benzamin Alvarez, Nora Ancarola, Luis Cadarso, Andrès Cobo, Santi Erill, Jésus Etxarte, Tito Inchaurralde, Xerco Nercé, Joan Pallarés, David Tarancón, José Antonio Troya, Pernille Usterud-Svendsen, Marc Vilallonga.

7 La Capella de l'Antic Hospital de la Santa Creu

Carrer de l'Hospital 56, 08001
93-442-71-71 f: 441-16-64
www.bcn.es/icub
lacapella@bcn.es
Tues–Sat, 12–2 and 4–8; Sun, 11–2;
closed Mon
admission: free
metro: Liceu

Located on a busy street behind the central market (La Boqueria).

Once a major city hospital, this large stone building with beautiful courtyards is now shared by libraries (including the National Library of Catalonia) and cultural and educational institutions. Since 1996 the old chapel has been used as an alternative space for exhibitions by young, emerging artists. The work shown here is typically hot-off-the-press, adventurous and risky, albeit sometimes raw and derivative.

Recent exhibitions: *Experiences, Future Visions Festival, Guillermo Goméz-Peña, Gure Artea (Young Basque Artists), Milan–Barcelona Exchange, No Mound Used, Consol Rodríquez & Eugeni Güell, Francesc Ruiz.*

8 Palau de la Virreina

Rambla de Sant Josep 99, 08002
93-301-77-75
www.bcn.es
Tues–Sat, 11–9; Sun, 11–3
admission: variable (free–500 ptas)
metro: Liceu

This 18th-century rococo mansion now houses the offices and services of the Barcelona Institute of Culture. The information center in the lobby is a great place to get leaflets about current and upcoming events and exhibitions. The colorful posters and banners on and around the building advertise the big show of the moment taking place in the grandiose rooms of the Virreina Palace. These projects focus

La Capella

on a wide range of subjects of very diverse character. Contemporary art, or a topic related to the contemporary era, is often featured. Even if the theme is of little interest to you, seeing a La Virreina exhibition is worthwhile since it will invariably include many outstanding, unusual and unfamiliar works.

Recent exhibitions: *Adventure with Material—An Italian Line from Futurism to Laser Beams, Oriol Bohigas, Garden of Eros, Joan Guerrero, Image of the Time—Time of the Image, Eduardo Muñoz, Peruvian Photography, Yoko Ono.*

9 Joan Miró

Plaça de la Boqueria, 1976
Rambla Sant Josep
metro: Liceu

As you walk along La Rambla in the area near the Liceu metro entrance, look down at the cobblestone pavement and you'll see a large, circular composition by Miró, one of the city's favorite sons. The mosaic features a few simple shapes, linear elements and primary colors—characteristics of the artist's vocabulary.

10 Gran Teatre del Liceu

reconstruction: Ignasi de SOLÀ-MORALES, 1999
Rambla dels Caputxins
www.liceubarcelona.com
informacio@liceubarcelona.com
metro: Liceu

The Gran Teatre del Liceu is Barcelona's legendary opera house, renowned for its beautiful interior and as a gathering place for high society. It was recently rebuilt after a fire, caused by sparks from a welding torch, destroyed all but the main facade on La Rambla in 1994. Originally constructed in 1847, the Liceu had previously been rebuilt Because of a fire in 1861 and was again repaired after an anarchist threw a bomb into the orchestra during a performance in 1893.

Responding to the desire to re-create the former theater exactingly, the hall was positioned in the same place, its horseshoe shape and five balconies were retained, decorative ornamentation was reproduced and even the ornate metal bases of the red velvet seats were recast. Equipment, however, was elevated to state-of-the-art levels, and the space was expanded to include a side entrance and lobby, rehearsal halls, dressing rooms, offices and retail space. Now the Liceu stretches far back along Sant Pau Street with its extension looking like a modern building.

11 Palau Güell

architect: Antoni GAUDÍ, 1886–89
Carrer Nou de la Rambla 3–5, 08001
93-317-51-98
Mon–Sat, 10–2 and 4–7:30
admission: 400/200 ptas
metro: Liceu, Drassanes

The wealthy industrialist Eusebi Güell was an early and major patron of Antoni Gaudí—the architect whose name is virtually synonymous with Catalan Art Nouveau. This mansion, commissioned by Güell in 1886, was the architect's first important building in central Barcelona and the project that established his reputation. Although a bit tame compared with his later work, it's a superb example of modernista design and craftsmanship. What's more, it's the only Gaudí house completely open to the public.

Of note are the combination of many different materials—a Gaudí trademark—and the overwhelming amount and imaginative character of the decorative elements. On the street facade, two parabolic entrance doorways with sinuous, interwoven grills give a taste of what lies within. In the interior, a three-story-high vertical space, crowned by a dome embellished with sparkles of natural light, which create a star-studded ambience, serves as the main salon and organizational core of the house.

As you move through the living quarters, be sure to inspect everything. Look at ceilings, walls, floors and all the accouterments so you don't miss the impressive tile designs, stained glass, carved wood, gilded metal, stonework, wrought iron and, of course, the fanciful, colorful chimneys and ventilation pipes on the roof.

12 Centre d'Art Santa Mònica

▣ renovation: Helio PIÑÓN, Albert VIA-
⬛ PLANA, 1989
⬛ Rambla de Santa Mònica 7, 08002
▤ 93-316-28-10 f: 316-28-17
⬛ Mon–Sat, 11–2 and 5–8; Sun, 11–3
admission: free
metro: Drassanes

Located near the bottom of La Rambla.

This art center has an uneven track record, which is not surprising since its program seems to take a something-for-everyone approach. It's housed in a 17th-century convent that has undergone a hodgepodge of renovations and expansions. The major architectural conversion (late 1980s) resulted in an egregious, porchlike access ramp running across the front facade and a monumental, right-angled archway projecting from the side facade. Construction improvements (1999) revised the schema of the ramp, shifting the main entrance to the ground level.

The interior, a towering space flanked by stone arches, was also dramatically altered. Now it has an awninglike structure overhead for lighting, a labyrinth of temporary walls and giant doorways and arches covered with light green and lavender tile. In addition to this center space, exhibitions are installed in side galleries on the ground floor (these are largely devoid of eccentric renovations) and a walled-in balcony on the second floor. The first floor contains a popular video room (screenings are Tues–Fri, 6:30; Sat, 6) and a bookstore specializing in Spanish and Catalan art, architecture and photography. If you climb to the top of the main staircase, you'll come to a small area called the Annex, or Alexandre Cirici Center of Contemporary Art Documentation. Changing exhibits of archival books and historical photographs are displayed here.

At any given time there are several different exhibitions going on in the center. The focus tends to be on Catalan artists, though they span several generations and work in a wide range of styles and mediums. The mix includes both conservative figurative and landscape painters as well as very radical, conceptually sophisticated artists who are experimenting with advanced reproductive processes and unusual materials.

Recent exhibitions: *Eduard Alcoy, Boarding Time, Tom Carr, Club 49, Electronic Art, P. Formiguera, Maria Helguera, Alfredo Jaar, Enzo Mari, Jordi Mercadé, Norman Narotzky, Pere Noguera, Ramón Parramón, August Puig, Joan Rabscall, Realism in Catalan Art, Jordi Teixidor, Andrès Terrades.*

13 Fernando Botero

♋ Gat, 1989/92
◻ Plaça de Blanquerna, Carrer Portal de Santa Madrona
metro: Drassanes

Turn right at the corner of the Santa Mònica Art Center onto Carrer Portal de Santa Madrona. After you pass the very ugly office tower (Torre Colón) and go one block beyond Avinguda de les Drassanes, you'll come to a sidewalk-like plaza on the left side of the street.

Cat is a huge (2.4 ton; 2,200 kilo) bronze with a muscular body like a bear, a big round face with toothpick-like projections as whiskers, wide-open eyes and perky little ears. To some it may appear cute, though its enormous phallic tail adds a sexual tone, a trait common to most all Botero sculptures.

Barri Gòtic and La Ribera

The Gothic Quarter is the oldest part of Barcelona, dating back to Roman times. A medieval cathedral and royal palace (Palau Reial Major) lie at its center, complemented

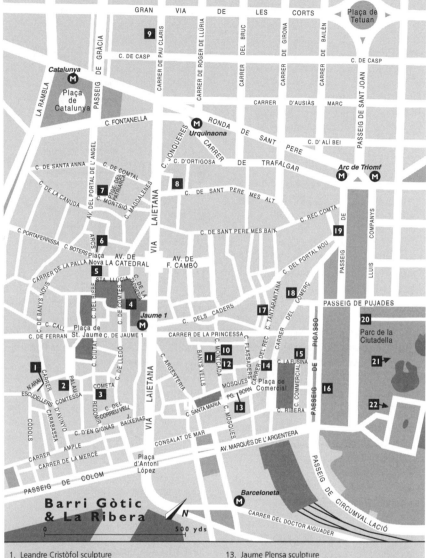

Barri Gòtic & La Ribera

0   500 yds

1. Leandre Cristòfol sculpture
2. Galería Antonio de Barrola
3. Centre Cívic Pati Llimona
4. Eduardo Chillida sculpture
5. Joan Brosso sculpture
6. COAC—Sala Picasso, J. Capell bookstore
7. Els Quatre Gats
8. Palau de la Música Catalana
9. Cafeteria Llibreria Laie
10. Museu Picasso
11. Sala Montcada
12. Galería Maeght
13. Jaume Plensa sculpture
14. Galería Berini
15. Metrònom
16. Antoni Tàpies sculpture
17. Espai Escènic Joan Brossa
18. James Turrell installation
19. Bernar Venet sculpture
20. Antoni Clavé sculpture
21. Parc de la Ciutadella
22. Museu d'Art Modern

by large public plazas and office buildings housing the major administrative departments of the city and Catalan region. The area also includes many charming streets whose restored or downtrodden, still-blackened dwellings give an eye-opening sense of the urban past. If you're inclined toward shopping, you'll find tiny passageways lined with specialty stores and craftsmen's studios as well as bustling avenues overflowing with boutiques of every variety.

The zone to the east of Via Laietana—La Ribera—contains some notable 14th-century mansions. You can best see the splendor of these on Montcada Street, where many of them have been restored and transformed into museums and upscale restaurants. Tourism also runs rampant here, so be prepared for flocks of tour groups and a plethora of shops selling schlock souvenirs.

A bit less trafficked and quite appealing is the small artsy haven called Born, located a bit southeast around the Plaça de Comercial. La Ribera district actually is a conglomerate of six neighborhoods, each with its own history. You can still see evidence of the artisan, aristocratic, working-class, fishing-industry and textile-merchant communities.

1 Leandre Cristòfol

Monument, 1935/91
Plaça de George Orwell
metro: Liceu, Drassanes

The easiest way to get here is by exiting La Rambla to the east at Plaça del Teatre onto Carrer dels Escudellers. Walk three blocks and continue on Escudellers as it turns to the right when the road forks. Plaça de George Orwell, named for the author of *Homage to Catalonia*, is located in the middle of these streets.

To add open space to a densely built neighborhood, an urban renewal project of the 1990s demolished an old apartment building and replaced it with a plaza. The site, particularized by Cristòfol's *Monument*, has become a popular gathering and events

spot. The sculpture is a tall, white concrete cylinder with a linear stainless-steel element circling down, around and above, bearing a wooden sphere at the highest point. The artist, who was active during the 1930s, originally made this Miró-like sculpture on a small scale. (The original is in the collection of the Reina Sofía Museum in Madrid.)

2 Galería Antonio de Barnola

Carrer de Palau 4, 08002
Tues–Fri, 5–9; Sat, 12–2 and 5–9; closed Mon
93-412-22-14 f: 412-19-31
gad00002@teleline.es
metro: Liceu, Jaume I

Located on a charming hill street in what was once the carriage and horse barn of a palace, this gallery has a spacious main room with high ceilings and old wood-and-stone arches. The basement, where works by gallery artists are on display, also exposes the raw structure of the building.

The strong architectural flavor of the space coheres with the architectonic sensibility in the work of many of the artists shown here—not surprising, since Antonio de Barnola is himself an architect. Describing the art as architectonic, however, doesn't imply that it's rigid, geometric or abstract. On the contrary, an artist like José Manuel Ballester paints compelling, enigmatic architectural environments or interiors that are also evocative studies of spaces and planes.

Exhibitions also reveal the gallery's proclivity for concept-based work of the installation, video or performance genre. The program includes both emerging and established artists. Shows by well-known international figures—Marlene Dumas, Joan Fontcuberta, Michael Graves, Arata Isozaki—add spice to the schedule, and collaborations with art critics, who are commissioned to organize exhibitions and write catalogue essays, further diversify the presentations.

Artists: José Ramón Amondarain, José

Josep María Martín, *Cold Days,* 1999

Manuel Ballester, Ester Baulida, Jordi Bressemer, Ana Busto, Luis Claramunt, Ester Ibarrola, Josep María Martín, Mireya Masó, Itziar Okariz, Lucía Onzain, Javier Peñafiel, Humberto Rivas, Manuel Saiz, Enrique Romero Santana.

Centre Cívic Pati
3 Llimona

Carrer del Regomir 3, 08002
93-268-4700
Mon–Fri, 9–2 and 4:30–8:30; Sat–Sun, 10–2
admission: free
metro: Jaume I

This community center is a good place to go for leaflets and announcements about exhibitions, performances and open studio events taking place in the Old City. Its own art exhibitions, on display in the Montserrat Roig room, tend to be rather conservative. But like most neighborhood spaces, especially those in areas where artists live and work,

they're the ones that occasionally present the first show of a future star.

4 Eduardo Chillida

Topos, 1986
Plaça del Rei
metro: Jaume I

The sculpture is located in a secluded courtyard but it's easy to find and convenient to meanderings in the area around the cathedral. Just walk down Carrer dels Comtes, the street flanking the left side of the cathedral, and turn left at the first crossing onto Baixada de Santa Clara. This passageway leads directly into Plaça del Rei (formerly the courtyard of Palau Reial Major).

Topos (*Site*) is an austere cube structure whose Cor-ten-steel walls are mutated by a few pronounced loops extending from the top and side edges. Although the loops echo the quatrefoil shape of the windows in the chapel behind, the sculpture was not specifically made for this location. It was part of a series first shown in Chillida's 1986 retrospective at the Fundació Miró. Thereafter, the artist donated the work to the city with the suggestion that it be placed in this plaza, juxtaposed to the 14th-century architecture of the surrounding buildings. Unfortunately, in this courtyard the sculpture seems both out of place and out of scale. It cries out for an open space, where it can stand alone and apart as an autonomous object.

5   Joan Brossa

Barcino, 1995
Plaça Nova
metro: Jaume I, Liceu

Using the Roman name for Barcelona, Brosso spells out "Barcino" in a row of bronze letters on the spot where the city walls once stood. (The ancient stone barrier and towers are still visible at the base of adjacent buildings.) In his customary mode, the artist has created a visual poem by shaping some of the letters into suggestive images—a sun, moon and pyramid.

6   Sala Picasso

Col·legi Oficial d'Arquitectes de Catalunya
Plaça Nova 5, 08002
93-310-50-00
Mon–Fri, 10–9; Sat, 10–2
admission: free
metro: Jaume I, Liceu

The building with the ugly Picassoesque engraved mural fronting Plaça Nova belongs to the Official Association of Catalan Architects (COAC). Its exhibition space on the ground floor, named Sala Picasso, presents informative, appealing shows related to the built environment of contemporary Spain. Even if you're not an architect or specialist, you're likely to find them quite interesting and relevant to your travels. In addition, there are usually photography exhibitions in the café-bar on the mezzanine level of the lobby.

Recent exhibitions: *Architecture in Iberia, Lluís Domènech i Montaner—Esteve Bonell—Josep Ma Gilal, Emergence—Three Teams of Young Architects from Madrid, Le Corbusier, Photographs of J. A. Coderch, Joze Plecnik, Recycling Madrid—Ábalos & Herreros, Robert Terradas.*

Joan Brossa, Barcino, 1995

Llibreria Cooperativa d'Arquitectes Jordi
6 Capell

📖 Col·legi Oficial d'Arquitectes de Catalunya
Plaça Nova 5, 08002
93-318-35-61 f: 318-69-51
www.arquired.es/eupalinos
eupalinos@arquired.es
Mon–Fri, 9–8; Sat, 10—2
metro: Liceu, Jaume I

Be sure to visit the superb architecture bookstore on the lower levels of COAC. It has an incredible selection of books and magazines on architecture, architects, urban planning, design, landscape, etc. You'll also find all sorts of architectural supplies and classy gift items on the bottom floor.

Els Quatre Gats
7 (Casa Martí)

Carrer de Montsió 3-bis, 08002
93-302-41-40
metro: Catalunya, Urquinaona

Located at the corner of Passatge del Patriarca.

This charming brick building of neo-Gothic design, with carved stone and wrought-iron embellishments, was the location of Els Quatre Gats (The Four Cats)—a popular bohemian hangout (1897–1903). The tavern was the brainchild of Pere Romeu, who envisioned an ambience similar to the Parisian cabarets of Montmartre and the Latin Quarter.

Leading modernista artists—Ramón Casas, Santiago Rusiñol, Isidro Nonell writers and musicians patronized the beer hall–styled tavern. Moreover, like their more famous compatriot, Pablo Picasso—who had his first exhibition on the walls of Els Quatre Gats in 1900—they memorialized each other and the setting in numerous compositions.

Although the heavy wood beams and art-covered walls (reproductions) replicate the historic past, Els Quatre Gats is now a chic, pricey restaurant. A lunchtime *men´ del día,* comprising two modest courses, pastry and wine, costs about 1,500 ptas.

Palau de la Música
8 Catalana

🏛 architect: Lluís DOMÈNECH I MONTANER, 1908
expansion: Òscar TUSQUETS and Carles DÍAZ, 1991
Carrer de Sant Pere més Alt 11 and Carrer de Sant Francesc de Paula 2, 08003
93-268-10-00
metro: Urquinaona, Catalunya

This concert hall is one of the great modernista buildings exemplifying the epoch's amazing fusion of architecture and craftsmanship in brickwork, stained glass, mosaic tile and stone sculpture. If you're impressed by the richly patterned columns and panoply of portrait busts and mythological figures on the

O. Tusquets & C. Díaz, Palau de la Música Catalana, 1991

facade, plan to tour the interior. Better yet, buy a ticket to a concert. The mind-boggling spectacle of design reaches a pinnacle in the auditorium, where a large, inverted, stained-glass dome spreads across the ceiling, infusing the space with natural light and dazzling tones of yellow, rose and blue.

The recent modernization and expansion efforts fortunately have not disturbed or altered the original building. Its exterior and modestly sized hall, created for the Orfeó Català choral society, remains intact. The annex, a reserved brick structure, supplements the old by providing a symphony-scale, technologically advanced auditorium, chamber music room, library (set in a glass-crowned tower), administrative offices, restaurant, shops and new entrance opening onto a small plaza.

9 Cafeteria Llibreria Laie

📖 Carrer de Pau Claris 85, 08002
93-302-73-10 f: 93-412-02-50
Mon–Sat, 10–9
metro: Passeig de Gràcia

Should you want to sit and relax in a non-touristy place in the center of the city, head for this café-bookstore. In addition to enjoying a pleasant atmosphere, you can peruse a large selection of books on architecture, art and film, many of which are in English. Tuesday nights during the spring, live jazz music is added to the mix.

10 Museu Picasso

🏛 Carrer Montcada 15–23, 08003
93-319-63-10 f: 315-01-02
📖 Tues–Sat, 10–8; Sun, 10–3; closed Mon
admission: 700 ptas; special exhibitions, 800/700 ptas; combination, 1,200/1,000 ptas; Wed, half-price; first Sun of each month, free
metro: Jaume I

Until the 18th century, the medieval houses on Carrer Montcada were owned by Barcelona nobility. Now the narrow street, which barely accommodates modern vehicles and the ceaseless streams of tourists, is home to various museums, art and commercial enterprises. The main attraction by far is the Picasso Museum, occupant of five contiguous stone mansions. (Casa Mauri and Palau Finestres at #s 21 and 23 are recent additions, open since October 1999.) Despite considerable renovation, the buildings retain their magnificent inner courtyards with classic diagonal staircases going from the ground to the first floor, vaulted rooms and ached support structures, diverse window designs and even a restored polychrome, coffered ceiling from the 13th–14th century.

The museum ensemble contains collection galleries, temporary exhibition space, multipurpose information rooms, a gift shop, bookstore, coffee shop, conference hall and back garden. There are two entrances from the street, at #15 and #23. Both have ticket desks, though the latter one is specifically for admission to the temporary exhibitions. Though you often have to wait on a long line to buy a ticket to see the art, which is displayed on the upper levels, the public has free access to the ground floor, where all other services line an interior boulevard crossing the museum transversely.

The permanent collection comprises paintings, drawings, ceramics and one sculpture by Picasso. Perhaps its greatest strength lies in early work from the 1890s. These holdings include a prodigious wealth of academic drawings, caricatures, street scenes, portraits, religious images and sketches. Even for scholars well versed in Picasso's output, there are many unfamiliar and unusual works. In addition, you see numerous versions of related works treating the same subject. While you marvel at his endless creativity, you have to pay tribute to his pack-rat habit of refusing to throw anything away.

As rich as the collection is in early work, the years after 1905 are represented by a spotty sampling of the artist's vast and varied production. Of note from the later decades are paintings from the extraordinary *Las Meninas* series (1957) and engravings, like *Suite 156* (1970)—witty, erotic scenes showing Picasso's exceptional facility with line, anatomical transformations and shiftings between male/female, artist/model, old/young and seeing/being seen.

Temporary exhibitions sometimes focus on a particular period or theme in Picasso's art or else they present the work of his friends and contemporaries. Recent exhibitions: *Robert and Sonia Delaunay, Raoul Dufy, Albert Gleizes, Picasso—Indoor and Outdoor Landscapes, Steinlen and 1900s.*

11 Sala Montcada de la Fundació "la Caixa"

Carrer Montcada 14, 08003
93-310-06-99 f: 258-13-08
www.fundacio.lacaixa.es
info.fundacio@lacaixa.es
Tues–Sat, 11–3 and 4–8; Sun, 11–3; closed Mon
admission: free
metro: Jaume I

This exhibition space, specializing in cutting-edge art, is part of the impressive "la Caixa" network. (See p. 173–174.) Each year the program comprises a cycle of exhibitions based on a particular theme proposed by a guest curator. Political life, the topic in 1999–2000, included shows by *Francis Alÿs, Martí Ansón, Antonio Ortega, Javier Peñafiel, Danika Phelps.* And the subject *Wandering Images* in 2000–2001 featured five artists who embrace cinematic references and the montage process in their work: *Eija-Liisa Ahtila, Conce Codina, Tacita Dean, Txuspo Poyo, Sergio Prego.*

Artists often take advantage of the space—a long, flexible gallery that easily accommodates creative installations and multimedia projects. Experimentation and the exploration of new ideas are encouraged and supported.

12 Galería Maeght

Carrer Montcada 25, 08003
Tues–Sat, 10–2 and 4–8; closed Mon
metro: Jaume I

In addition to its posh Montcada address, the

Tacita Dean, *Gellert*, 1992

aura within the gallery reinforces its blue-chip reputation. On entering, you see a lineup of oversize art monographs of the type that always seem to appear on the coffee tables of the rich and famous. Farther on are prints and posters by well-known modern masters. Though the gallery's exhibition program features these artists, it also presents the work of young artists and established Spanish names from the 20th century who haven't attained international stature. A visit here is therefore a good place to get a general overview.

Artists: Valerio Adami, Montomés Adela, Andreu Alfaro, Ana Andrés, Eduardo Arroyo, Joan Barbarà, Lluís Bartrina, Joan Bennassar, Georges Braque, Pol Bury, Alexander Calder, Lino Centi, Marc Chagall, Eduardo Chillida, Marco Del Re, Equip Crónica, Carles Gabarró, Joan Gardy-Artigas, Gérard Gassiorowski, Alberto Giacometti, José de Guimar,es,

Wassily Kandinsky, Christoph Kiefhaber, Aki Kuroda, Dominique Labauvie, Ricardo Mazal, Ruben Méndez, Juan Diego Miguel, Joan Miró, Andrés Nagel, Max Neumann, Paulo Palazuelo, Ramsà, Antoni Saura, Narcis Serinyà, Susana Solano, Antoni Tàpies, Manolo Valdès, Bram van Velde.

13 Jaume Plensa

Born, 1992
Passeig del Born
metro: Jaume I

Once dominated by a central marketplace (a picturesque glass-and-iron building from 1874, due to be converted into a city library), the Born neighborhood is still a lively gastronomic, leisure, art, craft, design, bar and cabaret zone. At its heart lies Passeig del Born, a broad, tree-lined avenue with a pleasant median strip. Functioning more as a local meeting place in a residential, small-business area than a busy thoroughfare crowded with strolling tourists, the atmosphere here is markedly different from La Rambla. (This boulevard is also only a few blocks long.)

A public sculpture by Jaume Plensa is located in the center section of the median strip but you're likely to pass by without seeing it if you're not alert. It tends to blend with the street furniture despite seeming utterly incongruous with it and the present setting. One part, positioned under a stone bench, comprises four solid iron balls imprinted with coded markings : 7 (BORN) E..., 4 (BORN) B..., etc. The second part, a simple, very weatherworn, locked chest sits atop a facing bench.

As is characteristic of the artist, the objects have a purity of form and an evocative, poetic presence. The imagery not only makes reference to the iron and shipping industries, but the balls, which have the appearance of munitions, also call to mind the anarchist trade unions that gutted civic buildings and churches, such as the beautiful Gothic church at the west end of Passeig del Born.

Jaume Plensa, *Born*

14 Galería Berini

Plaça Comercial 3, 08003
93-310-54-43 f: 319-56-40
berini@redestb.es
Tues–Sat, 10:30–2 and 5–8:30; closed Mon
metro: Jaume I

Renovated into one open space extending between two streets with entrances and windows walls at both ends, Galería Berini provides an attractive environment for showing art. The artists are mainly Spanish and Cuban, and the work ranges from disjunctive imagery in the enigmatic paintings by Isidre Monils, to comic-strip compositions by Enric Font, to exquisite scenes from Africa in the photography of José Antonio Carrera. What you may see in a given exhibition doesn't begin to indicate the gallery's direction, but each show provides an extensive, solid sense of a particular artist.

Artists: Franklin Alvarez, Pedro Alvarez, Vincench Barbera, José Ramon Bas, Paul Benny, Elena Blasco, Saidel Brito, Michæl Byron, Martin Carral, José Antonio Carrera, Cristóbal, Douglas Darnis, Alberto Donaire, Arturo Elizondo, Luisa Fernández, Enric Font, Inés Garrido, Antonio Girbes, Begoña Goyenetxea, Ciuco Gutiérrez, Werner Haypet, Hans Hedberg, Sara Huete, Ouko Lele, Chema Madoz, Isidre Manils, Antoni Marques, Juan Luis Moraza, Irïna Nakhova, Paloma Navares, Jaime Palacios, Sandra Ramos, Carlos Roche, Ramón Roig, Manuel Rufo, Oscar Seco, Antoni Sosa, Lillo Tatjer.

15 Metronòm

Caller de la Fusina 9, 08003
Tues–Sat, 10–2 and 4:30–8:30; closed Mon
tel/fax: 93-268-42-98
metronom@mx2.redestb.es
admission: free
metro: Jaume I

Metrònom is an interdisciplinary center focused on installation, video, Internet art, dance, music, film and other variants of time-based and new media creativity. Its name is meant to signify an important focal place that stays abreast of current activity. You can expect to see all genres except painting and sculpture, which are omitted because the center feels they are extensively shown elsewhere in Barcelona. Indeed, the

Mont Marsá, Untitled

program favors multidimensional projects, site-specific or performance work rather than the display of discrete objects. Artists are generally at a midcareer level with established reputations for experimenting with new themes, ideas, materials and technologies.

With its sweeping main space, Metrònom easily accommodates disparate art forms, including an experimental music week held each January, a Greek theater festival (summer) and other live presentations. Two small rooms on the ground floor and a gallery upstairs (Sala Nil) enable the presentation of several different exhibitions simultaneously.

The center is the brainchild of Rafæl Tous, a clothing textile engineer and collector of photography and conceptual art. It began in October 1980 and moved to this location in 1984. Tous rehabilitated the building, an old grocery store in horrible condition, and ran the entire operation until 1989, when he called it quits. Metrònom closed for about six years, reopening in 1995 as a city-sponsored space with Tous as director.

Recent exhibitions: *Margarita Andreu*, *Attraction*, *Txomin Badiola*, *Mercè Batallé &*

Tapies, Homage to Picasso

Chus García, Terry Berkowitz, Mira Bernabeu, Ana Busto, Daniel Chust, Mont Marsà, Silvia Martí Marí, Esther Mera, Santos Montes, Luca Pagliari, Vanessa Pey, Andrea Sunder-Plassmann, Francesc Torres, Yun.

Don't overlook the 1+1 bookstore located off the entrance lobby. It has a great selection of unusual publications and very helpful personnel.

16 Antoni Tàpies

Homenatge a Picasso, 1983
Passeig de Picasso
metro: Jaume I

Located on the periphery of Parc de la Ciutadella in front of Unbracle, a tropical plant conservatory housed in an unusual building with three ascending, barrel-vaulted wooden roofs. The work faces Passatge Mercantil.

This unconventional work of public art was commissioned from Tàpies, one of Barcelona's favorite sons, as part of the centennial celebration for Picasso, the city's lionized, adopted son. (Picasso was born in Málaga in 1881 but spent his formative years, 1895–1901, in Barcelona.) It's a huge glass cube containing an assemblage of steel beams, ropes, chairs, blankets, old paint rags and a huge piece of dilapidated furniture that oddly merges a couch and a sideboard. The disjunctive arrangement and incongruous collection of found artifacts is all the more eccentric because it sits in a shallow pool. In addition, water continuously slides down the glass plates, creating a fluid curtain through which you must view the assemblage.

Homage to Picasso embraces Picasso's unorthodox use of materials and revolutionary attitudes about art. Quotes from Picasso, printed on the draped fabric, reiterate this: "When I don't have blue, I use red." "What saves me is doing it worse every day." "No, painting is not done to decorate apartments, but is a weapon of war used offensively and defensively against the enemy."

Unfortunately, the quotes are impossible to

see or decipher, the glass cube has repeatedly cracked from the heat and the flowing water often doesn't function. Various attempts at remedying these conservation problems have thus far proved ineffective.

17 Espai Escènic Joan Brossa

Carrer Vermell 13, 08003
93-315-15-96 f: 310-13-64
metro: Jaume I
Located off Carrer de la Princesa on a newly formed plaza bordered by Carrers Vermell and de l'Allada.

Joan Brossa (d. 1998), who has several public artworks in the city, also produced conceptual performances before they were chic and wrote film scripts, plays and poems. His deep interest in popular theater traditions—*commedia dell'arte*, magic, mime, shadow puppets, silent-gesture acting—led to his creating this small playhouse. The tone is immediately apparent on the building's facade, where a big red B, positioned sideways, lies on the edge of the roof, and a harlequin appears to be falling out of a window.

The theater presents works by Brossa and others in his circle or those he admired. Sometimes performances take place on a stage in the public plaza out front, a delightful place to relax and observe neighborhood activities.

18 James Turrell

Compartiment igualat, 1992
Carrer del Comerç 36
metro: Jaume I, Arc de Triomf
If you can't find this work, don't despair; it's not always turned on. Should this be the case, ask for help in an office on the main corridor. Another difficulty is that the interior component of the project can only be seen during the day when the building is open, but the perspective into the space from the outside is best seen after dark.

Turrell, an American who has created light

James Turrell, *Equal Compartments*

and color installations worldwide, designed this one specifically for a renovated old convent (Antiga Caserna de Sant Agustí), that now houses a civic center, the administrative offices of Ciutat Vella, and a chocolate museum. (There is also talk of locating a pastry school here in the near future.) His intervention occurs along two intersecting hallways in the entrance area, one of which leads from the street through a sequence of three doors to the inner courtyard.

Using neon tubes to produce mystical auras of red, yellow and blue and pencil-thin lines, Turrell modulates the surfaces of the whitewashed walls even as he accentuates the geometric elements of the architecture. He further draws attention to the entrance by allowing vertical bands of colored illumination to shine through narrow cuts in the dark-toned steel doors.

19 Bernar Venet

Arc de 44.5°, 1992
Placeta de Comerç
metro: Arc de Triomf

Formerly the Portal Nou (new entry) to the walled city was located here. Now this periphery to the Old City is a chaotic conjunction of streets merging into a wide, traffic-laden avenue running alongside the pompous Arc de Triomf esplanade. Venet, a distinguished French artist, makes the most of a tiny paved corner in this setting.

His sculpture is a primary structure—a vertical line made of Cor-ten steel. But instead of appearing as an expressionless object, its taut, bowed shape echos the tension of the

Bernar Venet, *44.5° Curve*

modern urban environment. It also stands in marked contrast to the staid horizontals and verticals of nearby buildings.

20 Antoni Clavé

Homenatge a l'Exposició Universal del 1888, 1991
Parc de la Ciutadella
metro: Jaume I, Barceloneta
park hrs: 8–8; summer, 8–9

If you enter Parc de la Ciutadella from the north on axis with Passeig de Luis Companys (the esplanade in front of Arc de Triomf), you'll come upon this sculpture almost immediately at the first turn off to the left.

The title of this work calls attention to the fact that the World's Fair of 1888 was located in, and responsible for, the elaborate development of Parc de la Ciutadella. The work itself recalls the city's industrial past. It's composed of a tall, vertical frame covered by a collage of crushed, cut, corrugated, studded or painted metal elements. The panel sits atop a post behind a gear mechanism positioned between two huge wheels. When turned on, the frame rotates.

This is the only abstract sculpture in the park and was added to the concentration of figurative statues as a gesture toward the present era. Clavé (b. 1913), however, is an artist rooted in early-20th-century concerns with form and composition. And despite the object's tenuous alliance with the kinetic, mechanical objects of Jean Tinguely, it has none of the dynamic or iconoclastic character of his work, nor does it reflect qualities associated with late-20th-century, vanguard art.

21 Parc de la Ciutadella

daily: Oct–Mar, 8–8; Apr–Sept, 8–9
metro: Ciutadella Vila Olímpica, Arc del Triomf

In 1716–20 Felipe (Philip) V sought to ensure Bourbon rule over Barcelona, which he had captured after a 14-month siege, by demolishing the eastern part of the Ribera district and constructing a huge fortress, the Ciutadella, on the terrain. The citadel remained until 1868, when the city finally began to tear it down, replacing the fortifications with a park. It was Barcelona's first park and became a major site for the World's Fair of 1888, an event that significantly opened the city to the outside.

Parc de la Ciutadella is lush, tropical in places, with a large boating lake, gardens, orange groves, lots of 19th-century monuments, a zoo, various museums, palm trees inhabited by parrots, a network of meandering paths, and delightful places to sit, picnic or listen to a never-ending concert of bird sounds. A popular highlight is *Cascada* (Josep FONTSERE with Antoni GAUDÍ, 1875–81), a triumphal arch and viewing platform set in the midst of a waterfall, cascading steps, greenery, a pool with water jets and baroque sculptures.

Even if you're jaded by tourist spots, this park is a wonderland in which you can actually find a secluded patch of grass and get away from it all. The landscape design here is far superior to what you'll find in the major city parks elsewhere in Spain or Europe.

22 Museu d'Art Modern

Arsenal de la Ciutadella
Parc de la Ciutadella, 08003
93-319-57-28 f: 319-59-65
www.gencat.es/mnac
mnac@correu.gencat.es
Tues–Sat, 10–7; Sun, 10–2:30; closed Mon
admission: 500/250 ptas
metro: Ciutadella Vila Olímpica

This museum is part of the Museu Nacional d'Art de Catalunya (MNAC) conglomerate whose individual units are spread around the city (e.g., Palau Nacional de Montjuïc). The building, erected as the arsenal in Philip V's citadel, also houses the Catalan Parliament. Though the museum entrance is not immediately evident, should you try to enter the government section, you'll be stopped by guards and directed to the far left of the facade, where you'll find a garden courtyard at the rear of which is the proper door.

The collection of this museum contains Catalan art from the 19th century through the 1930s. It's especially rich in objects from the modernista era (Spanish Art Nouveau), including spectacular examples of furniture, jewelry, sculpture and works by Gaudí. Paintings by Santiago Rusiñol and Ramón Casas, friends of Picasso from his Barcelona years, give a telling sense of bohemian life in the city about 1900. A chapel altar by Frederic Vidal from the Casa Bertrand (c. 1900) and paintings by Isidre Nonell (1900–1908) further reveal the best of a dominant phase of Catalan creativity.

The sculptures of Julio González and Pablo Gargallo form another major segment of the permanent collection, denoting significant art activity in Catalonia during the interwar years. One of the region's most famous artists, Salvador Dalí, who developed his brand of Surrealism during these same decades (1920s–30s) is also represented by a few paintings. The sampling is not very strong, but it includes a very curious, cubist work, *Portrait of My Father* (1925), that was shown in Dalí's first exhibition at the Dalmau Gallery, Barcelona, in 1925.

The museum also presents temporary exhibitions. Often these feature unfamiliar artists whose work provides an interesting Spanish perspective on modern art.
Recent exhibitions: *Toni Catani, Ángel Ferrant, Meadows Museum Collection, Isidre Nonell*.

Eixample and Gràcia

"Eixample" means extension or enlargement and refers to the city's growth into an area roughly north of Ciutat Vella from about 1860 to 1936. The district, precisely organized as a grid of square blocks whose corners are trimmed diagonally, contains lots of fashionable stores, banks, corporate offices and historic buildings of Modernisme. It's an easy walk from Plaça Catalunya to the zone where a cluster of galleries is located. Just head up Passeig de Gràcia, an avenue of irresistible charm. To get a good taste of stylish Catalan socio-culture, plan a slow stroll with enough time saved for window-shopping and people-watching from a sidewalk café or street bench. (On the tree-lined Rambla Catalunya, one block to the west, you'll also experience the cosmopolitan flair of Barcelona.)

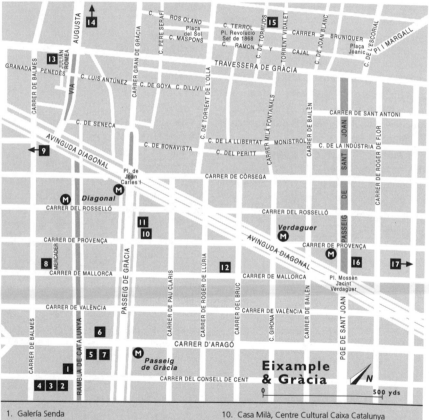

1. Galería Senda
2. Galería Senda—Espais 292
3. Galería Taché
4. Galería Toni Tàpies
5. Galería Joan Prats
6. Fundació Antoni Tàpies
7. Casa Battlo
8. Galería Estrany—De la Mota
9. Filmoteca
10. Casa Milà, Centre Cultural Caixa Catalunya
11. Vinçon
12. BD Ediciones de Diseño
13. Galería Alejandro Sales
14. Interlibro
15. Galería Metropolitana
16. Centre Cultural de la Fundació "la Caixa"
17. Sagrada Família

Gràcia is the area above the middle of Eixample on the other side of Avinguda Diagonal. (It's sometimes considered a subsection within Eixample.) Retaining the old-world ambience it had when it was a separate village, the narrow streets, lively plazas, markets, boutiques, craft workshops, restaurants and bars are like Barri Gòtic—but without the touristy veneer. Bohemians congregated here in the 1960s–70s and today it's home to some spunky art galleries.

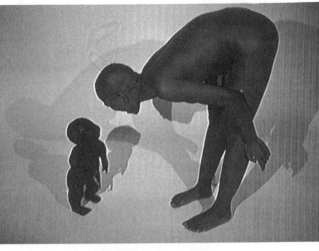

Luis Vidal, *I Want to Be Pretty, III,* 1999

1 Galería Senda

Consell de Cent 337, 08007
93-487-67-59 f: 488-21-99
galeriasenda@jet.es
Tues–Sat, 11–2 and 5–8:30; closed Mon
metro: Passeig de Gràcia

Gallery Senda moved into this chic storefront on the corner of Rambla Catalunya in 1995. With its glazed entry and three-tiered space, it's a pleasant, open environment with intimate pockets. In addition, the personnel and director, Carlos Duran, are very friendly and helpful.

Artists shown here are both midcareer and young, innovators and followers who have a good grasp of modern and contemporary issues. Ask to see work by Luis Vidal, an up-and-coming Barcelona talent who is hardly known yet outside Europe. From time to time, a historical exhibition, like *Picasso Drawings* in 1999, adds icing to the schedule.

Artists: Jean Michel Alberola, Juan Navarro Baldeweg, R. G. Bianchi, Martín Chirino, José Pedro Croft, Jane Hammond, Karin Kneffel, Anna Malagrida, Manel Margalef, Henri Michaux, Manu Muniategiandikoetxea, Jean-Michel Othoniel, Guillermo Perez Villalta, Augusti Roqué, Gino Rubert, Adrienne Salinger, Susana Solano, Juan Suarez, Jaime Súnico, Jordi Teixidor, Darío Urzay, Luis Vidal, Hélène Yousse.

2 Galería Senda–Espai 292

Consell de Cent 292, 08007
93-487-57-11 f: 488-21-99
Tues–Fri, 5–8:30; Sat, 11–2 and 5–8:30; closed Mon
metro: Passeig de Gràcia

Located on the upper floors and sometimes the roof, this space was Galería Senda's main address before it moved across the street. Now it serves as an annex where Senda presents photography exhibitions, emerging artists, site-specific projects or additional space for artists showing in the main gallery.

Recent exhibitions: *Franklin Cassaro, Carmen Mariscal, Pedro Mora, Miquel Navarro, Realidades, Susana Solano, Jordi Teixidor, Curro Ulzurrun, Eduard Valderrey.*

3 Galeria Carles Taché

Consell de Cent 290, 08007
93-487-88-36 f: 487-42-38
galeria@carlestache.com
Tues–Sat, 10–2 and 4–8:30; closed Mon
metro: Passeig de Gràcia

Midcareer artists with international reputations and abstract painting play a major role in this gallery's program. You can also expect to find refreshing work in video, multimedia

Jordi Colomer, *Simo*, 1998

and photography by young artists. Particularly impressive are the unsettling installations of Jordi Colomer, a rising star on the Spanish scene. Confronting viewers with odd settings, fragments of old objects or fetishistic behavior, he focuses on the potency of place, especially environments that are very private and unknowable. If you are unfamiliar with his work, take the opportunity to look through available catalogues or slides and inquire about current exhibitions in the area.

Artists: Chema Alvargonzález, Frederic Amat, Eduardo Arroyo, Jordi Benito, Juan Brossa, José Manuel Broto, Carmen Calvo, Miguel Ángel Campano, Jordi Colomer, Manel Esclusa, Xavier Guardans, Jannis Kounellis, Catherine Lee, Lluis Lleó, Malcolm Morley, Carlos Pazos, Georges Rousse, Antonio Saura, Sean Scully, Vicenç Viaplana.

4 Galería Toni Tàpies Edicions T

⌷ Consell de Cent 282, 08007
93-487-64-02 f: 488-24-95
galttapies@mail.cinet.es
Tues–Fri, 10–2 and 4–6; Sat, 11–2 and 5–8:30; closed Mon
metro: Passeig de Gràcia

Yes, Toni is related to Antoni, the venerated Spanish artist. They're father and son.

Edicions T was established in 1988 with a focus on producing prints and multiples by blue-chip international artists. When the gallery moved to its current location in 1994, it expanded its program to include exhibitions of unique works and young Spanish artists. It thus became one of the foremost galleries in the city. Special shows of work by John Baldesarri, Georg Baselitz, Mario Merz, Robert Ryman and Sean Scully have complemented exhibitions of the prestigious artists officially represented by the gallery. If you're an art buff, you're sure to recognize many of these names. You may not know others like Susy Gómez, a neophyte Mallorcan whose reworked fashion photos reveal a conceptual and visual acuity.

Artists: Marti Anson, Christine Borland, Susy Gómez, Ann Veronica Janssens, Sol LeWitt, Antoni Llena, Julia Montilla, Jaume Plensa, Jana Sterbak, Antoni Tàpies.

Editions by: Ana Laura Alàez, Eduardo Chillida, Victoria Civera, Barry Flanagan, Ferrán García-Sevilla, Susy Gómez, Sol LeWitt, Antoni Llena, Julia Montilla, Jaume Plensa,

Susy Goméz, Untitled 63, 1999

Arnulf Rainer, Thomas Ruff, Sean Scully, José María Sicilia, Jana Sterbak, Antoni Tàpies, Francesc Torres.

5 Galería Joan Prats

Rambla de Catalunya 54, 08007
93-216-02-84 f: 487-16-14
www.galeriajoanprats.com
galeria@galeriajoanprats.com
Tues–Sat, 10:30–1:30 and 5–8:30;
closed Mon
metro: Passeig de Gràcia

The space is deceptively modest since you initially perceive only two small rooms. But the gallery extends way back, organized in the old style as a sequence of intimate rooms with a pseudo-domestic cast.

Indeed, Joan Prats is one of Barcelona's stalwart contemporary art enterprises, dating back to 1976. It has an established history of supporting Spanish artists and bringing their work to international attention. Well-known foreign artists are also represented. In addition to exhibitions of gallery artists, recent one-person shows have featured Georg Baselitz, Julião Sarmento, Ray Smith, Hiroshi Sugimoto and Sue Williams. Often catalogues accompany these projects.

Artists: J. Biro, Alfons Borrell, Joan Brossa, Christo, Hannah Collins, Enzo Cucchi, Ferrán García-Sevilla, Joan Hernández Pijuan, Robert Longo, Luis Macías, Joan Miró, Robert Motherwell, Miquel Navarro, Perejaume, Victor Pimstein, Albert Ràfols-Casamada, Riera i Aragó, Edward Ruscha, Antoni Tàpies, Zush.

6 Fundació Antoni Tàpies

renovation: Roser AMADÓ, Lluís DOMÈNECH GIRBAU, 1986–90
Carrer d'Aragó 255, 08007
93-487-03-15 f: 487-00-09
museu@ftapies.com
Tues–Sun, 10–8; closed Mon
admission: 700/350 ptas
metro: Passeig de Gràcia

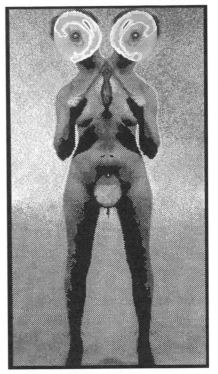

Zush, *Ita Docan,* 1990

Located between Passeig de Gràcia and Rambla Catalunya.

Since its opening in 1990, the Tàpies Foundation has established itself as a world-class center for contemporary art. Like the Miró Foundation, it bears the name of a single artist but has a broad-based program promoting the study, recognition and understanding of contemporary art and culture. Special exhibitions (usually one-person shows or installations) feature challenging artwork in traditional or alternative media, video and film. Often they bring to Spain the first in-depth showing of a significant aspect of contemporary art. The artists tend not to be the trendy, top 10 favorites lionized by other art institutions; rather, they are true innovators and conceptualists admired by other artists and professionals in the field.

Fundació Tàpies is located in an early modernista building designed by Lluís

DOMÈNECH I MONTANER (1880–85) for the Montaner i Simón publishing house. The decorative facade of Islamic-inspired brick and stained glass has been exactingly restored except for the eye-catching structures on the roof. Prohibited from changing the historic exterior, but wanting to enhance the building's stature to compensate for its neighbors that dwarf it, the architects positioned eight steel-and-screen partitions on top, perpendicular to the facade. Tàpies then used these as the support for an eccentric roof sculpture, *Cloud and Chair* (1990–91). The cloud imagery, formed of mesh and a massive tangle of aluminum tubing (actually, a single, 3,000-yd-long tube!), is crowned in the middle by the in-air delineation of a chair. Though industrial in appearance and suggestive of found, discarded matter, the motifs allude to meditation and artistic contemplation.

Contrasting with the exterior, the interior has been considerably remodeled and

Antoni Tàpies, *Cloud and Chair* (roof sculpture) 1990–91

enlarged. The layout retains front and rear atria and highlights elements of architectural decor from the original building. Totally new are the vast, flexible spaces on two levels below ground that serve as temporary exhibition galleries. An auditorium and outdoor terrace provide additional display and activity areas.

On the upper levels, high ceilings and natural light from above create a spacious environment for a display of work by Tàpies. These come from the foundation's permanent collection, donated by the artist and his wife and representing all phases of his career. Due to their large size, relatively few works are on public view, except during the summer, when a full-scale Tàpies exhibition occupies the entire museum.

Be sure to walk to the back of the atrium in the collection galleries to get a close look at the beautiful library. It's a simple, comfortable space with elegant wood-and-glass stacks filled with superb holdings on modern, contemporary and Asian art and culture. (Tàpies's personal interest determined the Asian component.)

The bookstore, to the left of the main lobby, focuses mainly on Tàpies with a limited selection of publications related to other artists. The most valuable item to get is the small brochure (free or 100 ptas) accompanying the current exhibition. These provide an excellent introduction to an artist's work plus up-to-date thinking about art forms and content. If you want to learn more, try to attend one of the foundation events: performance, symposium, conference, etc.

Recent exhibitions: *Abstract Cinema (1960–1980), Architectures of Discourse, Archive Cultures, Art and Language, Victor Burgin, James Coleman, Merce Cunningham, Hans-Peter Feldmann, Dan Graham, Renée Green, Insideout—Federico Guzmán, Chris Marker, Matt Mullican, Rainer Oldendorf, Eulàlia Valldosera, Andy Warhol—Cinema, Video and TV.*

note: It has become increasingly evident in today's art world that an outstanding

Matt Mullican, Untitled, 1996

exhibition program is the result of particular individuals, and when they leave a place its entire tenor and nature radically changes. Since the director of Fundació Tàpies recently moved to MACBA, both institutions will undoubtedly shift gears and pursue different paths to lesser or greater effect.

7 Casa Batlló

architect: Antoni GAUDÍ, 1905–7
Passeig de Gràcia 43
metro: Passeig de Gràcia
When asked to remodel a conventional, six-story apartment house, Gaudí transformed it into this decorative palace embedded with figments of his wild artistic and architectural imagination. The relative flatness of the upper levels and rectangularity of the windows still exist. But the facade is now dominated by projecting, curvilinear balconies, a surface studded with glittering fragments of colored glass and wavy, winding, sculptural window frames on the lower levels.

The streams of flowing rhythms and naturalistic patterns are endemic to French Art Nouveau and Spanish Modernisme. Gaudí's personal imprint is most notable in the fantasy roof design, whose high ridge of tiles has been variously identified as a hat, cockscomb, dorsal comb of a lizard or dragon splayed around the heraldic tower representing St. George.

8 Galería Estrany—De la Mota

Passatge Mercader 18, 08008
93-215-70-51 f: 487-35-52
estranydelamota@teleline.es
Tues–Sat, 10:30–1:30 and 4:30–8:30; closed Mon
metro: Passeig de Gràcia, Diagonal
Although this gallery is a bit removed from others, it's not to be missed. Located on a wonderful small street defying the square grid of the Eixample district, it occupies a huge space on the basement level. Don't

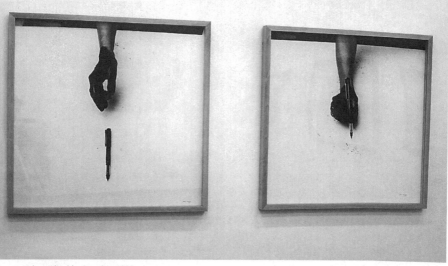

Helena Almeida, *Drawing,* 1999

expect to see run-of-the-mill or seductively beautiful painting and sculpture, since work shown here tends to be radically venturesome, if not expressly provocative. Against-the-grain imagery and materials, as well as a conceptual underpinning, predominates. This is one of the best places in Spain to see current and future art stars who have a real cutting-edge sensibility. A 1999 exhibition by José Antonio Hernández-Díez, for example, presented an abundance of brightly colored plastic forms similar to the ubiquitous packaging elements that come with electronic equipment.

Usually two different artists have one-person shows at the same time, or else there's a thematic, group show (e.g., *Indoors, In the Meantime, Ragtime*). The directors—Antoni Estrany and Àngels de la Mota—are very knowledgeable and willing to answer questions. An artist who's worth pursuing is Helena Almeida from Portugal. She creates remarkable conceptual photographs based on her own body and the process of painting.

Artists: Antoni Abad, Ignasi Aballí, Pep Agut, Helena Almeida, Tonet Amor's, Richard Artschwager, Natividad Bermejo, Christian Boltanski, Jean-Marc Bustamente, Nuria Canal, Daniel Canogar, Javier Codesal, Tony Cragg, Eugenio Dittborn, Alicia Framis, Douglas Gordon, Thomas Grünfeld, Andreas Gursky, José Antonio Hernández-Díez, Donald Judd, Thomas Locher, José Maldonado, Esko Männikkö, Cori Mercadè, Bruce Nauman, Gabriel Orozco, Ana Prada, Sigmar Polke, Jorge Ribalta, Joan Rom, Thomas Ruff, Montserrat Soto, Richard Venlet, Jeff Wall.

9 Filmoteca

Cinema Aquitània
Avinguda de Sarrià 33, 08029
93-410-75-90 f: 419-27-65
filmotecagc@correu.gencat.es
metro: Hospital Clinic

As with most cinemas with a historical bent, the program here features thematic cycles and film series focused on a particular director or actor. Recent programs: *East Germany Today, Gay and Lesbian Festival, Ritwik Ghatak, Andrzej Wajda.*

10 Casa Milà

architect: Antoni GAUDÍ, 1905–10
Carrer de Provença 261–65, 08008
93-484-59-79

daily, 10–8; summer: Fri, Sat, 9–midnight

admission: apartment, attic & roof—each 600/350 ptas, both 1,000/500 ptas; summer evenings (incl. roof music)—1,500 ptas

metro: Diagonal

You're bound to stop dead in your tracks when you come upon this eccentric building. Still today, nearly a century after it was constructed, the vanguard character and creative potency of Gaudí's design stand out, unequaled by many modern edifices. The project was the architect's largest residential venture, and its wavy walls and fantasy rooftop have become trademarks of his style.

Casa Milà is a seven-story apartment house named for the businessman who commissioned it and lived with his family in a palatial space encompassing the entire main floor. (This space is now used for art exhibitions. See below.) At the time, the ground level, not the top, was the preferred space in a multiunit dwelling since it received the best water pressure and didn't require walking up flights of stairs as was necessary in the pre-elevator era. The upper floors each contained four, differently sized apartments.

Although officially termed Casa Milà, the more popular name, La Pedrera, meaning "the quarry," designates the building as a rich source of stone and plays with the facade's resemblance to an open excavation. Not only is Gaudí's use of stone, rather than the stucco of most Art Nouveau architecture, distinctive, but his fabrication of the whole exterior as if it were a single, flowing mass is masterful. Swelling forms and curving rhythms billow down one street frontage, around an obtuse corner and along a second frontage without interruption. What's more, the undulating surfaces seamlessly incorporate doors, windows and balconies.

To appreciate the consistency and extent of the curvilinear formations, walk into one of the two inner courtyards. (Even if you don't buy a ticket to enter the upper levels, you can look at the main courtyard from where the admission booths are located.) Shaped as roughly ovoid spaces with no straight lines or sharp corners, these atria reiterate the character of the street facades. Unfortunately, the surfaces were so badly deteriorated that it was impossible for the restorers to tell how they originally appeared. It seems the stone walls may have been painted, but the rose color that now exists is a hypothetical choice. On the whole, the building has been judiciously restored to its original condition.

Gaudí's penchant for imagery associated with nature and the forces of nature is expressed here by evocations of the ocean in the wave patterns. The hammered stone is also suggestive of erosion by weather and time, and the decorative ironwork hanging from openings bears a strong likeness to seaweed or proliferating vines.

Although the stone facade of Casa Milà lacks the glittery, colored ceramics and ornamental details that tend to characterize Gaudí's aesthetic, in actuality, the masonry itself is pure hyperbolic decoration. The support system is based on the elephantine columns at the ground level and an invisible structural frame within.

In 1986 Fundació Caixa Catalunya (this is different from Fundació "La Caixa") purchased Casa Milà, restored it and rehabilitated it as a cultural center. The apartments are still occupied by private tenants, but various spaces were turned into public areas dedicated to art and culture. You can visit an apartment, furnished in period pieces (some are reproductions) that give you a sense of the early-20th-century life of a well-to-do Catalan family. You'll also see the curving ceilings, round-edged large windows and spacious rooms laid out around the two inner courtyards. Educational displays provide good background material on the reconstruction of the residence as well as the social, cultural and technical transformations that occurred around the time Casa Milà was built. (The slide presentation is a bit much, but other elements are illuminating.)

Most valuable to those interested in Gaudí's architecture is a visit to the attic. Restoration of the *golfe* (attic) entailed removal of apartments that had been added in 1954. Now the space, named Espai Gaudí, is a wide-open area containing diaphragmatic, parabolic arches supporting the roof. If you have no idea what these terms connote, don't worry, you'll quickly grasp the concept and marvel at Gaudí's genius when you see the parade of curving forms. In addition to exposing a phenomenal structure, Espai Gaudí serves as a resource center. It exhibits architectural models, floor plans, sketches and photographs of all Gaudí's projects. If you like modernista design or want to enrich your visit to Barcelona, plan to come here at the beginning of your stay in the city.

Of course, a tour of Casa Milà would not be complete without seeing the rooftop. This is the only part of the building decorated with Gaudí's handcrafted mosaics. The fanciful chimney towers and winding, rolling pathways are also classic exemplars of his unfettered imagination. As an added bonus, you get an incredible view of the city from the roof. Try to go after dark, when the sparkle from the street lights makes the tree-lined boulevards, grid plan and shoreline come alive. If you're in town during the summer, you can enjoy live music (jazz, flamenco, opera, etc.) and a bar on the roof, escaping from the crowded, noisy streets below.

Though not often recognized, Gaudí's development of the roof terrain on residential buildings was innovative, predating by decades the widely esteemed designs of Le Corbusier. His construction of an underground ramp for carriages and cars was another novel idea.

When Fundació Caixa Catalunya refurbished the building, it created a café-bar, Gaudí-oriented bookstore and souvenir shop on the ground floor. It also added an auditorium on the basement level for concerts and conferences.

10 Centre Cultural Caixa Catalunya, La Pedrera

Passeig de Gràcia 92, 08008
93-484-59-00 f: 484-58-89
daily, 10–8
admission: free
www.caixacat.es/fund cat.html
fcc@funcaixacat.com
metro: Diagonal

The exhibition entrance on Passeig de Gràcia is around the corner from the one used for visiting the upper floors of Casa Milà. The space was originally the Milà family residence.

Most exhibitions presented here feature notable artists and museum-quality objects. Many are from the modern epoch but not the contemporary decades. In addition to brochures (available in English) and catalogues, various special events and activities complement each project.

Recent exhibitions: *Chagall, The Fauve Years (1904–1908), From Impressionism to the Avant-Garde, Goya's Engravings, Thyssen-Bornemisza Collection, Joaquin Torres-García.*

11 Vinçon

Passeig de Gràcia 96, 08008
93-215-60-50 f: 215-50-37
vinconbcn@globalcom.es
Mon–Sat, 10–2 and 4:30–8:30
metro: Diagonal

If you like to browse in museum gift shops or spend your lunch hours at Williams- Sonoma or Pottery Barn, then don't miss this amazing design emporium. Organized somewhat like a warehouse, it's chock-full of products for the home and things for every imaginable task and activity, including many you never knew existed! Don't overlook the little gadgets and common items cleverly fabricated in awe-inspiring forms! On occasion, the store devotes a space called Sala Vinçon to art exhibitions. Usually these occur in association with a city festival or promotion.

Although Barcelona's reputation as a center of avant-garde design suffered greatly during Franco's regime, intense efforts to revitalize and advance the industry took place soon after his death in 1975. By the 1980s creative ingenuity and technological innovation by Spanish designers were attracting international attention. Enthusiasts even promoted a rivalry between Barcelona and Milan as the European capital of design.

12 BD Ediciones de Diseño

Carrer de Mallorca 291, 08009
93-458-69-09 f: 207-39-97
www.bdbarcelona.com
Mon–Fri, 10–2 and 4–8; Sat, 10–2 and 4:30–8
metro: Passeig de Gràcia, Diagonal

Located between Carrer de Roger de Ll'ria and Carrer del Bruc.

The great architect Lluís DOMÈNECH I MONTANER constructed this residence, Casa Thomas, in 1895–98 and enlarged it to accommodate a shop for the owner's graphic arts business (1912) on the ground and semi-basement floors. The exterior is still pure Modernisme with the original stained glass and wrought-iron railings restored and protected by a large sheet of plate glass. A touch of the present, and the only indication of the current occupant, is a spare neon light running the length of the glass and discreetly outlining the letters "bd" in the center.

When BD (Bocaccio Design, often mistakenly interpreted as Barcelona Design) remodeled the shop in 1979, it created an impressive space. Still using two floors, it brought natural light into the subterranean area via skylights interfacing with a courtyard in the middle of the building.

BD is a showcase of high-end, international design. Apart from the finely made, creative merchandise, the displays are captivating, well worth a visit in and of themselves. But this is not so surprising, since BD was launched in 1972 by a group of daring, young architects and design professionals who aimed to produce and exhibit innovative objects exemplifying an independence from conventional criteria. The company's products—furniture, lamps, rugs, domestic and decorative accessories—thus derive from experimental ideas and imaginative designs. Moreover, the objects aren't all manufactured in the same, anonymous factory, but each is "published" by the best craftsperson or technological process for the particular job.

The products are either historical designs from figures like Salvador Dalí, Antoni Gaudí, Josef Hoffmann, Adolf Loos, Charles Rennie Mackintosh, Alessandro Mendini and Giuseppe Terragni; or they are contemporary designs from such talents as Pep Bonet, Christian Cirici, Lluís Clotet, Javier Mariscal, Rafæl Moneo, Mireia Riera, Álvaro Siza, Ettore Sottsass, Robert Stern and Òscar Tusquets. In its displays, BD sets its own objects side by side with esteemed examples of other, world-renowned manufacturers. Though the work is for sale and customers are encouraged to feel, smell and try the items, the showroom has the look of a museum. Indeed, BD has organized exhibitions and competitions as part of its goal to stimulate the imagination. These have included *Alessi's Tea and Coffee Piazza*, *Ellen Gray's Designs*, *Loewe's Shop Windows*, *Loo's Lamps*.

13 Galería Alejandro Sales

Carrer Julián Romea 16, 08006
93-415-20-54 f: 415-65-33
www.artbarcelona.es
asales@compuserve.com
Tues–Sat, 11–2 and 5–8:30; closed Mon
metro: Diagonal

A visit here takes you to a tiny street, a block west of Via Augusta and just above Avinguda Diagonal, in a bourgeois section of the Gràcia district. The gallery occupies two spaces: a

Mabel Palacín, Untitled, 1998-99

large, open area well suited for big objects and a small room called Blackspace. Don't be inhibited from entering the office zone, since this is where you'll find a narrow door at the end of a wall of bookshelves connecting the two spaces.

Promoting young artists with growing reputations is a goal of Galería Alejandro Sales. Among them you'll find one who pursues abstract, geometric work (Arbós), one who creates mixed-media installations (Palacín), one who produces eery computer-generated images and one who disturbs reality by manipulating photographs (Peral). You may also see an exhibit of Richard Long or David Nash, renowned sculptors who have recently been added to the gallery roster. And since Blackspace is dedicated to international artists whose work has had little exposure

in Barcelona, every visit is a twofold experience.

Artists: Alfonso Alzamora, Eduard Arbós, José Cobo, Susanna Coffey, Estrada, Iñigo Güell, Ignacio Hernando, Richard Long, David Nash, Mabel Palacín, Alberto Peral.

14 Interlibro

Ronda General Mitre 211–213, 08023
93-418-38-08 f: 434-02-00
www.interlibro.com
metro: Lesseps

If you're interested in architecture, this bookstore specializes in books and magazines covering all facets of the subject. The selection is international and the texts are in various languages.

15 Galería Metropolitana de Barcelona

Carrer Torrijos 44, 08012
93-284-31-83 fax: 210-60-86
www.galeria-metropolitana.com
mail@galeria-metropolitana.com
Mon–Fri, 11–1:30 and 5–9; closed Sat
metro: Fontana, Joanic

Located just above Travessera Grácia, around the corner from Plaça Revolució Septembre 1868.

Open since 1995, this gallery features tough art, variously high-energy, irreverent, severe, disquieting, socio-culturally impacted, media-based or concept-oriented. It spans the gamut from painting and sculpture to photography, installation, performance, Internet work and experimental music. The space itself, comprising two rooms, has a chic appearance. If this description turns you off, you'll miss seeing the most maverick, un-Spanish gallery in Barcelona. You'll also miss a chance to walk around the heart of old Grácia village.

Recent exhibitions: *Jordi Abelló, Roberto Delgado, Joan Fontcuberta, Alberto Gárcia-Alix, Jürgen Klauke, Eloi Puig, Lorena Valldepérez.* Artists: Francesc Abad, Akané, Darya von Berner, Francesc Bordas, Cruspinera, Xavier Déu, Jesús Galdón, Elena Gascón, Matei Glass, Manolo Gómez, Bigas Luna, Toni Moranta, Oscar Muñoz, Mario Pasqualotto, Vanessa Pey, Fernando Prats, Ricard Salvatella, Elmar Thome, Erich Weiss.

16 Centre Cultural de la Fundació "la Caixa"

Passeig de Sant Joan 108, 08037
93-456-89-07 f: 458-13-08
www.fundacio.lacaixa.es
info.fundacio@lacaixa.es
Tues–Sat, 11–8; Sun, 11–3; closed Mon
admission: free
metro: Verdaguer

For years, this large mansion, richly decorated with tiles and fresco-painted designs, has been the preeminent cultural center of "la Caixa" Foundation. At any given time, the schedule has featured at least one major exhibition, usually of blockbuster caliber, plus a photography show and numerous other activities.

Beginning in 2001, the new Fundació "la Caixa" Headquarters in Montjuïc will serve as the major location for the foundation's exhibitions and events in Barcelona (see pp. 173). The center at Passeig de Sant Joan will close completely when the new center opens. Check local listings for up-to-date information on the change of location.

17 Sagrada Família

architect: Antoni GAUDÍ,
1883–(unfinished)
Plaça de la Sagrada Família, 08013
93-455-02-47
daily: Apr–Aug, 9–8; Sept–Oct, 9–7; Nov–Feb, 9–6
admission: 800 ptas
metro: Sagrada Família
Enter from the west off Carrer de Sardenya and Plaça de la Sagrada Família.

It's almost impossible to visit Barcelona and not be drawn to Sagrada Família. The sheer spectacle of the soaring spires rising high above the city's skyline and the wondrous magnitude of the artistry and originality are irresistible. Since the building was never finished, what you see induces speculation about what might have been and stimulates personal fantasies about uncharted possibilities. If only all public monuments had such visual-conceptual power!

In 1882 construction began on the Atonement Temple of the Holy Family (Expiatori de la Sagrada Família) as conceived by the architect Francesc de Paula del VILLAR. It was to be a modest, neo-Gothic church. But when Antoni Gaudí was appointed helmsman in 1891—he had already been working on the project since 1883—he scrapped the old plans and designed a much more ambitious building. It was to have three monumental facades, 12 towers (signifying the 12 Apostles), a supreme spire surrounded by four towers (the Evangelists) and a long nave able to seat 13,000 people. When he died in 1926, Gaudí had spent almost 40 years working nearly continuously on the project, even residing on the site in near destitution for the last 16 years. Quite appropriately, he was buried in the crypt, and Sagrada Família has become a Barcelona treasure.

From the current entrance, you can pass through to the apse, the first part finished by Gaudí. According to his plan, the center of the cross-shaped ground plan crowned by the highest spire (unrealized) would be straight ahead, and the grand facade, envisioned as the main portal (also unrealized), would lie at the opposite end of the nave (now partially constructed). The crypt down below was built by Villars and now contains a small museum in addition to Gaudí's tomb.

If you turn east (left), you'll come to the most outstanding part of Sagrada Família, the Nativity facade. Gaudí concentrated his efforts here during the 1890s, producing a mind-boggling array of sculpture. Using symbolism derived from Christianity or inspired by nature, he developed the three-part portal with representations of Hope (left), Charity (center) and Faith (right). Figures, narratives (scenes from Christ's birth and childhood), flora and fauna all appear. Sometimes the imagery is representational. But it also loses its identity, merging and melting into abstract forms and rhythms that vitalize the whole. So, too, architectural frames, like the steep gables of Gothic origin, get lost in the profusely decorated surface.

Rising above the facade are four majestic towers. Their scale and design are riveting, utterly magical, perhaps Gaudí's most conspicuously fantastical, eccentric production. Shaped as tall, tapered cones with openwork surfaces encrusted with sculptural elements, they are clad in mosaic tiles near the top and capped with bedazzling finials. If you're not subject to acrophobia or claustrophobia and have the stamina and strength to climb 400 steep steps in a spiral staircase, you can enter the towers, see the craftsmanship close up and enjoy panoramic views. Otherwise, you can take the elevator, assuming it's a good day when they're up and running!

Gaudí's plan was to complement the Nativity facade with the Passion facade (west) and the Glory facade (south), thereby dedicating all three to the life of Christ. At the time of Gaudí's death, only one portal, one tower, the apse walls and the crypt were finished: a very fragmentary, incoherent building. Although he left plans, his working method was fairly unstructured, susceptible to continuous change and elaboration. Moreover, anarchists destroyed the drawings and models during the Civil War.

Since Gaudí's death, construction has continued despite a never-ending controversy over the attempts of others to emulate his architectural schema and his extremely personalized decorations. Three towers were added to the east (Nativity) facade by 1930, restoration work was undertaken in the 1950s, and the west (Passion) facade, including its four towers, was begun in 1978 as a project of the sculptor Josep SUBIRACHS. Not only are Subirachs's figures angular and far less expressive than Gaudí's, but now concrete rather than stone is being used. Some changes are obviously stylistic and others result from economic circumstances. Indeed, construction is totally dependent on private funds, and these mainly come from admission fees.

The main facade (Glory) and central crossing towers have yet to be started, but parts of the nave walls and columns now exist. Already the scope of the project, especially the height of the towers, has been reduced. It remains to be seen if and what other changes take place and how they affect Gaudí's conception of the church, as best we know it.

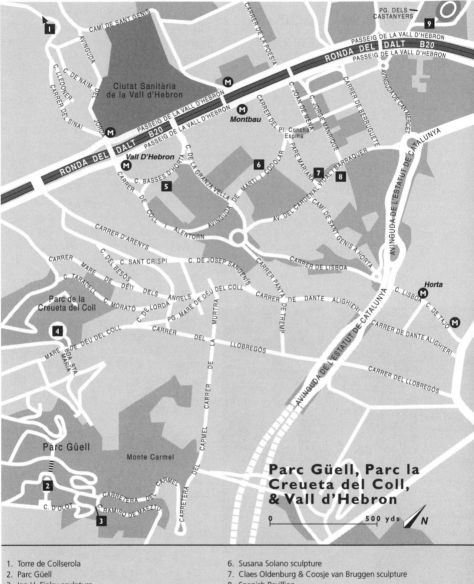

Parc Güell, Parc la Creueta del Coll, & Vall d'Hebron

0   500 yds   N

1. Torre de Collserola
2. Parc Güell
3. Ian H. Finlay sculpture
4. Parc la Creueta del Colle
5. Camp de Tir amb Arc
6. Susana Solano sculpture
7. Claes Oldenburg & Coosje van Bruggen sculpture
8. Spanish Pavillion
9. Joan Brossa sculpture

Parc Güell, Parc la Creueta del Coll, Vall d'Hebron

1 Torre de Collserola

architect: Norman FOSTER, 1989–92
Carretera de Vallvidrera al Tibidabo,
08017
93-406-93-54 f: 406-93-23
Jan–Apr, Nov–Dec: Wed–Fri, 11–2:30
and 3:30–6; Sat–Sun, 11–6; closed
Mon–Tues
May–June, Oct: Wed–Fri, 11–2:30
and 3:30–7; Sat–Sun, 11–7; closed
Mon–Tues
July–Sept: Wed–Fri, 11–2:30 and 3:30–8;
Sat–Sun, 11–8; closed Mon–Tues
admission: 500/350 ptas
Ferrocarrils de la Generalitat from Plaça
de Catalunya, exit at Peu de Funicular;
take funicular Vallvidrera then bus 211
(30–45 min).

Antoni Gaudí, *Dragon*

If you don't like heights or are faint of heart, this is a place you might want to avoid. The funicular will take you to the highest hill above the city (1,680 ft; 512 m), and then a glass elevator, speeding up the side of the Collserola Tower (945 ft; 228 m), delivers you to an observation deck on the 10th floor, seemingly in a distant ethereal zone. The ride itself will take years off your life! Of course, you can simply look north from most places in and around Barcelona and see this skyline tower without ever taking your feet off the ground.

A site visit will, however, afford incredible panoramic views and an up-close look at the innovative design of one of the world's foremost architects, Norman Foster from Britain. Unlike many telecommunications towers, this one fulfills high-tech needs without producing a visual blight atop a city. The slender tower has a concrete shaft with a core structure in the middle and a needlelike mast as the apex. Three cables connect the peak to the core and three sets of cables secure the core to the ground. Though the center structure appears cylindrical from a distance, it's actually a stack of 13 triangular steel platforms with curved sides. Like many architectural highlights in Barcelona, Collserola Tower was constructed for the Olympic Games. It now emits virtually all the television and radio broadcasts in the metropolitan area and is the main link for the whole Catalan network.

2 Parc Güell

architect: Antoni GAUDÍ, 1900–1914
Carrer de Larrad and Carrer Clot,
08024
daily: June–Sept, 9–9; Apr–May, Oct,
9–8; Mar, Nov, 9–7; Jan–Feb, 9–6
admission: free
metro: Lesseps
From the metro, circle around Plaça Lessups
to Travessera de Dalt, a major roadway; go
east for several long blocks until Carrer de
Larrard; turn left (north); walk to the top and

you'll reach the cross street, Carrer d'Olot, and the park's entrance. It's a hearty 10–15 min walk from the metro.

Situated up high on Montaña Pelada, Parc Güell provides spectacular views of Barcelona, made all the more appealing because of Gaudí's development of the site. Count Eusebi Güell had wanted to create a garden city (a landscaped middle-class suburb) on the hilly, desolate terrain, but none of the houses ever got built. By 1914, when the project was terminated because of World War I, his visionary architect had created only a gatehouse and a grand stairway leading to a cavernous covered market with a resplendent terrace above. The only other completed building, Gaudí's house, constructed by Francesc Berenguer, was a spired, fairy-tale dwelling to the right of the entrance. It is now the Casa-Museu Gaudí. Güell's estate replete with Gaudí's virtuoso designs became a municipal park in 1922.

Given the chance to indulge in town planning and landscape architecture, Gaudí created the beginnings of a pre-Disney Disneyworld, except that here the exotic images and ecstatic feelings refer to nature, and the natural setting has virtually shaped the constituent parts.

At the base where you enter, castlelike gates with turrets and decorated walls engender a wondrous atmosphere. You're immediately drawn toward the stunning, white mosaic-tiled, wide, curving stairway just ahead. All sorts of greenery and palm trees extend up and over its borders; cascading down the center is a multipartite rock garden and sculpture-enriched fountain. Halfway up the steps is the popular *Drac* (Dragon), a symbol of the park (usually obscured by posing tourists). Like Gaudí's other figures and forms, it has a rubble masonry core embellished by complexly patterned ceramic and glass fragments (*trencadís*)—a colorful and weather-resistant surface.

The steps split in two, forming paths to Sala Hip—stila, a deep, irregularly shaped, undulating hall (the prospective town's marketplace) populated by a forest of Doric-like columns. Continuing up the staircase paths, you arrive at the projecting terrace-plaza formed from the roof of the hypostyle and stretching way back to an esplanade and entrance to the walkways that meander around the park. Originally this platform space was intended as an open-air stage or arena. In addition to the panoramic views, the highlight is now the mosaic wall molded into a continuous bench around the serpentine perimeter of the plaza. It's yet another extraordinary Gaudí decoration that's simultaneously functional.

Should you venture into the park grounds, you'll walk on paths that follow the natural contours of the terrain, with bridged segments supported by buttresses in the guise of petrified tree trunks.

3 Ian Hamilton Finlay

L'ordre d'avui, 1999
Carretera del Carmel, Parc dels Tres Turons
metro: Alfons X, bus: 24

Located east of Parc Güell on a high lookout point within a recently designated park.

The city commissioned *Today's Order* from Ian Hamilton Finlay—a Scotsman well known for his political, poetic art—when his retrospective was taking place at Fundació Miró in 1999. The sculpture is a Catalan version of a monumental work using a quotation from Saint-Just, one of the most extreme French revolutionaries of the 1790s. Each word of the quotation and the author's name is carved atop one of nine blocks of granite lying flat on the ground like fallen tombstones. The message reads: "Today's order is tomorrow's disorder."

4 Parc la Creueta del Coll

architects: Josep MARTORELL, David MACKAY with Oriol BOHIGAS, 1987
metro: Vallcarta, bus: 25, 28

Located at the southeast section of the park. Enter from Passeig de la Mare de Déu del Coll. If you try to cut through the park from the west, massive stone cliffs will block your way. Taking the peripheral road is also not a good idea, unless you hanker for a very long hike up and down a rugged hillside with little to offer in terms of interesting vistas, lush landscape or local flavor.

After you pass through the entrance gates, a ramp leads to the developed area of the park. At the top of the ramp, standing like a beacon or signpost, is *Tòtem* (1987) by Ellsworth KELLY. The weathered Cor-ten-steel form—a slender, tall monolith (more than 30 ft high) with edges slightly bowed—is a majestic presence. And yet, it is perturbingly impenetrable.

Eduardo Chillida, *Eulogy to Water*

The park, which occupies an old quarry, was designed to take full advantage of the rock cliffs. They form a backdrop for the main plazas, a lake and an 80-ton hanging sculpture by Eduardo CHILLIDA (1987). Created from reinforced concrete and suspended over the water by steel cables, *Elogi de l'aigua (Eulogy to Water)* is an awesome sight. Its image is a cluster of clawlike, concave shapes that both enclose space and make it accessible. Thus, a dialogue between solid and void, form and formlessness occurs in the midst of a rebellion against gravity.

The superb placement of the two sculptures is equaled by the sensitive structuring of the terrain and layout of the recreation areas. The architects have terraced the area around the lake with steps, sloping paths and esplanades connecting the levels. Each section is tree-lined or planted with Mediterranean vegetation, and zones are equipped for toddler playgrounds or configured for particular sports or social gatherings. An unstructured, wooded area accommodates picnics and exercise trails. Unlike many contemporary parks, this one has lots of benches and the design is commodious for people of all ages. Moreover, it's clean, devoid of graffiti and kept in good condition, probably because the gates are locked at night.

If you want to spend time outdoors and prefer a non-touristy place with a couple of artworks to kept you attuned, this is a perfect choice.

5a Camp de Tir amb Arc

architects: Enric MIRALLES and Carme PINÓS, 1989–92
between Carrer de Basses d'Horta and Avinguda de Martí i Codolar
metro: Val d'Hebron, Montbau
Located just south of highway B-20 (Ronda de Dalt), across from Ciutat Sanitària de la Vall d'Hebron.

The Vall d'Hebron region, which spreads across the lower slopes of Collserola, the northernmost part of Barcelona, underwent a

Susana Solano, *Tell Me, Tell Me, Dear*

radical transformation as part of its development for the Olympic Games. Landscaping, parks and sport complexes were integrated with existing and new housing, roads and other urban structures. Although the archery fields created for the 1992 games are now used for soccer and rugby, the facilities (dressing rooms, bar, warm-up and training areas) remain, their vanguard design typical of work by Miralles and Pinós.

The architecture consists of five elongated units of differing lengths composed of precast concrete shells, tile walls and industrial screen pergolas (canopies). Most striking is the disorderly, zigzagging layout that accentuates angles, curves, axes, planes, contours, geometric shapes, voids and contrived plays of light and shadow. The molded retaining wall behind the facilities was formed using earth removed to flatten the fields.

6s Susana Solano

Dime, dime, querido, 1986/92
Avinguda de Martí i Codolar
metro: Montbau, Vall d'Hebron

The bold, Cor-ten-steel sculpture titled *Tell Me, Tell Me, Dear* is located at the bottom of a walkway running alongside the Municipal Tennis Center. It is an intriguing conjunction of disparate, planar forms assembled around a central void. With their sharp silhouettes and upright, slanted, angled and tilted positions, the component parts and the whole object possess multiple, changing images depending on your point of view.

Susana Solano is one of Spain's best-known contemporary artists, and this work does justice to her reputation.

Claes Oldenburg & Coosje van Bruggen, *Matches*

7 Claes Oldenburg and Coosje van Bruggen

Mistos, 1991–92
Avinguda del Cardenal Vidal i Barraquer
and Carrer del Pare Mariana
metro: Montbau

Witty, grand-scale public sculptures depicting everyday objects are a specialty of Claes Oldenburg and Coosje van Bruggen. Typically, they splay out imagery with extraordinary panache while cleverly taking the particularities of settings into account. Here, they situated *Matches*, a sculpture of painted steel and fiberglass, on the corners and adjacent roadsides of an intersection. That is to say, the main image—a giant matchbook containing five yellow matches, one with a blue flame gleaming atop its red tip—occupies one corner and four discarded matches lie nearby.

Often the artists choose an image because it has meaning for a particular population or location. Perhaps in this case the matches bear witness to the ubiquitous smoking habit of Spaniards.

8 Spanish Pavilion, Paris World's Fair of 1937

architect: Josep Lluís SERT with Luis LACASA; reconstruction 1992
Avinguda del Cardenal Vidal i Barraquer
metro: Montbau

Located one block east of the *Matches* sculpture.

This symbolically important building is worth noting if you're looking at other things in Vall d'Hebron. The original was constructed at the height of the Spanish Civil War to assert the resolute legitimacy of the Republic in the face of Franco's militant regime. Displays emphasized educational and social aims, defending ideals of peace and solidarity. Wrenching images in photomurals, news reports and poems revealed the suffering of the Spanish people and the war-torn landscape. In addition, works of art expressly created for the pavilion called attention to the Republican cause.

A columnar sculpture by Alberto Sánchez, *The Spanish People Follow a Way That Leads to a Star*, stood on the path leading into the building, and *Montserrat*, the heroic, life-size image of a peasant woman created in sheet iron by Julio González, greeted visitors at the entrance. *Spanish Mercury from Almaden*, a fountain-mobile by Alexander Calder, filled the center of the foyer; Joan Miró's *El Segador* (*The Reaper*), a 27-ft-high mural depicting a defiant Catalan, commanded the space in the open stairwell; and a program of documentary films on the war, organized by Luis Buñuel, was continuously screened in an outdoor auditorium. Of course, the big attention-getter, hung on a wall flanking the entrance, was Picasso's *Guernica*. It had been painted in response to the horrific bombing of a Basque village and came to represent the brutality and insanity of war.

The Republic's decision to participate in the Paris fair was made only a few months before the opening. Therefore, Josep Lluís Sert, a young architect who had studied with

Le Corbusier, did not have much time to create a design. He produced a modernist, rectangular building totally oriented to display. Even sections of the exterior most visible from the adjacent esplanade were covered with large photomurals of soldiers and slogans. Sert's role did not go unnoticed: he was declared "unfit to practice his profession" by the Franco government in 1939. As a result, he moved to the United States, where he became dean of Harvard's Graduate School of Design, a position he retained until the mid-1950s.

There was no particular association between Barcelona and the Spanish Pavilion, but the city decided to reconstruct the building as part of the renewal efforts spurred by the 1992 Olympics. Piecing together imprecise information, the reconstruction attempted to be faithful to the original, although an office annex was added. The building serves as the headquarters of the Jaume Figueras Archive and Library, dedicated exclusively to the Civil War, and the International Institute for Historic Studies.

9 Joan Brossa

Poema visual, 1984
Jardins de Marià Cañardo, Velòdrom d'Horta
metro: Montbau

Located on the north side of the B-20 highway (Ronda de Dalt) off Passeig dels Castanyers.

As you walk up the broad flight of steps that is the main approach to the Velòdrom stadium, on your right you'll see a grass plaza planted with olive trees. In its midst, standing at the head of a path like an entrance gate, is a monumental letter "A" made of stone blocks. Scattered on a slight hill set among increasingly scruffy vegetation are various punctuation marks. At the top you come to

Joan Brossa, *Visual Poem*

a clearing surrounded by a wooded thicket. The giant letter "A" again appears. But now only its lower legs remain upright; its other parts lie broken as ruins on the ground below.

Brossa's three-dimensional visual poem thus conveys the evolutionary process by means of a metaphoric journey through a real landscape.

Espai Fotogràfic Can Basté

▭ Centre Cívic Can Basté

Passeig Fabra i Puig 274, 08031
93-420-66-51 f: 420-17-97
www.noubarris.net/cccanbaste/espaifoto/index
globalid@lix.intercom
Mon–Fri, 4–9:30
metro: Virrei Amat

The entrance is off the small plaza between Passeig Fabra i Puig and Carrer de Pere d'Artés, a block above the Virrei Amat metro.

The oddly modernized white building (formerly a private house) standing out like a sore thumb on a busy avenue bordered by high-rises is the Can Basté Civic Center. Its program concentrates on photography with meritorious exhibitions complementing educational activities and studio-darkroom facilities.

Sala Cava, a barrel-vaulted gallery with high walls and natural light, serves as the main exhibition space. Projects of young, emerging artists receive special attention, though shows of established artists take place intermittently. The span of work includes traditional lens-based photography as well as experiments in digital imagery and other new media. Sala Golfes on the second floor provides another exhibition space, but its location in a narrow, unkempt corridor is a disservice to the art.

The center is best known for *Photographic Forum*, an annual conference (November/December) promoting contemporary photography. Recent exhibitions: *Georg Aerni, Amparo Fernández, Anna Junyer, Iñaqui Larrimbe, Tina Modotti, Xavier Padrós, Miguel Romero, Gorka Salmerón, Enric Servera, Jean-Louise Tornato, Patric Tato Witting*.

Plaça del Virrei Amat

🏛 architects: Andreu ARRIOLA and Carme FIOL, 1999
ⓜ metro: Verrei Amat

As part of an urbanization project to create an open space around the Virrei Amat metro, Andreu Arriola and Carme Fiol designed a walk-through type of plaza with bold lighting and architectonic structures. Spread across the area fronting Passeig Fabra i Puig are six very conspicuous, imposing large objects fabricated from laminated wood. Like trees, they have solid trunks that branch out, bifurcating to form a triangular space filled with a checkered surface of void and planar elements. Half of the "trees" stand upright, shielding metal light poles. The other half bend over, becoming canopies producing shade and flickering sunlight effects.

Off to one side of the plaza is a slotted rooflike structure with trees growing through and under it. And in the rear, a shallow pool with jets of water stretches across the space. Arriola-Fiol also created lighting fixtures for contiguous sidewalks. Using a floral inspiration from nature, these have three petallike elements set at different heights, folded down or up and facing this way and that.

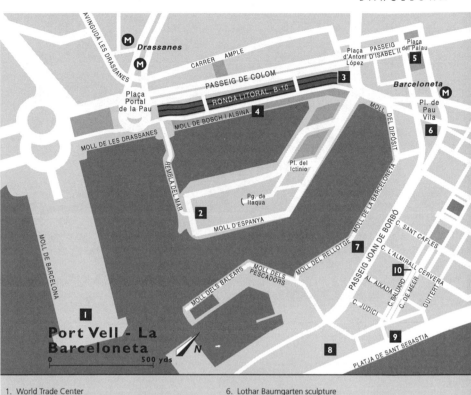

1. World Trade Center
2. Moll d'Espanya
3. Roy Lichtenstein sculpture
4. Moll de Bosch i Alsina
5. Ulrich Rückriem sculpture
6. Lothar Baumgarten sculpture
7. Mario Merz sculpture
8. Juan Muñoz sculpture
9. Rebecca Horn sculpture
10. Jannis Kounellis sculpture

Port Vell–La Barceloneta

Formerly an unattractive shipping and industrial zone totally cut off from the city by a multilane highway, Port Vell (Old Port) at the bottom of La Rambla is now a bustling environment abounding with leisure hot spots, office and business plazas, promenades and enchanting marinas. The radical conversion occurred because the city made a high priority of redevelopment projects to reintegrate the waterfront into the urban landscape and convert the old docks into a people-oriented seashore.

1   World Trade Center

architects: Henry COBB (Pei Cobb Freed), 1999
Moll de Barcelona
metro: Drassanes

Taking full command of its location at the head of Moll de Barcelona (Barcelona Wharf) with unimpeded views of the old city, Montjuïc and the sea, this enormous business complex and cruise center has brought a distinctively different class and character to the waterfront.

The building, shaped like a ship when viewed straight on, adds a striking profile to the horizon. In fact, the edifice is circular, composed of four separate units (a hotel and

Piñón & Viaplana, Moll d' Espanya

three office segments) set atop a common base (a self-contained shopping and restaurant plaza). Formal gardens with fountains stretch in front of the building, creating a regal setting along the length of the pier. Further enhancing the visual and economic dynamics of the World Trade Center are the luxury cruise liners that use both sides of the wharf as a mooring place. Greatly favored because its dock opens onto an appealing waterfront and is in close proximity to the center city, Barcelona is now one of the leading destinations for cruise ships on the Mediterranean.

2 Moll d'Espanya

architects: Helio PIÑÓN, Albert VIA-
PLANA, 1990–95
metro: Drassanes

Although you may not be much interested in the youth-and-tourist-saturated shopping plaza that is a prominent segment of Moll d'Espanya, do at least take a stroll along Rambla del Mar, the floating walkway whose wooden gangplank has a stream of wave lines on posts intermittently attached to its edges. Bulging out from the middle of the path is a double-tiered terrace furnished with benches and protected from the wind by glass walls. If you're lucky you may even see the walkway swing open to allow boats in and out of the harbor.

Should you continue to the end of Rambla del Mar and venture onto the main pier, you'll find two yacht clubs, Maremagnum (recreation, shopping, restaurant, bar, disco, multiplex film theater and convention center), IMAX (wide-screen cinema) and L'Aquàrium. In addition, you'll see an assiduously designed environment. Areas are partitioned and activities are defined by the diversification of paving materials, the creation of slopes and mounds, tree groupings, and alignments of sculptural elements and lighting columns. Unfortunately, the results are a bit excessive and verge too closely to the appearance of a miniature golf course.

3 Roy Lichtenstein

Cap de Barcelona, 1992
Passeig de Colom/Pas de Sota Muralla
metro: Barceloneta

Located at the end of Moll d'Espanya where it meets the shoreline. This corner is a wide-open space and a jumble of converging streets and street names.

Barcelona Head is a colorful, jubilantly configured large object positioned to be visible from various city streets, waterfront paths and to cars speeding along the Ronda del Litoral superhighway. Indeed, it was created with intersecting parts as a sculpture in the round whose image is dynamic no matter what the perspective or approach of the viewer. Recognizable as a head, the components are nevertheless jazzy, abstract elements in their own right. Many derive directly from voluminous brushstrokes and some bear Lichtenstein's trademark dot patterning, an enlargement of the offset printing technique associated with comic strips.

In homage to the masterful craftsmanship of Gaudí, Lichtenstein chose to fabricate this sculpture using concrete covered with broken ceramic tiles.

4 Moll de Bosch i Alsina

architect: Manuel de SOLÀ-MORALES, 1987
between Passeig de Colon and Plaça de Palau
metro: Drassanes, Barceloneta

Transforming the quayside, named Moll de Bosch i Alsina, previously known as Moll de la Fusta, was the first phase of the grand-scale rejuvenation project for the waterfront. Attacking this strip of land involved a complex restructuring of the road network, most particularly the superhighway, Ronda del Litoral. A raised platform was built over it, thus putting the high-speed traffic lanes and new parking facilities out of sight and underground. This opened up prime "people" space above ground and effected a better connection between city and sea.

The space has two levels. The lower one at the water's edge is a traditional, cobbled esplanade and wide stretch of parkland planted with lines of palm trees. Benches encourage people to use this area for relaxing, socializing or enjoying the view. The upper level has terrace cafés, bars, restaurants and walkways embellished by architectural elements. Red vernacular bridges, like the ones in Van Gogh's paintings from Arles, span sections of the uncovered underground roadway, and rows of blue-and-orange tile benches, protected from the sun by white trellises, add color and charm to the area. Despite the blight of graffiti and vineless trellises, not only has the area been made accessible and appealing, but the design has also accommodated a diversity of uses and ambiences.

Roy Lichtrenstein, Barcelona Head

La Barceloneta

The triangular-shaped area with a long, narrow tail-strip jutting far out to sea was first inhabited by people moving there to escape the increased density in Ciutat Vella following Philip V's construction of La Ciutadella. The original residents lived in huts on the beach. After 1753, however, military authorities, concerned about defending the city, organized the area into small housing parcels on narrow streets running parallel to the port. Soon industrial warehouses moved into the northern quadrant, and before long the district was heavily populated by fisherman, sailors and factory workers.

Redevelopment projects for the waterfront and Olympic Games spruced up La Barceloneta. The last of the old warehouses became Palau de Mar, a complex of bars, restaurants and cafés with the Museum of Catalan History upstairs. A yacht marina occupies the harbor along the eastern side of Port Vell and the land fronting this landscape was designed as an esplanade and plaza.

A unique aspect of the redevelopment of La Barceloneta was an exhibition organized by the Cultural Olympiad, called *Urban Configurations* (1992). For this, eight renowned artists from various countries were commissioned to create permanent art projects in the neighborhood. Exemplary works were produced, and though they suffered wear and tear or vandalism over the years, most received conservation treatment by 1999.

5 Ulrich Rückriem

Untitled, 1992
Pla del Palau
metro: Barceloneta

This work by Ulrich Rückriem, a highly regarded German sculptor of minimalist persuasion, was commissioned for the section of La Barceloneta cut off from the waterfront by the highway. More particularly, it faces the street that traverses the middle of Pla del Palau—a tree-shaded, flat plaza bordered by neoclassical buildings. Composed of four wedges of Finnish granite

Ulrich Rückriem, Untitled

set in pairs framing a center axis, the sculpture is like an entry gate. Though solid, simple blocks of stone, they are rough-cut and retain clamp markings along their edges as witness to the industrial processes entailed in their creation. These are signature features of Rückriem's work and characteristic elements of art from the late 20th century that rejected the purist, idealized mode of abstraction.

6 Lothar Baumgarten

Rosa dels vents, 1992
Plaça de Pau Vila
metro: Barceloneta

The art of Lothar Baumgarten often concerns itself with shifts in language, especially as these relate to sociopolitical history. Here his subject is *Wind Rose* (predecessor to the compass rose), an ancient navigational instrument used to indicate directions of the winds. Developed from lines drawn across the Mediterranean between coastal ports to chart paths for ships, the original device had eight points. Baumgarten makes reference to a wind rose by setting the wind terms into the pavement in cast iron—a material recalling the industrial past of the area. Using Catalan words to name the winds also manifests the post-Franco determination of the region to revive its unique culture and language.

Instead of placing the names close together so they are all visible at once and read as a single image, Baumgarten has spread them across the stepped area in and around Plaça de Pau Vila. Each designation has been positioned exactingly to correspond with its directional current: "tramuntana"–north, "migjorn"–south, "ponent"–west, "llevant"–east, "gregal"–northeast, "mestral"–northwest, "xaloc"–southeast, "garbi"–southwest.

Subsequent to the installation of this artwork, which was somewhat rushed to meet Olympic Game deadlines, the city completed the road network and construction around Palau del Mar. In the process, several letters of the wind names were destroyed. (So much for the integrity and value of public art!)

7 Mario Merz

Creixent en aparença, 1992
Moll de la Barceloneta
metro: Barceloneta

Like the Baumgarten work, the project by Mario Merz—a leading figure in the Italian Art Povera movement—spreads over the ground. It consists of numbers following the mathematical progression known as the Fibonacci series, in which each number is the sum of the two proceeding terms (1, 2, 3, 5, 8, 13 . . .). The numbers are handwritten and appear as neon lights set into the ground, protected by glass plates. As the numerals increase, they are set farther and farther apart. *Increase in Appearance* plays with the conundrums of temporal and spatial, logical and illogical, visual and conceptual systems.

In all there are 21 "windows." Number 1 is located on the triangular plaza (fronted by Moll del Rellotge) at the southern end of Moll de la Barceloneta. The series continues along the stepped area extending out toward Passeig Joan de Borbó and ends with number 10,346. The sculpture has unfortunately had many technical problems caused by water getting inside the glass-covered boxes containing the neon lights. You may therefore find the boxes boarded over and the lights nonfunctional—the entire work thus nullified.

8 Juan Muñoz

Una habitació on sempre hi plou, 1992
Plaça del Mar
metro: Barceloneta

At the end of Passeig Joan de Bordó, where it curves to the right, cross the street and enter Plaça del Mar. Walk across the plaza to the right toward the Institut de Ciències del Mar.

The sculpture *A Room Where It Always Rains* is situated on a quiet patch of land shaded by four trees and opening to the sea. The room named in the title is actually a large

Juan Muñoz, *A Room Where It Always Rains*

cage containing five bronze figures whose lower bodies are in the form of spheres, not legs. The figures are thus doubly immobilized, confined within a cell and unable to walk. Four are grouped facing one another and the fifth stands apart, turned outward. Regardless of their positions, there is no interaction among them or with outside viewers. All are self-absorbed, eternally suspended in an indeterminate time and place. What makes this sculpture particularly evocative is the incongruity of figures who are simultaneously imprisoned and yet situated in the open air with poetic seaside vistas.

A constant in the work of Juan Muñoz is the charged, melancholy atmosphere in which figures are utterly alone, even if physically together, estranged from their surroundings, incapacitated, and divested of individualizing features, albeit compellingly human. As in the play *Waiting for Godot* by Samuel Beckett, the scene is set, the characters are in place, but nothing happens.

9 Rebecca Horn

L'Estel ferit, 1992
Platja de San Sebastia near Carrer de Meer
metro: Barceloneta

From the Muñoz sculpture walk to the beach, turn left, and go toward the tower of boxes just ahead surrounded by white sand. *The Wounded Star* by the German artist Rebecca Horn was created in homage to the small restaurant owners who used to do business here before the land was gentrified. Constructed as a helter-skelter stack of four, windowed and rusted-steel cubes, it conveys the vibrancy of the past even as it suggests a derelict collection of discarded objects. The image also calls to mind a place of refuge, watchtower, lighthouse or fantasy elevator to the stars.

When the audio-electric systems are operating, flashes of light dart through the interior and a soft voice speaks the names of the people who had to leave.

10 Jannis Kounellis

Untitled, 1992
Carrer de l'Admiral Cervera
metro: Barceloneta

On the short walk from Horn's sculpture to Kounellis's, you traverse the residential zone of La Barceloneta made quaint by the colorful laundry strung across balconies and the nonstop chorus of chirping birds that populate multitudinous cages on these same little facade extensions of otherwise nondescript buildings. Any street off the beach will do, but the most direct is down Carrer de Meer, taking the second left onto Carrer de l'Admiral Cervera. There's a tiny plaza with a food stand and café tables just ahead between Carrer de la Mestrança and Carrer del Baluard.

The sculpture by the revered Italian artist Jannis Kounellis hangs from a raw wall at the back of the plaza. This wall was exposed and the plaza developed when the building in front was demolished. The site had natural appeal for an artist who favored raw industrial materials and appropriated, time-worn objects. (He, like Mario Merz, p.133, was a member of the radical Arte Povera group.) As one who had grown up near the port of Piraeus, Greece, Kounellis also had an inborn sensitivity to the maritime environment. In his work, images allied with commerce, travel and the exchange or diffusion of cultures (e.g., beans and grains) can be traced to these roots.

In the Barceloneta object, a weathered I-beam as high as the six-story building behind it forms the structural support for the work. Suspended from it at the top is a chain of seven steel shelves bearing burlap sacks of coffee. For Kounellis, coffee and the smell of coffee were linked to harbors and the import-export theme. Although shipping no longer takes place in Port Vell, coffee (and cocoa) beans are a specialty of many shops in La Barceloneta.

Rebecca Horn, *The Woonded Star*

Jannis Kounellis, Untitled

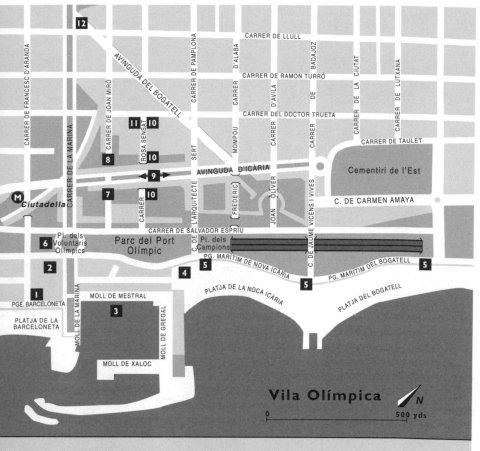

1. Frank O. Gehry sculpture
2. Hotel Arts
3. Port Olímpica
4. Servicio Meteorológica
5. Antoni Roselló sculpture
6. Antoni Llena sculpture
7. Central Telefónica
8. Eurocity 1
9. Enric Miralles & Carme Pinós sculpture
10. Eurocity 2, 3, 4
11. Tom Carr sculpture
12. Luis Ulloa sculpture

Vila Olímpica

From Barceloneta it's a pleasant walk, about 3/4 mi (1.25 km), along the seashore promenade (Passeig Marítim) to Vila Olímpica. If the soothing natural vistas don't hold your attention, you'll have the bonus of being drawn forward by the mesmerizing image of Frank Gehry's giant fish sculpture seemingly swimming through space in front of two shoreline skyscrapers.

It's hard to imagine that not so long ago (pre-1992) this prestigious stretch of beautiful beaches was a dreary landscape of obsolete warehouses and railroad sidings. The renewal project could have easily produced a concentrated hotel-resort district with the typical vacation-tourist ambience. But Barcelona expressly developed a diversified community combining the 2 1/2 mi (4 km) of reclaimed beaches with residential complexes, office buildings, corporate headquarters, a grand hotel, retail shops, business services, leisure and sports facilities. In addition, parks and pedestrian zones proliferated, replacing highways, which were put underground, and large infrastructure elements were extensively remodeled or relocated.

Although the village was initially created to house the Olympic athletes and the port designed for Olympic water competitions, the conversion into an urban neighborhood was built into the original master plan (developed by Martorell, Bohigas & Mackay).

1   Frank O. Gehry

Peix, 1990–92
Passeig Marítim and Carrer de Ramón Trias Fargas
metro: Ciutadella Vila Olímpica

From afar the wavy shape and glittering surface of *Fish* (sometimes called *The Golden Fish*) create a spectacular landmark. From close up, the huge size, mesh exterior and

rigorous framing system reorient it from a figurative sculpture to being an architectural structure joined to the adjacent hotel. At 115 ft tall and 177 ft long (35 x 54 m), the form is monumental. And yet, it is only a non-volumetric skin whose underlying support scheme of steel beams, painted white (like the exoskeleton of the hotel tower) is fully exposed. Moreover, the skin is bronze color–dipped stainless steel—a reflective screen with transparent, luminous properties. By positioning the fish high above the ground, Gehry further endows the image with buoyancy, and by adding a pair of upturned wings to its belly he presents it in fantasy terms (quite appropriate for the hometown of Gaudí and Miró) as a flying fish.

The fish image developed out of a trellis Gehry initially designed as a shading device over the courtyard of the hotel's retail center. As the architect recollects, the scheme needed "an accent piece that would challenge the tower and create a tension with it. The trellis evolved to a wave form and slowly became

Frank O. Gehry, *Fish*

what is—an abstract flying fish." He wanted to name the sculpture *Sardana* after the Catalan dance performed in front of the cathedral, for although the hotel tower is not a cathedral, "it has a dominating presence and the sculpture dances in front of it."

2 Hotel Arts

architects: Bruce GRAHAM (Skidmore, Owings & Merrill), 1992
Carrer de la Marina 19–21, 08005
metro: Ciutadella Vila Olímpica

Hotel Arts and Torres Mapfre, the skyscraper pair on the Olympic waterfront, are the tallest buildings in Barcelona. Indeed, the city purposefully made an exception to height regulations to give the new district a distinctive character. The choice of architect, Bruce Graham—the leading American designer of high-rises, including the John Hancock and Sears towers in Chicago—furthered this goal.

Apart from its prominence as the home of Gehry's *Fish*, Hotel Arts stands out as the building whose framework of modular steel is on the outside and painted white. Not only does its crossbeam design provide structural support for the 45-story tower, but it also emboldens the underlying stone-and-glass block with an emphatic linear pattern.

3 Port Olímpica

architects: Oriol BOHIGAS, David MACKAY, Josep MARTORELL, Albert PUIGDOMÈNECH, 1992
metro: Ciutadella Vila Olímpica

If you cross Carrer de la Marina, the esplanade between the two high-rises, you'll come to Port Olímpica, an impressive marina bordered on four sides by piers and promenades. A vast range of pleasure craft are docked or leave from this harbor, and you can enjoy the scene from various locations. Perhaps Moll de Gregal, the two-level pier on the east side of the port, has the most to offer. It has four terraced restaurants at water's edge and

a pergola running the length of the upper walkway as it extends out to sea. Located at the end of this pier is a cluster of white tile, cuboid buildings with slanted-roof turrets designed to accommodate a sailing school and maritime offices.

4 Servicio Meteorológica

architect: Álvaro SIZA, 1990–92
Carrer de Arquitecte Sert 1, 08071
metro: Ciutadella Vila Olímpica

Located just beyond the north end of Moll de Gregal and on the south side of Passeig Marítim de Nova Icària.

You can't miss this striking, cylindrical building by Portugal's preeminent architect and Pritzker Prize laureate, Álvaro Siza. Characteristic of his style is the utter simplicity of form; the precise articulation of curves and lines; and the use of incisions and voids to assert spatial and functional relationships.

Siza does away with all nonessentials, concentrating on core structures and primary shapes. But his buildings are far from bland or commonplace. Here, for example, he dramatically disrupts the circularity of the whole by cutting out two sharply angled segments on opposite sides of the ground level. He also pierces the surface plane with deep hollows, each shaped to bring natural light into several interior spaces and to add verticality to the exterior image. Tonal differentiation between the concrete base and white marble of the upper facade is a more subtle means of altering the cylinder without embellishing it. Notably, Siza develops the meeting point between the two materials as a razor-edged, continuous line.

If a round building situated near the shoreline reminds you of the ancient defense towers located all along the Mediterranean coast, this is no accident. Consideration of the appropriateness of a particular form for a specific place is a seminal part of Siza's creative process.

5 Antoni Roselló

🏛 *Torres d'il·luminació*, 1992
Passeig Marítim
metro: Ciutadella Vila Olímpica

The three parts of this work are spread out along Passeig Marítim. One is behind the Siza building and the other two are at intersections with Carrer de Jaume Vicens i Vives and Carrer de la Llacuna.

As part of the reconfiguration of the road system and enhancement of the waterfront area in Vila Olímpica, the city commissioned the Catalan artist Antoni Roselló to create a sculpture for the seaside promenade. He developed *Towers of Light*, three tall, thin, angled columns with slanted tops. The forms are nicely punctuated with ridges and other markings, and divided vertically with rusted steel on the side facing the sea and stainless steel on the city side. At night, the constellations Aquarius, Taurus and Pisces are delineated in blue lights on the towers.

6 Antoni Llena

🏛 *David—Goliat*, 1993–94
Parc de les Cascades
metro: Ciutadella Vila Olímpica

A sequence of parks, each created by a different designer, runs the length of Olympic Village on the city side of Passeig Marítim. Underneath is the Ronda del Litoral beltway. Turn left (west) as you enter the parkland and you'll soon be at Plaça dels Voluntaris Olímpics—a focal-point plaza whose centerpiece is a spherical water-jet fountain. Traversing the plaza is Carrer de la Marina, a major north-south axis and grand esplanade that passes between the skyscrapers and terminates on the Marina Pier.

Despite their obvious concern with vistas, landmarks, a preponderance of green space and a pedestrian-friendly environment, the planners created this monumental intersection where cars reign supreme. You'll be hard-pressed to view the fountain close-up, but if

Alvaro Siza, Meteorological Services

you walk around the periphery of the traffic circle, you'll come to a sculpture by Antoni Llena at the entrance of Parc de les Cascades. It features a large, rectangular sheet of white-painted metal configured with holes to suggest the image of a mask. This element floats high in the air, supported by three, irregularly twisted steel tubes, one of which has a black crushed form wrapped around it. Unfortunately, it predominately appears as spindly tubes until the wind blows strongly enough to slant the face upward so it becomes visible. It undoubtedly was more effective in its original form as a small object made from wire and paper.

To the north of the park area, across Carrer de Salvador Espriu, is the residential sector of Vila Olímpica. Various architects were commissioned to create the apartment buildings (most are seven stories high), which are laid out around interior courtyards and private spaces with greenery. It's worth walking around the neighborhood to see the variations, though none are cutting-edge designs.

7 Central Telefónica

architects: Jaume BACH, Gabriel MORA, 1989–92
Carrer de Joan Miró, Avinguda d'Icària
metro: Ciutadella-Vila Olímpica

The planners of Olympic Village sought to locate office buildings of architectural prominence on major traffic axes within the residential area. One of these, designed for Central Telefónica, actually comprises two structures connected by a bridge over the street passing between them. An oval unit sheathed in corrugated aluminum with narrow rows of windows circling it houses offices. In contrast, the other unit—a technical facility—is angular, windowless and clad in stone. To add a bit of zap to its boxy form, the architects tapered it at the base. The slanted sides are quite subtle, just enough off to cause a double-take and perhaps some worry about your eyesight. The bridge is also positioned on a slight incline.

8 Eurocity 1

architects: Roser AMADÓ, Lluis DOMÈNECH GIRBAU, 1992
Carrer Joan Miró, Avinguda d'Icària
metro: Ciutadella Vila Olímpica

Like Central Telefónica, this office building crosses Carrer Joan Miró. But here the main structure in its entirety, not just a skybridge, is held aloft. Suspended over a zone of open space with the street running through the middle, it sits four stories above the ground in the form of a narrow (two-stories high) square box with a small square cutout in the center. Two nondescript service towers and steel poles positioned around the perimeter support the building. Though a grid of glass and granite patterns the exterior walls of the upper structure, the austerity of the design reiterates the reductive, geometric appearance of the whole.

Antoni Llena, *David–Goliath*

9 Enric Miralles and Carme Pinós

Pergoles, 1990–92
Avinguda d'Icària
metro: Ciutadella Vila Olímpica

Commissioned to create a work for the esplanade of Avinguda d'Icària—the main east-west artery crossing the village—Miralles and Pinós created a two-block-long parade of eccentric pergolas (from Carrer de Arquitecte Sert to Carrer de Joan Miró). Composed of a wild, disjunctive assortment of steel elements and wood slats, these structures sometimes bend over like arched trees, sometimes form roof screens, but mainly resist categorization, regimentation and anything verging on structural purity. Appearing more like gestures than objects with each thrust going off in a different direction, they stand in marked contrast to the rather staid ambience of the new district.

10 Eurocity 2, 3, 4

architects: Helio PIÑÓN, Albert VIA-PLANA, 1992
Carrer Rosa Sensat
metro: Ciutadella Vila Olímpica

Located at the intersections of Avinguda d'Icària and Carrer del Doctor Trueta

Three "gateway" structures of identical appearance create an interesting alignment on Carrer Rosa Sensat. They largely follow the modernist, urban aesthetic that uses a reductive rectangular form with a nondecorative, geometric point of focus—here a cutaway segment with a stepped profile running across one-third of the building's length. But the architects added vigor to the design by having the middle of the structure span a street such that the lowest step of the void serves as the entrance and the right-angled zigzag frames a perspective view down the street. Since the seaward side of the building is mirror-glazed (the other sides are clad in marble), a view of the port is pronounced no matter which direction you're actually facing.

E. Miralles & C. Pinós, pergolas

11 Tom Carr

℞ *Cilindre*, 1992
⌂ Carrer de Rosa Sensat
  metro: Ciutadella Vila Olímpica

Located on the corner of Carrer de Rosa Sensat and Carrer Estocolm.

This huge minimalist sculpture seems oddly placed, tucked away on a grassy hillock at the back corner of a housing zone. It's a bright blue cylinder, 36 ft long and 13 ft high (11 x 4 m) with one slanted and one flat end. Walking around it, you discover its location is even stranger than initially perceived: it's set over a ramp entrance to an underground garage. In fact, this very conspicuous object was designed to look like a sculpture but function as an extractor for automobile fumes.

12 Luis Ulloa

℞ *El pla de la nostàlgia*, 1992
⌂ Avinguda del Bogatell
  metro: Bogatell

Located on an unnamed plaza at the end of Bogatell Avenue where it crosses Carrer de Llull and abuts Carrer de Marina.

This area, just two blocks north of Olympic Village, is a mix of old, run-down warehouses, renovated buildings and neighborhood redevelopment projects. The plaza itself resulted from the clearing away of derelict elements and creation of an open space.

Luis Ulloa developed his sculpture, *Field for Nostalgia*, as a point of interest in an otherwise monotonous landscape. Indeed, Ulloa takes advantage of the space by making a three-part work and spreading it out across the plaza. Each section is differently scaled and all incorporate intersecting or adjacent elements that encourage viewing the work from multiple directions. Though borrowing strongly from a minimalist aesthetic, the sculpture has its base in diversity more than repetition. It includes barrier wall and open archway forms, linear and planar segments, angled and curving rhythms. The use of Cor-ten steel and concrete makes reference to the area's industrial past.

Hopefully the city's art maintenance crew will have removed the unsightly graffiti by the time you see this well-designed, nicely placed object.

Luis Ulloa, *Field of Nostalgia*

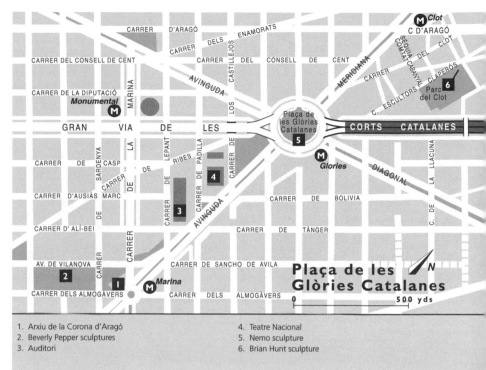

1. Arxiu de la Corona d'Aragó
2. Beverly Pepper sculptures
3. Auditori
4. Teatre Nacional
5. Nemo sculpture
6. Brian Hunt sculpture

Plaça de les Glòries Catalanes

1 Arxiu de la Corona d'Aragó

architects: Roser AMADÓ, Lluís DOMÈNECH GIRBAU, 1990–93
Carrer de la Marina
metro: Marina

Located across the street from the metro station and Marina bridge.

The landscape in this area used to be utterly unsightly when major rail lines going to the now defunct North Station dominated the environment. Redevelopment brought in a mass of roadways (not a great improvement) but also added green space and the striking building designed for the Archives of the Crown of Aragon. Indeed, the library was relocated here as part of the plan to decentralize the city's cultural resources.

The extreme angularity and irregular form of the building make it intriguing from all approaches and views. It sits atop a flat expanse like a sculpture in the round without an explicit front, side and back. In fact, it's composed of two structures, one basically triangular sheathed in stone with a glass rim around the roof, and the other shaped like a square with a missing quadrant clad in silvery metal. The two parts nest together with a passage and common plazas in between. Though the architecture has a windowless character—a necessity to protect archival materials—a few carefully placed, geometrically designed openings on the exterior walls and a tentlike peak on the roof are sources of natural light.

Beverly Pepper, *Sun and Shade*

2 Beverly Pepper

Sol i ombra, 1986–91
Parc Estació del Nord, 1986–91
metro: Marina

Located to the west of Arxiu de la Corona d'Aragó with its main entrance off Carrer dels Almogàvers.

Beverly Pepper, an American artist from the David Smith generation, created an outstanding example of site-specific public art for a new park developed on several acres of land previously occupied by railroad tracks. Her design includes three sculpted areas and park furniture. Created in collaboration with landscape architects—Andreu ARRIOLA, Carme FIOL, Enric PERICAS—it camouflages environmental blights and provides links to surrounding facilities, most of which were constructed or renovated as part of the neighborhood renewal plan (e.g., adjacent sports fields and the district sports center, police station and intercity bus terminal that now occupy North Station).

Pepper demarcates the entrance path from Carrer dels Almogàvers by setting it off between walls—not upright, planar barriers but molded forms covered with a mosaic of white ceramic tiles whose intricate shapes generate a web of flowing lines and swirling patterns. (Needless to say, Gaudí was an inspiration here.) One of the walls is a sinuous curve that sweeps up from the ground to a height just below the thicket of trees and bushes planted behind its enveloping contour. The other is a long, wavy mound with the peaked profile of an obtuse triangle. As with most of Pepper's outdoor sculptures, the forms are scaled to the setting and shaped to accommodate the physical and sensorial responses from people. In this case, some of the walls invite touching and readily adapt as seats or backrests.

Fallen Sky, the second land sculpture located in the middle of the park, is a rolling hill that snakes across a carpet of grass. Like the walls, the tile surface is delineated with streaming rhythms. Here they are accentuated in a few places by the addition of colored tiles. And similar to the mound, the hill's shape has undulating slopes and a sharp ridge along the top. Surrounding this main form and further modulating the flat ground are groupings of low-lying, ripplelike forms again defined by a tile surface.

Before heading to the east side of the park to see the third sculpture, be sure to look at Pepper's furniture designs. Light fixtures, made from Cor-ten steel, are totally reduced to an upright post of modest height with the light embedded into the top of the form. In contrast, the benches are cast from concrete, round and arranged in clusters. With their upturned curves circling a gently sloped core, they have the semblance of the swirling skirts worn by Spanish dancers. Though more comfortable and visually pleasing than conventional benches, the concave seats unfortunately have no drainage and therefore are useless after it rains.

Pepper borrowed the title of her park ensemble from the terminology for bullfight seating—*sol i ombra*, sun and shade. While the entrance and *Fallen Sky* sections are mostly sun oriented, *Spiral of Trees* is a shade zone. It is an amphitheater-like land sculpture formed from an aquamarine-and-purple-tiled step coiling around a spiral of spindly trunked trees on terraced ground.

3   Auditori de Barcelona

architect: Rafæl MONEO, 1999
Carrer de Lepant 150, 08013
93-247-93-00
www.auditori.org
info@auditori.org
metro: Marina, Monumental

Located on the west side of Plaça de les Arts off Avinguda Meridiana.

The exterior appearance of this building suggests an office center or school—anything but a major concert hall in a European culture capital. There is no grandiose entrance and none of the classical trappings used to signify an important edifice. It's also a long, low, austere structure without the monumental presence that typically characterizes performance auditoria. And yet, this is one of the largest city buildings and contains a symphony hall with 2,340 seats, a chamber-music hall with 700 seats, a multipurpose hall for an audience of 300–500, rehearsal rooms, offices and the potential for housing the Conservatory for Catalan Music and the Barcelona Music Museum. No matter what your taste in music, you're sure to find an appealing performance since the program

Beverly Pepper, *Spiral of Trees*

includes classical, jazz, rock, pop, soul, blues, electronic, new music, ethnic, flamenco and anything in between.

Rafæl Moneo, Spain's preeminent living architect (chosen in 1999 to renovate and expand the Prado), explicitly understated the scale and outward character of Auditori by forming the whole as if it were a single, cubic volume and cladding it with a modulated grid of narrow Cor-ten-steel and glass panels outlined by the white concrete of the base structure. The building actually comprises two sections, each housing one of the main auditoria, separated by a large, open-air patio. Functioning as a public entrance, this square-shaped space contains a drive-through passageway for drop-offs and access to the theaters and underground garage. It is unpretentiously denoted on the front facade by a concrete canopy and low-lying staircase. In the back, a detached ticket office marks the location. Although unenclosed, the central area is a dark, cold space, traversed by a plethora of lines and angles. In its midst, another square-shaped space, extending from the second floor to the roof and positioned at a 45 angle to the surrounding square, creates a light zone. This structure, designed by Pablo PALAZUELO, has been described as a translucent lantern or floating sculpture. Fabricated from frosted glass, it is paneled with the same grid as on the building's exterior except that here diagonal streaks yield additional rhythms.

Unfortunately, the building's starkness is negatively amplified by the harsh, flat plaza surrounding it. Only a few small trees offer a touch of nature, though the in-process development of the area as a new cultural center is enhancing the environment with green spaces and other improvements.

Rafael Moneo, Barcelona Auditorium

Ricardo Bofill, National Theater of Catalunya

4 Teatre Nacional de Catalunya

architect: Ricardo BOFILL, 1995–97
Plaça de les Arts 1, 08013
93-306-57-06 f: 306-57-03
www.tnc.es
metro: Glòries

Barcelona's decision to spread out its cultural and leisure magnets as part of the neighborhood revitalization process resulted in the creation of Plaça de les Arts (a grass and olive tree plaza that insulates the new buildings from surrounding roads) with the Barcelona Auditoria on one side and the Catalan National Theater (TNC) on the other. Not only did this construction radically transform a run-down area but the city acquired two distinctive public edifices in the process. Notably, the pair couldn't be conceptually or stylistically more different.

Borrowing from classical imagery, Ricardo Bofill, a leader in postmodern and high-tech architecture, designed a majestic templelike structure for TNC. Gigantic columns, a gabled roof and grand staircase in front make conspicuous reference to the Greco-Roman tradition. The glazed curtain walls, however, are pure contemporaneity and the interior layout is pure Bofillian ingenuity. Since the lobby areas are open during the day, be sure to go inside and walk around.

The initial eye-catcher within the spacious and airy glass-enclosed, skylit lobby are the four, autonomous little buildings of classical demeanor. These contain visitor services—information desk, ticket booth, telephones, etc. There is also a glass cube housing a bookshop. The large palm tree growing through its open roof complements others set elsewhere in the lobby and around the exterior. Furthering the sense of being in an inside-outside environment is the presentation of the theater itself as a building within a building. The circular facade bearing classically shaped window and door reliefs appears like an ancient coliseum except that modern escalators and glass elevators are located on the sides to carry patrons to the upper level of seating and the "rooftop" restaurant. The "roof" extends over the auditorium but is far below the actual roof

Ricardo Bofill, National Theater of Catalunya (interior)

of the building. It overlooks the lobby and offers views of the city beyond.

As a big proponent of mass-production processes, Bofill used precast concrete to effect the look of carved stone as the main building material. And as the exposed ceiling in the lobby reveals, the support system derives from large steel beams resting on the 26 perimeter columns.

The main auditorium of TNC has 894 seats arranged in steeply sloped rows with no balconies, as in historic amphitheaters. Classical articulations occur throughout and the use of sycamore and marble adds an aura of refined luxury. In contrast, the design of the 500-seat auditorium, located on the lower level, is decidedly informal. Geared to experimental productions, it has movable, bleacher-type seats that permit diverse arrangements and total flexibility in the use of the space. The building also includes a bar, café, school, rehearsal rooms, dressing rooms, television studio and underground parking garage. An annex in the rear houses workshops and storerooms.

Since Tony Kushner's Angels in America inaugurated the TNC building, it has hosted an impressive, highly varied and successful program of traditional and innovative plays.

5 Nemo (François Scali, Alain Domingo)

Meridià, 1992
Plaça de les Glòries Catalanes
metro: Glòries

Located in the center of the plaza near a children's play area.

Plaça de les Glòries Catalanes outdoes the Arc de Triomphe in Paris in being the most humongous conjunction of boulevards and transportation systems. The plaza itself leaves a lot to be desired. It seems to serve mainly as a cross path for people going to the metro, buses or parking garages located in (or under) it.

Meridian is a low-lying sculpture that doesn't stand out from a distance, but as you pass by, its image and enigmatic markings make you stop and take notice. The form is a long wall of Cor-ten steel, about 16 in (.40 m) thick, that stretches across the ground, its top curved like the edge of a sphere. The smooth curvature, however, is broken by a section of jagged, mountainous eruptions. Along the bottom of one side, the wall has meter markings. On the other side, the markings are Dunkerque, 50°; Paris, 45°; xx°, Barcelona.

Two French artists known as Nemo created Meridian to commemorate the bicentennial of the meter. As history records, two other Frenchmen, Délambre and Méchain, measured the distance of a geodesic cleft running from the North Sea through France and the Pyrenees mountains down to Barcelona and were thus able to calculate the extent of the earth's circumference from which they derived the metric unit. Amazingly, Nemo incorporated all this in a simple, appealing public sculpture. An accompanying sign detailing the historical background would be helpful for people who aren't science buffs or fact wizards (or readers of this guidebook!).

6 Bryan Hunt

Ritus de primavera, 1986
Parc del Clot
metro: Glories, Clot

Parc del Clot is to the east of Plaça de les Glòries Catalanes and this sculpture is at the northernmost end of the park, near the corner of Carrer del Municipi and Carrer de Rossend Nobas.

This charming neighborhood park, superbly designed by Daniel FREIXES, has ball fields, a playground area, a large central square, elevated walkways, grassy hills and a grove of shade trees. Architectural fragments from an old railroad station and workshops are highlights of the setting. They feature an expanse of brick arches, now enhanced by a fountain with water cascading down into a pond.

The American sculptor Brian Hunt chose a roomlike space within the vestigial arched framework as the location for *Rites of Spring,* a tall bronze object whose flowing, rippling surface suggests a waterfall. Indeed, the work stands in a shallow pool like a mystical figure in an ancient temple. The spiritual-sublime

Nemo, *Meridian*

Bryan Hunt, *Rites of Spring*

aura is furthered by the rich greens of the ivy that envelop the architectural remains.

Viewing this work in the Parc del Clot setting provides an interesting example of the potency of context. If it were seen within the white box of a museum or gallery, it would appear as a cool, minimalist-derived sculpture; here it becomes a highly metaphorical, sensual object.

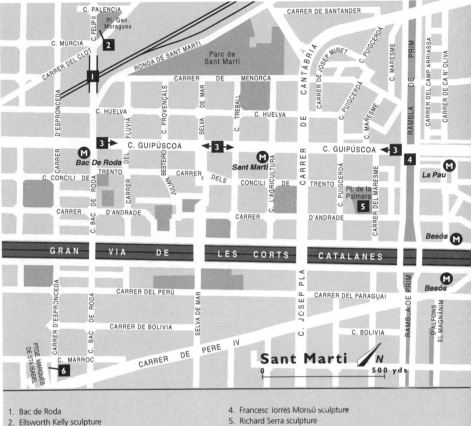

1. Bac de Roda
2. Ellsworth Kelly sculpture
3. Francesc Torres sculpture
4. Francesc Torres Monsó sculpture
5. Richard Serra sculpture
6. Hangar

Sant Martí

1   Bac de Roda Bridge

architect: Santiago CALATRAVA, 1987
metro: Bac de Roda

Located where Carrer de Bac de Roda changes its name to Carrer de Felip II.

Exemplifying Barcelona's unusual efforts in neighborhood revitalization was the decision to locate a landmark bridge by the world-class architect-engineer Santiago Calatrava in a derelict landscape. The bridge, a pedestrian and automobile crossing over railroad tracks, was also created as a vital link between two separated districts. Though the magnificent structure that resulted more than fulfills these goals, the immediate surroundings are an unsightly mess of graffiti-covered walls, weed-infested barren ground and chain-link fences. Only the residues of green lawns, trees and walking paths developed as parklands in tandem with the bridge project remain. If you can overlook the environs, the bridge itself—an extraordinary gem of contemporary creativity—is worth a visit.

Painted white, the steel structure has an elegant sculptural quality with two parabolic arches sweeping up and over a horizontal stretch of roadway. Both the vertical and

Santiago Calatrava, Bac de Roda Bridge

diagonal tension cables within the enclosed curve of the arch and the spread of the arch at the bottom that accommodates stair and ramp access routes produce additional rhythms without upsetting the harmonious flow of the whole. Details, like the slant of the railings or design of the lights, reinforce the form and lines even as they modulate the bridge's overall structure.

2   Ellsworth Kelly

Untitled, 1987
Plaça de General Moragues
metro: Bac de Roda, Sagrera

Located on the north side of Calatrava's bridge at the intersection of Carrer de Felip II and Carrer del Clot (the name changes here to Carrer de la Sagrera).

The interplay of triangular formations underlay Olga TARRASÓ's design for this plaza and Ellsworth Kelly's sculpture. Both are rooted in a minimalist aesthetic that pays extreme attention to shapes, edges, corners, scale, perspective dynamics and tonal relationships. It's quite difficult to appreciate this, however, because children's play equipment of a totally different stylistic character has been installed in the very midst of Kelly's two-part sculpture, where they also detract from the triangular-shaped ramps and walls of Tarrasó's simple but refined entrance schema. Community needs were obviously not incorporated into the initial program, and this resulted in a band-aid solution that has sadly degraded what could have been a notable public art project.

The sculpture Kelly devised for this triangular plaza situated a tall (50 ft; 15 m), slightly tapered column—a stainless-steel version of *Totem* (see p. 124)—at the foremost end of the property. Facing this at a distance is the juncture line (20 ft high; 6 m) of an acute-angled object comprising two curve-edged planes fabricated in Cor-ten steel. The work thus presents unlike forms linked by the specificity of their placement and their relationship to the space and shape of the plaza.

Ellsworth Kelly, Untitled

3   Francesc Torres

La línea de la Verneda, 1999
Carrer de Guipúscoa
metro: Bac de Roda, Sant Martí, La
Pau

If you're not in the mood for the 1-mi (1.6 km) walk that encompasses the full length of this public art project, you can hop on two or three metros and see the beginning, middle and end. If you're really strapped for time and energy, go to the metro stop at Sant Martí or La Pau and combine a viewing of a section of this work with the sculptures of Serra and Torres Monsó (see below).

Along the center esplanade of Carrer de Guipúscoa, Francesc Torres (a Barcelona native with ties to New York and Berlin) created The Verneda Line, a sculpture conceptualized around the history of the local area. A large letter "A," resting on the ground with a slanted top, establishes the beginning (Carrer de Bilbao); a broken band with intermittent text passages and occasional waves in the air, unfurls down the long boulevard; and the sculpted letter "B" marks the end (Rambla de

Prim). The line relays both official and unofficial historical data about the area, covering a period of 1000 years. One statement notes: "In 1933, the anarchists in the Verneda neighborhood abolished money. The experience, unfortunately, lasted only a few hours."

Frrancesc Torres, *The Verneda Line*

Frrancesc Torres, *The Verneda Line*

By presenting the line as a discontinuous stream, Torres conveys the idea that history is full of gaps with many unremembered and unrecorded parts. By setting the final "B" upside down, he also suggests that history can be read in reverse without changing its content.

4 Francesc Torres Monsó

El llarg viatge, 1992
Rambla de Prim
metro: La Pau

Located at the intersection of Carrer de Guipúscoa.

Rambla de Prim is one of those delightful European promenades—a wide, tree-lined medium strip where you can walk at a leisurely pace or sit for hours without interruption. Since the surrounding area comprises block after block of bland, 20th-century apartment buildings, the rambla is even more of a respite.

The Long Voyage by Francesc Torres Monsó, a sculptor from Girona, adds a nice headpiece to a long, shallow pool running down the middle of the boulevard. Standing

tall, the square column of weathered Corten steel has two cubic blocks tenuously balanced off its top front edge. As in the paintings of Kasimir Malevich and other Russian constructivists, primary geometric forms create animate compositions, especially when shapes and perspectives are disconcertingly off-kilter.

5 Richard Serra

El mur, 1984
Plaça de la Palmera
metro: Sant Martí, La Pau, Besòs

Located on the east side of the plaza near Carrer de Meresme.

In an early phase of its revitalization program, Barcelona commissioned Richard Serra to create a work for vacant acreage in the midst of a neighborhood overrun by dull, Mediterranean-modern apartment blocks constructed during Franco's reign. The artist designed a grand-scale wall sculpture in the genre of *Tilted Arc* (1981), the public artwork that aroused intense controversy, ultimately being removed (1989) from what was to have been its permanent location in New York's Federal Plaza.

The situation in Barcelona was unique since the artist didn't have to relate his work to an existing setting. Instead, he had the opportunity to create a setting coordinated with his sculpture. More precisely, his sculpture could shape and define the space and character of the land. (The architects Bernardo de SOLA and Pedro BARRAGÁN assisted with the landscape aspects of the project.)

Taking a solitary palm tree as a point of departure, Serra positioned it at the midpoint between two concrete walls, each about 171 ft long (52 m) long and 9 ft high (2.7 m). The walls form an emphatic barrier across the plaza. They also divide it into two opposing sections, one a sand-covered playing field and the other a cobblestone park lined with shade trees and furnished with benches and a bandstand. Although an autonomous object, the sculpture simultaneously relates to and separates itself from the surrounding environment.

The Wall is an utterly planar, massive blockage of space. Its form, though seemingly simple and self-evident, is actually confounding and visually unpredictable when viewed from various perspectives. It demands that you don't just look at it but move all around it so you can physically experience its potency. It appears variously straight, then curved; intimating, then protective; as a single, continuous structure and as two structures separated by a wide passageway. Most especially, you become attuned to the ways it molds and manipulates space.

Similarities with other Serra sculptures notwithstanding, this work is distinctive in being fabricated from concrete, not Cor-ten steel. Perhaps this project led the artist to focus subsequently on steel because concrete seemed too architectural a material for his aesthetic. Insofar as his public sculptures are inevitably marred by graffiti, the use of concrete, which can be more readily restored, has proved to be pragmatic.

Richard Serra, *The Wall*

6 Hangar

Passatge del Marqués de Santa Isabel
40, 08018
93-308-40-41
www.hangar.org
metro: Poblenou

From the Poblenou metro station walk north along Carrer de Lope de Vega for three streets; turn right onto Carrer de Pere IV at the intersection with Avinguda Diagonal; just after this, turn left into Marqués de Santa Isabel, a small street.

Hangar is an industrial building, modestly renovated for use as studios, workshops and meeting rooms. It began in 1997 as an artists' initiative under the umbrella of Fundació AAVC (Catalonia Association of Visual Artists), an organization with over 700 members. Currently there are 12–13 private studios, which accommodate both local artists and foreigners participating in a residency exchange program sponsored by art centers in Marseille, Lisbon, Rotterdam, New York (P.S. 1) and elsewhere.

Beyond its function as a studio facility, Hangar offers courses, lectures, technical assistance and equipment for use by artists. These support artistic experimentation and growth, especially in new realms, like video, multimedia production and electronic art. Although there's no formal exhibition space in the building, artists sometimes organize events and installations. On the last Friday of each month (8 pm), two or three artists who have studios in Hangar present their work to the public in a program called Showroom. Keep an eye out for posters and announcement cards that have been distributed around town to find out about the various activities.

The area around Hangar, an industrial zone with low rents in old factories and warehouses, is home to many artists. As in many cities, artists open their studios to the public annually. In Poblenou (the name of this district), the open studios event takes place for three days each June.

Map labels:
Plaça de Sants · C. DE VIRIAT · Sants Estació · Entença · Montserrat · CARRER · DEL · ROSSELLÓ · C. SANT ANATONI · Estacio Barcelona Sants · Pl. Països Catalans · CARRER · DE · PROVENÇA · C. L'AUTONOMIA · C. RIEGO · DE SANTS · C. PREMIA · C. WATT · C. MUNTADAS · Parc Espanya Industrial · AVINGUDA · DE · ROMA · C. MASNOU · C. D'ERMENGARDA · CARRER DEL RECTOR TRIADO · TARRAGONA · C. LLANÇA · Tarragona · C. D'ENTENÇA · C. ROCAFORT · CARRER · D'ARAGÓ · C. DE LLOBET · C. CALLAO · ST. NICOLAU · DE · CARRER · C. CALÀBRIA · Hostafrancs · C. DEL CONSELL DE CENT · CREU · COBERTA · 2 · Parc Joan Miró · C. DE VILAMARI · CARRER · DE · CARRER · DE · DIPUTACIÓ · Rocafort · GRAN · VIA · DE · LES · Plaça d'Espanya · CORTS · CATALANES · Espanya · AV. DE LA REINA MARIA CRISTINA · AVINGUDA DEL PARAL·LEL · AVINGUDA DE MISTRAL · CARRER · DE · ROCAFORT · SEPÚLVEDA · CARRER · DE · ROCAFORT · C. CALÀBRIA · Sants · N · 0 · 500 yds

1. Lawrence Weiner sculpture
2. Joan Miró sculpture
3. Plaça dels Països Catalans

4. Parc de l'Espanya Industrial
5. Plaça Joan Peiró
6. Jorge Castillo sculpture

Sants

1 Lawrence Weiner

Park Mistral, 1994–96
Avinguda de Mistral 46
metro: Espanya, Rocafort

Located to the southeast of Plaça d'Espanya near the intersection of Carrer d'Entença and Carrer de Floridablanca.

As part of its urban revitalization program, the city pedestrianized Avinguda de Mistral and developed it as a community space featuring a public artwork by Lawrence Weiner, a first generation, conceptual artist. In the segment of the street where grass now alternates with playground equipment, Weiner positioned three long cubes of concrete, creating a zigzag rhythm across the area. The cubes are painted red, blue and yellow respectively, and bear texts related to "mistral," the name of the street.

Although "mistral" can refer to the strong, cold, northerly wind in southern France, Weiner links it to Frédéric Mistral, a Frenchman awarded the Nobel prize in literature in 1904. Notably, the author wrote volumes on the language of d'Oc, which he sought to save and revive as the main tongue in its homeland, the Provençal region in the south of France. His efforts (though unsuccessful), share a likeness to Catalunya's fight to make Catalan

Lawrence Weiner, *Park Mistral*

the primary language of its territory.

In his signature manner of using texts to establish a conceptual, contextual orientation to a place, Weiner placed quotations from Mistral's writings (1845) on plaques at the ends of the cubes. In addition, he inscribed the following phrases in block letters in Catalan, English, Spanish and Provençal along the sides and tops of the cubes:

& SOMETHING WOVEN
& SOMETHING FORGED
& SOMETHING GIVEN TO THE SEA

2   Joan Miró

Dona i ocell, 1983
Parc Joan Miró
Carrer de Tarragona and Carrer d'Aragó
metro: Tarragona

If you walk north on Carrer de Tarragona from Plaça d'Espanya, you first pass the old bullring (Plaça de Braus Les Arenes), an impressively patterned, brick-and-tile structure from 1899, now used for pop music concerts. Behind this is Parc Joan Miró, a large square plot, previously occupied by a municipal slaughterhouse. If you have the time to walk through the park, rather than along the street lined with mundane office towers, you'll find a trellised vineyard, playground, library, grid of palm trees, and areas for outdoor bowling, hockey and table tennis.

In the northwest corner, set within a shallow pool presiding over a wide-open, paved plaza, is *Woman and Bird,* one of the city's favorite landmarks by its beloved native son, Joan Miró. This 72-ft-high columnar sculpture made from concrete and broken-tile mosaic was designed, fabricated (by the esteemed ceramicist Joan Gardy Artigas), installed and dedicated during the last two years of the artist's life. (He died at age 90 on December 25, 1983.) It's a classic Miró image combining playful, childlike elements, bright colors and burlesque eroticism. A bird, signified by a hollow cylinder bearing whimsical little yellow wings in the form of a crescent moon, is perched atop the head of a phallic-shaped woman whose body is defined by three dark concavities: a circular one in the middle of her face, another circular one in the back of her lower torso and a long, open slit running all the way up the front of her figure.

3 Plaça dels Països Catalans

architects: Helio PIÑÓN and Albert VIAPLANA with Enric MIRALLES, 1983
metro: Sants Estació

Having routed most major train lines to the new Barcelona Sants station, the city went about revitalizing the surrounding district. A critical priority was transforming a vast wasteland in front of the station into an impressive plaza. Bounded by congested roads and dreary, block buildings, the setting left a lot to be desired. Moreover, a profusion of railway tunnels located just beneath the surface restricted the weight and depth of materials or vegetation that could be used.

The resulting plaza, inspired by Wassily Kandinsky's 1926 essay on visual language—"Point and Line to Plane"—has an austere, utterly reductive character. It is devoid of any plants and all color, except for the pinkish tone of the granite pavement. The architects have also minimalized the functional elements—lampposts, benches, tables, canopy, walkways, fountain—into discrete entities (points), alignments or long pathways (lines), flat shapes or geometric shadows (planes). This is not to say that the plaza appears standardized for, in fact, there are considerable diversity and eccentricity. For example, a prominent oddity is a 49-ft-high (15 m) flat roof held up by thin poles. This uncommon object is intended as a shade area under which people can take shelter from the heat or rain. An undulating band running above the ground across the length of the huge plaza turns out to be a pergola covering the main pedestrian path. And two rows of descending-height steel pipes jutting up from the pavement are actually fountain components, only identifiable as such when the water is turned on (a seemingly infrequent occurrence). Although they designed to be functional, these pipes, like virtually all the objects, appear as pure compositional elements on a grand plane, which is the plaza.

As an abstract composition or conceptual program, the design is masterful and has received due praise. As a public space, however, it is an extremely harsh and barren expanse that is unwelcoming and doesn't invite human interaction. Indeed, the scarcity of seating is problematic and surprising considering the location adjacent to a place where waiting is a constant. In terms of ambience, the lack of volumetric elements

Joan Miró, *Woman and Bird*

H. Piñón and A. Viaplana, E. Miralles, Plaça dels Països Catalans

is also critical for it intensifies the aura of an uncomfortable, denaturalized space. (Notably, Kandinsky's essay concentrated exclusively on painting, and creativity removed from real-world space and forms.)

4   Parc de l'Espanya Industrial

△ architects: Luis PEÑA and Francesc RUIS, 1981–85
□ metro: Sants Estació

Located on the south side of Barcelona Sants.

Pressure from the local blue-collar community was greatly responsible for converting this large spread of land from an industrial, textile-mill complex into a park for public recreational use. As a result, it contains diverse activity centers for people of all ages. Functional needs notwithstanding, it is also an outstanding, environmentally sensitive design.

The architects explicitly wanted to separate the park from the train station and surrounding traffic hub. To accomplish this they took advantage of the sloped terrain to ensure that each zone would be a self-contained entity. Indeed, the park is virtually invisible from the station. To see it you must cross Carrer Sant Antoni and look down from a barrier punctuated by nine grandiose light towers. Appearing like border guards, their bombastic scale and architectonic form relate to the urban scene lying behind. In contrast, the long span of white stone steps, descending from the row of towers, segues into the landscape ahead—an Arcadian setting with ponds, fountain, lawn, trees, paths and benches. (Could anything be more diametrically opposed to the plazas around the station!)

Railings and/or a steep drop prevent entry from this periphery, but if you walk left toward the monumental sculpture situated atop the northeast corner of the park, you can angle around to gain access to pedestrian paths. *Dragon* (or *Dragon without St. George*, 1987) by Andres NAGEL, serves variously as an artwork, water slide and play object for kids. Cleverly configured to be theatrical and intriguing in appearance from multiple perspectives, its steel form is also well integrated with an architectural base shaped from curving steps and a fountain.

Within the park, areas are specifically developed for basketball, soccer, tennis, racquetball and other sports. There is a large indoor sports center. Sectors are harmoniously linked by pathways even as they are differentiated into open and closed terrains, places for socializing (there are numerous benches and tables) and quiet realms. Water, which is a dominant presence throughout, creates various ambiences and activity settings.

Sculptures are also scattered around the park. Most notable are two weathered steel objects located near the duck pond and racquetball courts. *Alto Rhapsody* (1984–85) by Anthony CARO is a disjunctive conglomerate of discrete curved and angular parts, many of which look like scraps found lying about a steel yard. A focal point is a

deep half-cylinder with pieces thrust into its hollow and positioned around its rim. As with most Caro objects, each segment and each viewpoint offer a distinctive motif, and they never add up to a unified whole.

In contrast, Pablo PALAZUELO organizes the flat and bent planes of *Landa V* (1985) around a central void. Although no two shapes are the same, the ensemble has a unifying core and knowable order.

If you follow the old stone wall and take the bridge over the lake, you'll exit the park at the west end, having meandered through the component sectors.

5 Plaça Joan Peiró

architects: Helio PIÑÓN and Albert VIAPLANA, 1990–91
metro: Sants Estació, Plaça de Sants
This plaza replays some of the features of Plaça dels Països Catalans (see above), but here eccentricity is more visible and more quirky, hence more compelling, even a bit

Anthony Caro, *Alto Rhapsody*

H. Piñón & A. Viaplana, Plaça Joan Peiró

surreal and witty. And because the land area is not as immense, the reductive aesthetic isn't so somber. The enhanced suggestion of volume is also a welcome change.

A flat canopy suspended high above a walkway is the centerpiece. In contrast to similar designs in the other plaza, this one has a half-wall on one side with windowlike cutouts. The construction appears like an unfinished building or relic, especially when related to adjacent objects. On one side there's a polished granite platform with four corner pillars. The slanted tops of the posts suggest useless absurdity, confirming the platform's appearance as a forsaken object, except that it is exactingly propped up to lie flat and hover above the ground just high enough to be used as seating and a table. Another odd seating-and-table structure on the other side is made of narrow wood slats (the same as are found in the roof) bound to a steel frame. This time, the base is slanted and a high back wall with a top ledge provides extra seating for those with a penchant for climbing and heights.

Notably, many architects and city planners involved with revitalization projects in Barcelona have been mindful of climate particularities. Not only do new or redesigned urban plazas contain pergolas that add shade areas to open spaces, but the shape and character of the canopies are adventurous and innovative.

6 Jorge Castillo

El ciclista, 1986
Plaça de Sants
metro: Plaça de Sants

From Plaça Joan Peiró it's a short walk west along the pedestrianized Passeig de Sant Antoni to Plaça des Sants, a major traffic intersection.

The Cyclist image, shaped by cut planes and silhouettes within a large steel plate, is appropriately located at ground level along the edge of a road. When seen from front or back, it shows a whimsical depiction of a man astride his bicycle followed by a bird. Alternatively, side views present fragmented shapes fanning out at the bottom as if the image of the figure were captured in a flurry of speed.

While calling attention to the popular sport of cycling, the work also pays tribute to this particular neighborhood's role, via the Sant Sporting Union, in establishing the Catalonia Cycling Tours (1923).

A flat surface in a prominent urban setting is a tempting bulletin board, and unfortunately this sculpture is often so plastered with posters that you can't see the image at all.

Gorge Castillo, *The Cyclist*

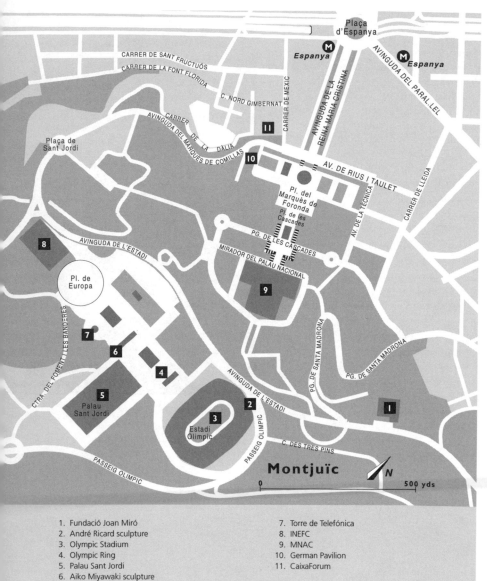

1. Fundació Joan Miró
2. André Ricard sculpture
3. Olympic Stadium
4. Olympic Ring
5. Palau Sant Jordi
6. Aiko Miyawaki sculpture
7. Torre de Telefónica
8. INEFC
9. MNAC
10. German Pavilion
11. CaixaForum

Montjuïc

This grand hill overlooking the ports and cityscape was always popular with Barcelonans for Sunday outings. Since 1992 the plethora of Olympic-related development has turned Montjuïc into a favorite leisure, culture and sports haven, visited by locals and tourists alike on both weekdays and weekends. Be prepared for crowds at virtually all the outdoor and indoor venues. Though the grand entrance to Montjuïc begins at Plaça d'Espanya and proceeds up a steep, terraced hillside embellished with fountains and cascading waterfalls, it's easier to start at the top and work your way down. You'll still be doing a fair amount of walking with a few hilly passages, but you'll eliminate the hefty climbs. If you plan to see most of the museum exhibitions plus the architecture and some parkland, be prepared to spend a full day.

The best means of public transportation to Montjuïc entails taking the metro to Espanya and then bus 50 up the mountain. You can also take the metro to Paral-lel and then ride the funicular to the top. (If you opt for the funicular, check about off-season curtailments of service on weekdays.)

1   Fundació Joan Miró

architect: Josep Lluís SERT, 1974; Jaume FREIXA, 1988

Plaça de Neptú, Parc de Montjuïc, 08038

93-443-94-70 f: 329-86-09
www.bcn.fjmiro.es
fjmiro@bcn.fjmiro.es
Oct–June: Tues–Wed, Fri, 10–7; Thurs, 10–9:30; Sun, 10–2:30; closed Mon
July–Sept: Tues–Wed, Fri, 10–8; Thurs, 10–9:30; Sun, 10–2:30; closed Mon
admission: 800/450 ptas
metro: Espanya, then bus 50; Montjuïc funicular

The road from Plaça d'Espanya winds around Montjuïc before reaching Fundació Joan Miró. Sit back, relax and take in the views. You'll know you've arrived when you see a white building on the left with curved roof projections and a few large sculptures on the front lawn.

Miró established his foundation in 1971 and opened this building four years later. His intention was to create it a major repository and display space for his own work and related archives. He moreover wanted it to be a dynamic center in which modern and contemporary work was exhibited, studied and discussed. From its inception, Fundació Miró supported and showed far-reaching and international modes of art, including objects, performances and productions using the most radical and at times unfashionable media, styles and subjects. Long before museums began to have special rooms devoted to emerging artists, and well in advance of the popularity of alternative spaces, Fundació Joan Miró was committed to promoting off-beat and experimental, investigatory work by relative unknowns.

Josep Lluís Sert, a close friend and fellow Catalan, designed the building. Similar to his widely acclaimed Maeght Foundation in France (Saint Paul de Vence, 1959–64), the architecture here bears witness to the hilltop setting and a preeminent concern with natural lighting. Although the building was expanded in 1986–88, the extension continues the form and conceptual orientation of the original. Its architect, Jaume Freixa, who worked with Sert on his design, was also commissioned in 2000 to develop a second extension to accommodate new gifts to the collection.

Despite being painted white, the austere, solid-concrete walls of the exterior give a fortresslike impression. This is contradicted, however, by the quirky, assemblage character of the whole, with its irregular sequence of closed and open cubic components and its eccentric silhouette of skylight protrusions. The wood-grain imprint on the surfaces, a residue of the casting process, and creative details, like the scalloped canopy over the main entrance, also temper the severity of the purist aesthetic without being decorative attachments.

Once inside, the impression of a window-less architecture is further challenged not only by skylights but also by the arrangement of galleries around two glass-enclosed courtyards. Sert's hallmark use of basic units composed to avoid a sense of repetition and uniformity is masterfully stated in variations of room height, shape and size and micro, nonlinear-oriented circulation routes. His assiduous coordination of interior and exterior is even more impressive. Windows and terraces in the notchlike areas, which are part of the building's periphery, provide visual or physical access to the surrounding park landscape, and a roof patio installed with sculptures offers spectacular city vistas.

Special exhibitions are located in the area to the left of the entrance. During a given year, the museum usually presents two thematic group shows, one monographic exhibition of a historical figure from the modern period and one show featuring a living artist, usually including work specially created for Fundació Miró.

Unlike virtually all major museums, this one has no in-house curators. Exhibitions are either commissioned from guest curators or organized by other institutions. It's an interesting setup, perhaps deserving credit for the high quality and broad-based character of the program. Recent exhibitions: *Art of Central Europe, Alexander Calder, Francesc Català-Roca, Ian Hamilton Finlay, Peter Greenaway, René Magritte, Sigmar Polke—On Goya, Reality and Desire, André Ricart, Mark Rothko, Thomas Schütte, Three Visions of the Landscape: Klee—Tanguy—Miró, Voices.*

Complementing the large special exhibitions are experimental projects by young artists within the series *Espai 13*. The titular *Open Space* refers both to the raw, semi-industrial gallery on the lower level and the free exploration of new paths and alternative perspectives. Since 1977 when it began (it was called *Espai 10* until 1988), there have been over 200 participants in the series. Each year a guest critic (of any nationality and usually a forward-thinking individual from a young generation) develops a thematic cycle comprising five shows, each of which features commissioned work(s) by a different artist or team of artists. The projects are wide-ranging from objects to on-site installations, actions, environments, performances and media productions.

Singular Electrics, the theme of *Espai 13* in 1998–99, focused attention on the latest

J. L. Sert (architect), J. Miró sculptures, roof of Miró Foundation

communications and imaging technologies as mechanisms for rereading the political, social and psychological patterns in our society. In 1999–2000, the artists Charles Juhasz Alvarado, Adam de la Croix, Ignacio Lang, Dhara Rivera and Chemi Rosado Seijo addressed issues of mobility and cultural exchange in the cycle *An Oasis in the Blue Desert—Young Caribbean Artists*. Without question, *Espai 13* presents some of the most compelling, fresh exhibitions of cutting-edge art that you're likely to find anywhere. Be sure to keep your eyes open for the staircase and elevator going down to the gallery since they are easy to miss, located in the back corner of the courtyard on the right.

The museum offers a full program of lectures, conferences, films, performances, concerts and other activities to accompany its large and small exhibitions. It also produces brochures, catalogues and other publications (in Catalan, Castilian and English) for most exhibitions and collection displays.

If you think you are already familiar with the art of Joan Miró, you're in for a pleasant surprise. The museum owns a rich selection of his paintings, tapestries, drawings, prints, ceramics, sculptures and notebooks, including choice objects from his prime surrealist years. You're sure to see many unexpected, fascinating aspects of Miró's creativity. Among the treasures are *Personage* (1930), a witty, erotic sculpture comprising found wooden elements, an umbrella and a tree branch, and *Man and Woman in front of a Pile of Excrement* (1935), the gripping little painting that captures the foreboding climate in Europe during the mid-1930s. Two series from Miró's middle years are also striking. *Paintings on White Ground for the Cell of a Solitary Man* (1968) reveal an incredible manifestation of line as expression, freedom, thought, meditation and endless meanings. And in *The Hope of the Man Condemned to Death* (1974), color, form and line triumph as abstract, formal presences even as they evince symbolic and figurative potency.

The collection began with a major donation

Thomas Schütte exhibition, 1999

from the artist and is still growing through purchases and gifts from his family and friends. Displays and special exhibitions from the collection are located in galleries behind the right courtyard on the ground floor and upstairs all around this courtyard. During the summer, the entire museum is devoted to Miró's art.

Rounding out the exhibitions is a display of art given to the foundation as a tribute to Miró after his death in 1983. Included are works by Balthus, Alexander Calder, Anthony Caro, Marcel Duchamp, Max Ernst, Sam Francis, Philip Guston, Fernand Léger, André Masson, Henri Matisse, Robert Motherwell, Claes Oldenburg, Robert Rauschenberg, Richard Serra, Yves Tanguy, Dorothea Tanning and others. For the most part these are not great objects, but the collection is interesting nonetheless for indicating the broad appeal of Miró's art across several generations of radically dissimilar artists.

In addition to galleries, the foundation building also contains an auditorium, library, bar-restaurant, huge gift shop and bookstore. The restaurant is a delightful, albeit often crowded and noisy place, and though the bookstore has a good selection of art magazines and monographs on modern artists and architects, the contemporary era is thinly represented.

2 André Ricard

Support for the Olympic Flame, 1992
Avinguda de l'Estadi
metro: Espanya, then bus 50

If you turn right when exiting Fundació Miró and continue along Avinguda de l'Estadi, you will soon come to the main Olympic Stadium. Perhaps the first thing you'll see, positioned outside the stadium at road's edge, is a tall steel sculpture with an elongated, curvaceous form topped by a bowl. Created by a Barcelona designer, André Ricard, this soaring image, somewhat resembling a torch, was the object that held the Olympic flame. In an amazing display worthy of Greek spectacles and contemporary showmanship, the lighting ceremony culminated in an archer shooting a flaming arrow into the sculpture's bowl.

3 Estadi Olímpic

architects: Vittorio GREGOTTI with Carles BUXADÉ, Federico CORREA, Joan MARGARIT, Alfonso MILÀ, 1990
Avinguda de l'Estadi
daily, 10–6
admission: free
metro: Espanya, then bus 50; Montjuïc funicular

Exemplifying the city's restore-and-revitalize spirit was its decision to make an old stadium the centerpiece of the 1992 Olympics. To be sure, the decision was impacted with symbolism. The structure had been built for the 1929 International Exhibition of Barcelona, where it was pridefully used for the inaugural

events and other activities. Six years later, it was again the focus of worldwide attention as the site for the "People's Olympics"—an alternative to the official 1936 games in Berlin, which many nations planned to boycott because of the Nazi rise to power. But then civil war broke out in Spain and the project had to be abandoned.

Having survived for over 60 years, albeit unused and in a horrible state of disrepair, the old stadium—a vivid reminder of Barcelona's glorious and defiant pastó was reborn for the Olympics as a signifier of the new Barcelona. Actually, only the greatly restored, neoclassical facade of the original remains. To increase the seating capacity to over 50,000 and to meet new security and safety requirements, the architects pared the stadium down to its shell, designed an entirely new infrastructure and added features like a metal canopy over the grandstand.

Olympic Stadium is now used for sports competitions, rock concerts and special events.

4 Anella Olímpica

architects: Federico CORREA, Alfonso MILÁ, Carles BUXADÉ, Joan MARGARIT, 1992
metro: Espanya, then bus 50; Montjuïc funicular

As you walk around the stadium, you'll enter an area known as the Olympic Ring. This monumental span of cleared, landscaped and park terrain, encompassing new and refurbished sports facilities, was the epicenter of the 1992 games. Its spinal core is a grand esplanade configured as a series of stepped plazas extending from the stadium to INEFC (a training hall). Shallow geometrically shaped ponds, a wall of cascading water, paved and grass-covered expanses and rows of tall lighting pillars divide and order this very refined but dauntingly formal space.

The setting with its panoramic views and projects by internationally renowned architects is well worth a visit. If the weather is nice, you might consider a picnic under the trees in the Jardí d'Aclimatació (Acclimatization Garden) on the upper side of the esplanade, or on one of the open-air terraces in the area.

5 Palau Sant Jordi

architect: Arata ISOZAKI, 1983–90
Avinguda de l'Estadi, 08038
metro: Espanya, then bus 50; Montjuïc funicular

Before walking around the entire esplanade, take a close look at the extraordinary Sant Jordi Pavilion by Arata Isozaki, one of leading architects of the contemporary era. (He designed the Museum of Contemporary Art in Los Angeles.) Set into the hill below the stadium on the left (south) side of the esplanade, this unobtrusive structure with a gracefully curved roof, often likened to a Japanese warrior's helmet, houses the largest indoor facility built for the Olympics. Though shaped by innovative technology, the exterior purposefully downplays a high-tech image in favor of contours in harmony with the natural surroundings and the old stadium.

A prime element of the design bravura is the space-frame dome. Formed by a geodesic structure covered with zinc sheets and glazed ceramic tiles, it was totally assembled on the ground and then raised into position by hydraulic jacks. From the inside, the lack of supporting columns and the ring of natural light encircling the upper section, which is also dotted with skylights, makes the roof appear ethereal and suspended in space. This airiness is also expressed on the exterior by the undulating rhythm of the glazed walls in the midsection.

The main hall can accommodate an ice rink or 200-meter track with seating for 17,000. The pavilion also houses four basketball courts, restaurants, offices and related athletic facilities, many of which are located in the flat-roofed, rectangular building that extends from the main structure on a lower level of the hillside. Though identified largely as a sports stadium, Palau Sant Jordi can also be used for commercial fairs, exhibitions, performances and conventions.

Arata Isozaki, Palau San Jordi

6 Aiko Miyawaki

Canvi, 1990
Avinguda de l'Estadi
metro: Espanya, then bus 50; Montjuïc
funicular

On the plaza in front of Palau Sant Jordi, 36 concrete columns joined by curving, swaying steel cables reiterate the reductive, grid aesthetic and industrial materials of contemporary sculpture even as they reject a focus on the object in favor of what Aiko Miyawaki has termed "a kind of intermediary." More than static form or compositional order, she is concerned with conceptual visualizations brought about by movement, sound, light reflections and other shifting emanations. The Japanese title U*tsuroi*, which translates into English as *The Moment of Movement or Change,* encapsulates the Eastern idea of evanescent nature. On viewing Miyawaki's art, Kenzaburo Oe, the 1994 Nobel laureate for literature, described it as "the eternal fleeting, the sustained transient."

Santiago Calatrava, Torre de Telefónica

7 Torre de Telefónica

architect: Santiago CALATRAVA, 1991–92
Avinguda de l'Estadi
metro: Espanya, then bus 50; Montjuïc
funicular

Just beyond the Miyawaki sculpture at the edge of the esplanade and overlooking the city is the sculptural Communications Tower by Santiago Calatrava, sometimes called the *Olympic Flame.* Set in a circular pool, the slender, white-painted steel mast rises up and connects with a horseshoe form swirled around a projectile-like element. Though commissioned by Spanish Telefónica to enhance digital communications systems in Barcelona, the tower was also designed as a sundial: the mast is slanted so it is at the same angle as the earth's axis.

The object, which actually has a functional interior, was a late, very controversial addition to the Olympic Ring. The appropriateness of its location within the sports complex, the nature of its design and its relationship to the environment were all topics of heated debate.

8 INEFC

architect: Ricardo BOFILL, 1989–91
Avinguda de l'Estadi, 08038
metro: Espanya, then bus 50; Montjuïc
funicular

Located at the far western end of the Olympic Ring.

If you're expecting a Bofill building with outrageous borrowings from classical architecture, the structure that functioned as a training center during the Olympics and is now the National Institute of Physical Education of Catalonia will be disappointing. Four stories high, it's organized as twin units laid out in an H-shape with the main public elements located in the center hall and cloistered courtyards on either side. The overtly classical exterior with its emphatic front stairs and prefabricated concrete elements made to look like carved stone are Bofill trademarks, but the design lacks his characteristic panache.

9 Museu Nacional d'Art de Catalunya

renovation: Gae AULENTI with Enric STEEGMAN, 1985–93

Palau Nacional, 08038

93-622-03-75 f: 622-03-74 (these are the new numbers)

www.gencat.es/mnac

mnac@correu.gencat.es

Tues–Wed, Fri–Sat, 10–7; Thurs, 10–9; Sun, 10–2:30; closed Mon

admission: 800/500 ptas; Thurs, 7–9, 350 ptas; special exhibition, 300–700 ptas

metro: Espanya, then bus 50; Montjuïc funicular

Built for the International Exhibition of 1929, the National Palace sits atop the north face of Montjuïc and is fronted by a succession of terraces, waterfalls and fountain displays all aligned on axis with the entrance towers in Plaça Espanya. Though staircases previously served as the only pedestrian route up the hill, these are now accompanied by escalators. It's still a hefty climb, and you'll undoubtedly find at least one escalator segment out of service. If you're continuing on from Fundació Miró or the Olympic Ring, or if you've taken bus 50 up the hill, you'll approach the museum from the rear via one of the paths off Avinguda de l'Estadi. These lead around to Mirador del Palau, the museum's front portico and a clearing with majestic views of the city.

Palau Nacional became the Museu Nacional d'Art de Catalunya (MNAC) in 1934 and now houses art from the Romanesque, Gothic, Renaissance and Baroque periods. Sometimes documentary photography (19th–20th century) is also exhibited here. Composed mainly of Catalan work, the museum is especially renowned for its extraordinary collection of 12th-century frescoes. These were saved from plundered, ruined churches in the Pyrenees and are displayed here in architectural settings replicating the originals. These paintings are a must-see not only for their cultural and artistic significance but also

because they bring telling relevance to bear on spatial and figurative issues addressed by modern artists.

The frescoes and related work from the Romanesque era are exhibited to the left of the main lobby; paintings and art from later periods is on the right side. A gift shop, restaurant and domed, oval space with a grand pipe organ (created for the 1929 fair and currently used for receptions) lie to the back of the lobby.

In addition to the art, Gae Aulenti's renovation of the building is an attraction at MNAC. Similar to the unconventional interiors she created for the Musée d'Orsay in Paris and Palazzo Grassi in Venice, she has set stark white contemporary walls as detached surfaces in front of old architectural elements. Cuts, in the form of geometrically shaped apertures, sharp angles and blunt borders, keep original features visible even as they create disjunctive juxtapositions and the complexity of a multilayered structure. Aulenti also divides or encloses space with stagelike settings created by adding walls, arches, doorways, platforms, projecting shelves, ramps and steps. Beyond functioning to individualize the shape and nature of a particular display or area, the new components often serve to open, block or confound views from one space to another. Indeed, Aulenti's architectural design is not a neutral backdrop but an assertive presence—for better and for worse.

In the Romanesque galleries where frescoes and mural fragments are placed in spare architectural environments (chapels, domes, vaulted ceiling structures, etc.) with subdued lighting the results are mesmerizing. The experience is enriched by related materials—models and floor plans of the original churches, photographs, maps and labels in three languages (Catalan, Castilian, English)—unobtrusively installed in an adjacent space.

10 German Pavilion at the International Exhibition

architect: Ludwig MIES VAN DER ROHE, 1929/1986

Avinguda del Marquès de Comillas, 08038

www.miesbcn.com

miesbcn@ysi.es

daily, 10–8

admission: 400/250 ptas

metro: Espanya

Located at the base of Montjuïc on the left (west) side of Plaça de Carles Buïgas and the circular fountain, La Font Màgica.

Though sometimes called the Barcelona Pavilion, this paragon of modern architecture was built as the headquarters for the German delegation at the 1929 International Exhibition in Barcelona. Soon thereafter it was dismantled, admired only through photographs by generations of architects and students of modern culture. A proposal to reconstruct it at the time of the fair's 25th anniversary (1954) received widespread support, including the agreement of its revered designer, Ludwig Mies van der Rohe, but circumstances were not advantageous. Finally, in 1981 the city undertook the project, and five years later the building was inaugurated on its original site. It now houses the Mies van der Rohe Foundation.

Still today, the architect's extraordinary design, premised on the simple interplay of planes, spaces and clear lines, has a radical edge. Clones and copies have been attempted, though they typically lack the finesse in proportional relationships and masterful use of materials that endow Mies's austere formalism with a serenity and elegance. It isn't just the glass curtain-walls—utterly unconventional in 1929—but a balanced embrace of transparency and the emphatic, rhythmic integration of inner and outer spaces. And though the overhanging flat, white roof was a conspicuous break with tradition, it was the turn away from bulky, concrete columns to high chromium–content (shiny) steel that reinforces the building's horizontality and gracefulness.

L. Mies van der Rohe, German Pavilion

Travertine floors, walls of dark green marble and golden onyx, and water—present in the long, shallow pool stretching across the front of the pavilion and in a second, interior pool—diversify the surfaces. Characteristically, Mies enriched the utterly reductive structure without adding decoration. Even the life-size nude sculpture, Georg Kolbe's *Morning* (1925), that he placed within the interior pool serves as a point of harmonious contrast, not embellishment. (The original sculpture in plaster, no longer extant, is here represented by a bronze replica.)

Mies's famous Barcelona chairs, designed specifically for the 1929 pavilion, are again included as part of the display. Constructed with a gently curving X-frame and fabricated from aluminum and leather, the chairs and ottomans—like the pavilion itself—epitomize the best of the unadorned, rigorously articulated forms that have come to characterize modernity.

11 CaixaForum

renovation: Roberto LUNA, Arata ISOZAKI, 1999–2001
Casaramona, Avinguda del Marquès de Comillas 6–8, 08038
93-423-88-06 f: 325-17-08
www.fundacio.lacaixa.es
info.fundacio@lacaixa.es
Tues–Sat, 11–8; Sun, 11–3; closed Mon
admission: free
metro: Espanya

Located across the street from the Mies pavilion at the foot of Montjuïc.

"La Caixa" is Spain's largest and richest bank with the familiar, ubiquitous symbol—a blue star, red spot, yellow dot created by Joan Miró. Fundació "la Caixa" (FLC), the philanthropic branch of the corporation, has developed impressive social, cultural, science, environmental and educational programs with outposts throughout the country. The building known historically as Casaramona will become CaixaForum by the end of 2001,

replacing the mansion in the Eixample district (see pp. 119) as the foundation's cultural center in Barcelona.

The visual arts division of FLC has become one of the premier promoters and supporters of contemporary art in Spain. Its stated goal is to increase public awareness and interest in contemporary and experimental art, photography, historic avant-garde artists and specific aspects of cultural history. CaixaForum has the space and resources to explore new ways to implement these goals, while continuing the enterprising, quality exhibitions and events it has developed in the past. Because it sees itself not as a museum but as a cultural center with a multidisciplinary base, it offers a spectrum of activities geared toward diverse audiences. Indeed, the performances, lectures, debates, concerts, poetry readings and workshops not only complement the art but are notable in their own right. Attending one of these, as well as spending time in the Mediateca, which has a superb collection of over 1,000 artist videos, will make your visit extraspecial.

Walking around the exterior and interior of the center is a great way to see one of the best examples of industrial Modernisme. The building was designed by Josep PUIG I CADAFALCH in 1911–13 as a textile and thread factory for Casimir Casaramona. During the Civil War (1940), it was appropriated for use as a horse stable and parking garage by the Policia Nacional and functioned as such until 1993. By the time the police moved out, the structure had severely deteriorated. Since it had been declared a historic monument in 1976, redevelopment of the site necessitated major restoration and conservation work.

La Caixa de Pensions had acquired Casaramona in 1963 but made no plans for it until 1992, when Fundació "la Caixa" actively explored the possibility of converting the large building into its main cultural center. This entailed replacing the decorative brickwork brick by brick, totally reconstructing the interior space, expanding the complex by excavating a new subterranean level and moving the main entrance. Despite all the

A. Isozaki (entrance) and R. Luna, CaixaForum (computer image)

changes, great care was taken to respect the exterior and original structure.

In both appearance and layout the old factory is distinctive. It fills an entire city block without being massive because it's only one story high, except for four corner segments, which have two stories, and two tall towers that look like campaniles but in the past contained water for fire protection. And though it appears to be a solid entity from the outside, it's actually a complex of separate units. As you will discover once inside, the whole is divided into three long zones with streets (initially designed as delivery routes) running between and across them.

The new entrance, designed by Arata Isozaki (the architect of the Palau Sant Jordi Olympic stadium), provides the sharpest contrast to the old building. It's a grand, minimalist glass prism extending across the facade and down into the new, subterranean reception area. Whereas the main gates were originally on Carrer de Méxic, now the entry frontage faces the Mies pavilion on Avinguda Marqués de Comillas.

In addition to public service areas, the subterranean level includes a gift shop, bookstore (with a good selection of catalogues, art books and magazines), library Mediateca (video library), auditorium and conservation labs. The ground level comprises the exhibition galleries, educational workshops, a café-restaurant and the restored modernista streets. Meeting rooms and administrative offices are housed in the four corner units. The spaces allocated to exhibitions are open, flexible expanses that can readily accommodate all sorts of contemporary artwork. One wing will be devoted to rotating shows of objects from the collection and the schedule will typically feature three or four different exhibitions at any given time.

A section of the FLC cultural center opened on November 29, 1999, for a special exhibition celebrating the centennial of the Barcelona soccer team, *100 Years of*

Blaugrana Passion. When the exhibition was over, the center closed again to finish construction work. It reopens officially in late 2001. Exhibitions will follow the pattern developed in the former location. That is to say, the schedule will include superb showings of work by leading contemporary artists (monographs and thematic projects), photography, creative dimensions of past epochs, non-Western cultures and Spanish heritage. Recent exhibitions (held in the Eixample space): *Arman, Aspects of a Collection, The Desert, Forms of the World (Photography from the New Objectivity Group), Gary Hume, Herbert List, Tracy Moffatt, Return to the Land of Wonders—Contemporary Art and Childhood Imagery, Miguel Rio Branco, Russian Symbolism, Shameless Gazes, Spirits of Water—Art of Alaska and British Columbia, Ed van der Elsken.*

In addition to organizing discerning exhibitions, FLC began developing an outstanding collection of contemporary art in 1985. Representing the dominant international currents of the past decades, it includes over 800 choice works (painting, sculpture, photography, video, installation) by such artists as Joseph Beuys, Sophie Calle, Francesco Clemente, Richard Deacon, Günter Förg, Katharina Fritsch, Bernard Frize, Robert Gober, Andreas Gursky, Gary Hill, Cristina Iglesias, Ilya Kabokov, Jannis Kounellis, Paul McCarthy, José Maldonado, Mario Merz, Tatsuo Miyajima, Shirin Nashat, Bruce Nauman, Jorge Oteiza, Sigmar Polke, Fiona Rae, Gerhard Richter, Thomas Ruff, Doris Salcedo, Susana Solano, Sam Taylor-Wood, Rosemarie Trockel, Richard Tuttle, Juan Uslé, Jeff Wall, Franz West, Rachel Whiteread. Though exhibitions focusing on different aspects of the collection will be an ongoing feature of the program in Barcelona, FLC will continue to circulate collection exhibitions around Spain. Should you come across an announcement for one of these in your travels, don't hesitate to see it. Guaranteed, you'll find an invigorating show with top-notch examples of recent art.

Col·lecció Testimoni, a second collection begun in 1987, specifically aims to keep track of the artistic panorama of Spain. Works are all purchased from regularly scheduled shows held in galleries across the country. Each year a new acquisitions exhibition takes place in a different location. This not only celebrates Spanish contemporary art but also affords an excellent overview of the preceding year's production and directions.

FotoPres, a biennial competition and exhibition honoring the best work by photojournalists in Spain, is yet another FLC program in the visual arts.

Outskirts Of Barcelona

Centre Cultural Tecla Sala

📧 Avinguda Josep Tarradelias 44
L'Hospitalet de Llobregat
93-338-57-71 f: 338-55-53
cultura@l-h.es
Tues–Sat, 11–2 and 5–8; Sun, 11–2; closed Mon
admission: free
metro: Torrassa
From the metro station walk down the hill of Carrer Rosalia de Castro and turn right at the first corner.

L'Hospitalet is an urban community bordering Barcelona on the southwest. Tecla Sala, its cultural center, formerly a textile factory, has housed an art exhibition space in an amenable but hampering, ground-floor area since 1986. In October 2001 exhibitions will move to a new space in an adjacent paper mill, an industrial stone-and-wood structure from 1855 being renovated by Albert VIAPLANA and Helio PIÑÓN. What is already one of the region's strongest art centers—and best kept secrets—will undoubtedly become stronger and better known.

Tecla Sala's spunky, risk-taking exhibition program shows young, imaginative artists and provocative, at times contentious work. Don't be surprised if you find works by some of the feisty rebels who are shaking up the international art world here rather than in Barcelona proper. It may be off the beaten track in terms of location, but the eyes and ears of this exhibition space are attuned to where it's happening. With its history of

Francesc Torres, *The Man Who Lost His Head,* 2000

producing joint projects with other institutions (both within and outside Spain) and having artists create special installation works on site, Tecla Sala offers compelling, impressive exhibitions. Be sure to put it on your list of must-see places. Should you be in the area at the time of a performance, poetry, music or film conference, try to attend. These, too, are memorable, energizing events with eminent participants.

Recent exhibitions: *The Eros Garden*, *Alberto García-Alix*, *Sarah Lucas*, *Manuel Ocampo*, *The Other Britannia*, *Alicia Ríos*, *Spanish Conceptual Art (Rafael Tous Collection)*, *Francesc Torres*, *Francesca Woodman*.

Walden 7

architect: Ricardo BOFILL, 1973–75
Avinguda de la Indústria, Sant Just Desvern
bus: 157 from Plaça des Sants or L57, L50, L51, L61, L62 from various locations in Barcelona; exit at Edifici Walden.

Sant Just Desvern, a growing suburb with a rural and industrial heritage, lies on the northwest periphery of Barcelona. Walden 7, the monumental apartment complex by Ricardo Bofill, is located on a site formerly occupied by the Sanson cement factory and bordering the N340 highway. The odd conjunction of this location and the utopian name of Walden suggests the bold nature of the project. Rather than a sylvan paradise it's urban architecture formulated with the individual, not the masses, in mind. If you're familiar with Bofill's flamboyant, high-density housing in France, you won't be surprised that here, too, he has created an eccentric structure challenging the regimented plan and bland appearance of the ubiquitous block building.

The design's idiosyncratic character is instantly visible in the colossal portals and tiny, half-circle balconies scattered across irregularly shaped facades. Looking somewhat like a medieval castle or fortress, its tile surfaces—variously colored rust, rose, blue,

Ricardo Boifill, Walden 7

green, violet, mustard—also bear witness to the spirit of Gaudí.

Bofill has described Walden as a vertical labyrinth. The term vividly conveys the reality of his 16-story building comprising 446 apartments with seven interior courtyards linked on all levels by vertical and horizontal circulation paths. The apartments in turn are composed of one to four modules arranged on one level or as a duplex, and accessed by a semiprivate corridor or staircase. A few shops, services and public spaces are located on the ground floor, and the roof terrace is developed as a leisure zone with two swimming pools.

As imaginative as the building was, it soon had the appearance of a disaster. The main problem related to the tile facing, where large sections progressively fell off, leaving an unsightly, bald surface. Finally, in 1993–95, the exterior was totally repaired and is now in pristine condition.

La Fábrica—Taller de Arquitectura

architect: Ricardo BOFILL, 1973–75
Avinguda de la Indústria 14, Sant Just Desvern
bus: 157 from Plaça des Sants or L57, L50, L51, L61, L62 from various locations in Barcelona; exit at Edifici Walden.

Located behind Walden 7. Because of the chain-link fence surrounding the property and the enormous amount of vegetation on and around the building, it's difficult to get a good look. It's best to walk along the bordering sidewalks, poking your head intermittently between the vines.

On the back part of the Walden 7 lot, Bofill developed a building that transformed the silos, subterranean tunnels, machine rooms and other segments of the abandoned cement factory into new spaces with very different uses. Not only did Bofill adapt, refurbish and add onto parts of the former factory, but he also used dynamite and a jackhammer to reveal hidden forms and create open spaces. Ultimately, he produced an incredible, surreal ensemble tailor-made as his family home and the headquarters of Taller de Arquitectura (his business). The unconventional work area includes offices, studios, a maquette laboratory, projection room, library, archive storage and a gigantic "cathedral" space for exhibitions, concerts, receptions and social functions.

Among the oddities in the layout and exterior design are stairs leading nowhere; old building fragments kept as ruins; refined, churchlike window slits in big concrete towers; cutout voids as independent shapes; unrestored walls, which look like bombed-out remains, juxtaposed with reconstructed volumes; and a seemingly unfinished structure composed of incongruous, autonomous units. Despite all this, the building has an Edenic aura because greenery climbs the walls and hangs down from the roofs in profusion, and a veritable forest of tall eucalyptus, palm, cypress and olive trees envelops it.

EXCURSIONS FROM BARCELONA

Lleida

The Castilian name of Lérida is often used for this inland Catalan city. Train from Barcelona, 2 hr.

Sala El Roser

Caller de Cavallers 15, 25002
97-327-09-95 f: 326-09-28
Mon–Fri, 6–8; Sat, 11–2 and 6–8; Sun, 11–2

From the train station walk straight through the city either on Avinguda de Françesc Macià alongside the river, or one street up on the pedestrian-shopping street that has various names. Turn right on Caller de Cavallers. El Roser is on the right side about halfway up the hill.

Built in the 18th century as a convent, this building now houses a museum, art school, library and Sala El Roser. Although the exhibition space—a center area flanked by six small, chapellike rooms enclosed with high arches—has historical resonance, it's hardly a flexible, neutral location for showing contemporary art.

The program focuses on young artists, not necessarily local or Spanish, some doing original, intriguing work showing a good understanding of recent art and art critical currents, and others producing pallid variations on the ideas and methods of the current superstar artists. As with many such spaces, you never know what to expect. If you're adventurous and like to explore untouristed territory, a visit here may be worth the trip.

Recent exhibitions: *Anna Busto, Daniel Canogar, Existential Times, Joan Rebull, Maite Villafranca.*

Girona

Although Girona (Gerona in Castilian) may not warrant a visit because of its contemporary art offerings, it's a delightful, picturesque place with lots of old European flavor. You can easily explore the city, particularly the medieval sector, which lies east of the Riu Onyar, on foot, but be prepared for a steep climb up the steps and winding passages to the gardens, Roman walls and other hillside sites. Even if you just stay on the flatlands, the narrow, arcaded streets (spanking clean) are filled with historical points of interest and shops selling local crafts and wares. The summer months are typically crowded with tourists from Germany, Britain and Scandinavia.

Train from Barcelona, 1 hr.

Espais, Centre d'Art Contemporani

Carrer Bisbe Lorenzana, 31–33, 17002
97-220-25-30 f: 220-84-98
Mon–Sat, 12–2 and 4:30–8:30

From the train station walk straight ahead for 2 1/2 blocks on Carrer Bisbe Lorenzana.

Located across from the four-star Hotel Carlemany, this chic exhibition space has a lively program of exhibitions and performances. Most of the artists are young Catalans who may not be big names but show a good grasp of contemporary trends and ideas. Recent exhibitions: *Jordi Canudas, Chema López, Pere Noguera, Quim Cantalozella—Jaune Geli—Elena Genís.*

Sales Municipals d'Exposició

Rambla de la Llibertat 1, 17004
97-222-33-05 f: 221-83-45
www.ajuntament.gi/ccm
ccm@grn.es
Tues–Fri, Sun, 6–9; Sat, 12–2; closed Mon
admission: free

Located alongside the Tourist Office at the

south end of the old city. From Espais, cross to the plaza (Plaça Miquel Santaló) and turn right (northeast) onto Carrer de Joan Maragall; continue to the river (three blocks); cross Plaça Catalunya, turn left and walk along the riverfront promenade, which becomes Rambla de la Llibertat.

Housed in a compact building with big copper doors, Girona's Municipal Exhibition Space puts on refreshing, noteworthy shows, favoring photography, mixed-media, video and installation art. The focus is on unusual or evocative modes of expression where creative talent merges with technical ability. Exhibitions are nicely presented in two modest rooms with just enough works to convey an artist's sensibility.

Recent exhibitions: *Daniel Canogar, Mim Juncà, Montse Lao, Torres Monsó, Antonio Muntadas, Teo Ortiz, Humberto Rivas, Mayte Vieta.*

Museu del Cinema

Sèquia 1, 17001
972-41-27-77 f: 41-30-47
June–Sept: Tues–Sun, 10–8; closed Mon
Oct–May: Tues–Sun, 10–6; closed Mon
admission: free

Go back across the river on Pont de Pedra (the bridge adjacent to the Tourist Office) and take the first right onto Carrer Santa Clara; at the next street, Carrer Perill, turn left; this short street hooks around and intersects with Carrer de Sèquia. The museum is on the corner.

In addition to being a repertory film theater, this cinema museum has the distinction of being the first of its kind in Spain. It opened in 1998. Permanent exhibitions derive from the collection of Tomàs Mallol, an extraordinary wealth of materials spanning the period from the mid–17th century to 1970. Included are 7,500 objects, apparatus and accessories from the precinema and early cinema period; 15,000 documents (posters, photographs, drawings, etc.), 800 films and 700 film-related publications. Complementing the historical

displays from the permanent collection are interactive displays, temporary loan exhibitions, lectures and conferences. If you're a film buff, this is a place you don't want to miss.

Banc d'Espanya

architects: Lluís CLOTET, Ignacio PARICIO, 1983–89
Gran Via Jaime I

Continue down Carrer de Sèquia, passing alongside Plaça de Constitució (on the right); turn right onto Gran Via de Jaume 1, a grand avenue. The bank building is just ahead and across the street on the corner of Carrer 20 de Juny de 1808.

The cylindrical brick form of this postmodern building, with its arcadelike openings running round the facade, recalls the Roman tradition of monumental structures created for amphitheaters, aqueducts and bullrings. The architectural team of Clotet and Paricio intentionally sought to emphasize the affinity with the region's historic roots even as they aimed to convey the incongruity of a bank looking like a bullring.

The building has many whimsical oddities that further stray from institutional bank design. Most pronounced are the encircling driveway looking like a moat and the suggestion that the outer brick wall is a false facade shielding a "real" building inside.

Figueres

Located 85 mi north of Barcelona. Train from Barcelona, 1 3/4 hr; from Girona, 30 min.

Teatre-Museu Dalí

Plaça Gala-Salvador Dalí 5, 17600
97-251-19-76 f: 250-16-66
www.dali-estate.org
July–Sept: daily, 9–8
Oct–June: Tues–Sun, 10:30–6; closed Mon
admission: 1000/800 ptas

The walk from the train station to the museum takes about 10 minutes; just follow the signs.

As you might expect, this is a very popular tourist attraction with busloads arriving continuously no matter what season of the year or time of day. Though Dalí's art is historically linked to classic Surrealism of the 1920s–30s, his conceptual approach, purposefully outrageous behavior, development of installations and environments, embrace of commercialism, merger of the classical and kitsch, egocentric eccentricity, ongoing art-life performance activities and his controversial subject matter dealing with eroticism and heroic figures from history, mythology, Hollywood and religion have all been adopted, whether directly or not, by the most prominent and revered artists of the current generation. A visit to this site, itself a Dalí creation, is thus imperative for anyone working in or trying to grasp the pulse of major tendencies in contemporary art. The unabashed formation of this museum as an entertainment center is also relevant in light of the character of present-day museums.

The building, which opened in 1974 as the Dalí Theater-Museum, lays claim to being the largest surrealist object in the world. Though constructed from the ruins of the Municipal Theater, destroyed at the end of the Spanish Civil War, the artist reconfigured parts and added his imprimatur to every nook and cranny. In fact, he felt a serendipitous bond to the building since he was baptized in the church facing it (he was born in Figueres in 1904) and had his first exhibition in the theater's lobby at age 14.

The exterior is painted a rose-fuchsia color, sharing an affinity with the color of a pope's or cardinal's robe. Blobs that look like turds but are meant to be odd little three-pointed loaves of bread create a polka-dot pattern across the outer walls, and an alignment of large eggs and trophylike statuettes borders the roof. The front facade has figures and objects created by Dalí on the balconies and a giant geodesic dome, which replaced the old cupola in 1998, atop the building. In addition, some large-scale sculptures are prominently installed in the plaza at the museum's entrance. Needless to say, the museum is hard to miss!

Once inside, you enter the interior courtyard, where the centerpiece is a zany ensemble, *Rainy Cadillac*—a version of the famous *Rainy Taxi* of 1938. The focus is a sleek, black 1941 Cadillac with an open-armed nude sculpture of the biblical Queen Esther on the hood. Stationed behind is a column of truck tires crowned by a figure in a boat with big blue drops of water hanging down from it and the umbrella overhead. Solemn music blares from the car, aggrandizing the imagery with a sound ambient. Forming a backdrop to this ensemble is a huge mural in the place of the stage curtain of the old theater's actual stage, which is now visible behind a glazed wall. The

Salvador Dalí, *Rainy Cadillac*

mural is an enlargement of a 1947 painting depicting a nude torso with a cavity in its abdomen, a cracked skull and an eery, desert landscape.

From the stage area you gain access to the various exhibition spaces spread around the three floors in the old theater building (rooms 1–18) and the expanded annex, Torre Galatea (rooms 19–24). The layout is not a continuous stream so keep track of the room numbers if you don't want to miss anything. Nearly every corridor and staircase is itself a fantasy art environment or else it leads to one.

The displays include work from all phases of Dalí's career. There are some early, experimental paintings in Cézannesque, fauvist and cubist styles and many late works, some of which feature remakes of imagery from the prime surrealist years. The museum owns very few of Dalí's most famous objects from the historically important interwar era. A popular favorite is the gallery featuring Dalí jewelry designs (room 18), and there are also exhibits of optical games, paintings for stereoscopic viewing and holograms by the artist.

By far, the preeminent creation in the Theater-Museum is the Mae West room (room 11). Expanding on a gouache of 1934–35, *The Face of Mae West (Usable as a Surrealist Apartment)* and an object from 1936–37, *Mae West's Lips Sofa*, Dalí and the architect Òscar TUSQUETS produced paranoiac furniture for the illusionary room. The star's voluptuous lips are transformed into a shocking pink sofa, her nose into a fireplace, her eyes into a pair of framed pictures and her blond hair into curtains framing the room. To view the image, you climb a narrow flight of stairs and peer through a magnifying lens positioned between the legs of a stuffed-camel sculpture on stilts.

Complementing the exhibition of Dalí's own work, the museum has installed one gallery (room 14) with art from his personal collection. The objects are by his favorite artists—William Bouguereau, Marcel Duchamp, Marià Fortuny, El Greco, Ernest Meissonier, Modest Urgell. The museum also devotes space to work by two Dalí followers of minor value, Antoni Pitxot and Evarist Vallés.

In addition to all else, a crypt (room 7) includes the tomb of the artist.

Salvador Dalí, *The Face of Mae West*

Port Lligat (Cadaqués)

Port Lligat lies just outside Cadaqués, a charming fishing village and seaside resort with vistas of the desolate, olive-grove landscape of the Pyrenees foothills near the French border. It is a 1-hr drive from Figueres along a winding, 25-mi (40-km) road. The best public transportation is the SARFA bus. It's a pleasant, 15-min walk from Cadaqués north to Port Lligat.

Casa-Museu Salvador Dalí

97-225-80-63 f: 225-90-30
www.dali-estate.org
pllgrups@dali-estate.org
June 15–Sept 15: daily, 10:30–9
Sept 16–Jan 6 and March 15–June 14: Tues–Sun, 10:30–6; closed Mon
admission: 1300/800 ptas
Visits by prior arrangement only.

If you want to broaden the scope of your knowledge about Salvador Dalí, a visit to his House-Museum will show you where he lived for long periods during his childhood, youth and later life. Beginning about 1930, this was the artist's major residence and the place where he created much of his artwork.

The house is a cluster of fishermen's huts, purposefully arranged by the artist and his wife, Gala, in the form of a labyrinth. The property includes a pool, gardens, a studio and library.

Púbol

This small village lies northeast of Girona and 25 mi (40 km) south of Figueres. Train from Figueres or Girona to Flaça, 15 min; from the train station to Púbol, it's 2 1/2 mi (4 km). If you take the SARFA bus from Figueres or Girona to Púbol, the distance from the station is only 1 1/4 mi (4 km).

Casa-Museu Castell Gala Dalí

Púbol, 17120 La Pera
97-248-82-11 f: 248-90-22
www.dali-estate.org
pbgrups@dali-estate.org
June 15–Sept 15: daily, 10:30–8
Mar 15–June 14 and Sept 16–Nov 1: Tues–Sun, 10:30–6; closed Mon
admission: 700/500 ptas

Dalí bought and decorated this 12th-century castle as a gift for his wife, Gala. She lived here during the summers in the 1970s until her death in 1982. The interior is flamboyantly outfitted with illusionary, camouflage or voyeuristic setups and transparent furniture, in addition to the "conventional" artwork on the walls. Highlights include a clear glass table built over a hole in the floor so you can look down to the entrance and see who's at the door; busts of Richard Wagner around the reflecting pools; and elephant-on-stilt sculptures in the garden. The aura of Gala permeates throughout by means of the "G" emblazoned on the doors, the majestic presence of her throne, the display of her couturier dresses and her tomb in a basement crypt watched over by a giraffe sculpture.

País Vasco

If you got confused in Barcelona with the prevalent use of Catalan as the spoken and written language, you'll be doubly confounded in Basque Country (Euskadi) with the shift from Castilian to Euskera, a language unrelated to other tongues. The use of Euskera in signs and place names is inconsistent and irregular. For example, Bilbao, rather than the Euskadi "Bilbo," is still the name of choice. And whereas written Basque is increasingly pervasive, the spoken language has yet to be adopted by the general population. Most sites visited by tourists provide Basque and Castilian in their signs and texts.

Basque Country comprises three provinces: Guipúzcoa (Gipuzkoa), a small, seaside zone including San Sebastián; Viscaya (Bizkaia), the area with Bilbao as its capital; and Álava (Araba), the inland region around Vitoria. However, Navarra (whose capital is Iruña/Pamplona) and sections of land within southwest France are also considered by some to be part of Basque Country. Control of the Basques and the notion of a separate, sovereign territory (diversely construed) have long been a cause of battle and political unrest, most recently in the terrorist attacks committed by militant Basque nationalists (ETA).

A small newsprint brochure, *El Diario Vasco*, provides a handy, bimonthly calendar of art exhibitions in the Basque region and elsewhere in Spain. It also contains short articles on various shows and numerous color illustrations. Alternatively, the contemporary art magazine *Zehar*, published in San Sebastián, offers articles and information on the current goings-on in the Basque region. It's available for free in various galleries, alternative spaces and other artsy places.

San Sebastián (Donastia)

It's easy to see why this town is such a fashionable resort once you meander through the lively old town and city center or walk along the beautiful beaches of the spectacular half-moon bay. Much of the central area is arranged in a grid and easy to get around on foot. If you're searching for a particular address, however, the street signs may drive you to distraction: some are in Castilian, some in Basque, some in both, some use confounding abbreviations and some display the official, multiword, unpronouncible, conglomerate name. You may also find the double set of numbers on the buildings bordering Plaza de la Constitución a bit baffling. That's because the street-level ones are addresses and the ones on the balconies are left over from the days when the square served as a bullring!

Like many seaside cities that attract well-to-do vacationers, San Sebastián has its share of touristy art galleries showing colorful landscapes and lush abstract paintings.

One of the most celebrated events that takes place annually in the city is the prestigious *International Film Festival*. Held in mid-September, it includes a thematic program, retrospectives of a contemporary and established director, a competition among new films and the ever-popular Open Zone (Zabaltegi)—films by new directors and features already presented in other festivals. Movie stars from all over the world attend the screenings, some serving as jurors and honorary guests. (See www.sansebastianfestival.com.)

During Halloween week, the city also hosts the *Horror and Fantasy Film Festival*. Comprising movies for both children and adults, features and shorts, new and old films, the program attracts serious scholars, Gothic fanatics and a you-name-it spectrum in between. (See www.donostiakultura.com/terror.)

Train from Barcelona, 8 1/4 hr; from Madrid, 5 3/4 hr. If time is a consideration,

Rafael Moneo, Convention Center & Kursaal Auditorium

there is direct air service that takes 1 1/2 hr from Barcelona and 1 hr from Madrid.

Palacio de Congresos y Auditorio Kursaal

architect: Rafael MONEO, 1999
Avenida de la Zurriola

Located on the east side of Puente de la Zurriola.

Just where the Urumea River, contained by stone embankment walls, connects with the Bay of Biscay, there's a plot of land that also fronts a newly made white sand beach and has magnificent views in all directions. This is where the Convention Center and Kursaal Auditorium are located. Rafael Moneo, the master of minimalist architecture, designed an utterly simple but edgy double-cube structure for the setting. It is rigorously geometric, although the box forms slant vertically and horizontally, thereby suggesting the propulsive nature of the sea rather than the fixity of man-made creations. Narrow panes of blue-green fluted glass, which

sheath the buildings, reinforce an association with the sea by echoing the translucence and rippling of water. Inspired by the sharp-angled, volumetric boulders and cliffs along the Bay of Biscay coast, Moneo also sought to evoke a fantasy image of two monumental glass rocks washed ashore.

Be sure to walk along the river toward the pier to appreciate the relationship between the architecture and the natural setting. You'll also see the dynamics of the two cubes—one large, one small—set at angles to one another fronted by stone terraces stretching out to the sea. A long bench is positioned for favorable viewing, and a tapering stone ramp runs the length of the complex, adding yet another perspectival energy to it.

The cubes house a large concert auditorium (1,850 seats) and a smaller, adaptable space (650 seats). They rest atop a long base containing street-front shops, meeting rooms, reception halls, banquet facilities, an exhibition space, restaurant-bar and parking. The architecture thus responds to the space and business needs of a convention-entertainment complex while also embracing the majestic character of the natural setting.

Galería DV

San Martin 5, 20006
94-342-91-11 f: 342-01-22
galeriadv@galeriadv.com
Tues–Fri, 5–9; Sat, 11–1 and 5–9; closed Mon

Located in the Centro district, three streets south of Avenida de la Libertad and just off the corner of Prim.

The name DV derives from *El Diario Vasco*, the local newspaper that supports the gallery. Of all the galleries in town, it's here you're likely to find challenging work by young Basque artists and occasional exhibitions of established European or American artists. If you leaf through the catalogues of past shows, you'll get a quick-and-easy overview of art in the region.

Artists: Javier Alkain, José Ramón Amondarain, Alfonso Berridi, Frédéric Bruly Bouabré, Jon Mikel Euba, Iñaki Gracenea, Mari Puri Herrero, Seydou Keïta, Ana Mendieta, Manu Muniategiandikoetxea, Alberto Peral, Ana Isabel Román, Sean Scully, Raúl Uruutikoetxea.

Koldo Mitxelena Kulturunea

Urdaneta 9, 20006
94-348-27-50 f: 348-27-55
www.gipuzkoa.net/kultura
sala@kultura.gipuzkoa.net
Tues–Sat, 10:30–2 and 4–8:30; closed Mon
admission: free

Located at the south end of the main plaza (Plaza del Buen Pastor) next to the post office.

Sharing an imposing, old masonry building, formerly the School of Engineers, with a library, this cultural center has been organizing a versatile, adventurous art exhibition program since opening in the mid-1990s. Don't be

Raul Uruutikoetxea, Untitled (Airport), 2000

Eduardo Chillida, *Wind Comb*

surprised to find visitors of all ages, especially in the main gallery space on the basement level. The shows are thematic or monographic, featuring young, local or international artists. Objects are carefully selected, and catalogues, which accompany each project, are well researched and interesting. Conferences and lectures are also part of the programs. Recent exhibitions: *Art as Resistance to Violence*, *Willie Doherty*, *Domestic Scenes*, *Festival of Performances*, *Concha Jerez*, *Tony Oursler*, *Qui Yu Fen*, *Soledad Sevilla*, *The Space of Sound*.

Ganbara, a second, more posh and intimate space on the top floor, offers interdisciplinary exhibitions often using documents, illustrated books and prints to explore a topic related to history, music, literature and the like.

Eduardo Chillida

Haize-Orrazia (Peine del Viento, XV), 1976
Paseo Peine del Viento
Located at the west end of La Concha Bay. If you don't want to take the somewhat lengthy but delightful walk around the cove from the city center to the cliffs at the opposite end, at least walk the stretch along Playa de Ondarreta.

Sculptors must dream of finding the ideal location for an artwork, a place where it would have a commanding presence and its potency as a creative object would be instantly felt by anyone coming upon it. Such sites are rare indeed. The possibility of realizing an artwork in them is even rarer. And the probability that the work would rise to the occasion is rarer yet. *Wind Comb* is one of those rarities. Consider a trip to San Sebastián just to see it.

The artist Eduardo Chillida (b. 1924), one of Spain's foremost sculptors, is a passionate Basque native and favorite son of San Sebastián. Many towns in the area and throughout the country have public sculptures by him, but none come close to the majesty of this one. Fixed to promontory rocks at the base of high, jagged cliffs, it is positioned to relate to both land and sea. A terraced setting, designed by Luis Peña

GANCHEGUI, makes the work accessible for close viewing from various perspectives. In fact, the sculpture isn't visible along most of the shoreline, and even as you draw near, it remains out of sight, hidden behind the last bend.

Wind Comb is a three-part sculpture of dark, rugged steel that accentuates Chillida's favored hook motif. But whereas the motif is often a flat, circular shape, here it is clawlike, expressive, if not menacing. Silhouetted against the sky, the parts gesture toward each other while also serving as spatial markers allied to the horizon.

Arteleku

Kristobaldegi 14, Loiola 20014
94-345-36-62 f: 346-22-56
arteleku@kultura.gipuzkoa.net
Mon–Fri, 8–9
suburban "Topo" train: exit at Loiola
Located on the outskirts of San Sebastián about 1 mi (2 km) southeast of the city center.

Opened in 1987 in refurbished industrial buildings, Arteleku has become a popular center for contemporary art activity. The complex includes studios, meeting rooms, a bookstore, library and exhibition space (used mainly for works produced on site). Young and established artists, critics, scholars and anyone interested in theoretical and interdisciplinary ideas related to the arts come here from all regions of Spain to attend courses, workshops, lectures and symposia. The programs are diverse and the atmosphere is open and friendly. Visitors are welcome.

Arteleku also publishes *Zehar*, the notable art magazine for the Basque region.

Hernani

Museo Chillida-Leku

Almudena Barcáiztegui
Bº Jauregui 66, 20120
94-327-12-79
www.eduardo-chillida.com
eduardo@eduardo-chillida.com
Apr–Oct 15: Wed–Mon, 11–6; closed Tues
Oct 16–Mar: Wed–Mon, 11–4; closed Tues
admission: 900 ptas
bus: Garayar G2 from Calle Oquendo (San Sebastián)
Located about 6 mi (10 km) south of San Sebastián.

In the summer of 2000 Zabalaga, a 16th-century farmhouse located on a 12-acre estate, opened as the Chillida-Leku Museum. Developed by the artist as a showcase for his work, it offers a handsome setting in which to see prime objects spanning his career.

The house has been fully renovated to expose the original structure of stone and wood beams. With all the residential elements and some room divisions removed, it is a stunning space in itself and an engaging backdrop for displays of Chillida's sculptures and drawings. The surrounding forests and fields create a very different ambience for about 40 large-scale works.

Bilbao

Bilbao (Bilbo), formerly a grimy industrial center, has skyrocketed onto the radar screens of culture aficionados and fun-loving tourists because everyone wants to see Frank Gehry's spectacular Guggenheim Museum. There's no denying that this building is one of the great 20th-century masterpieces and warrants all the attention it's been getting. However, don't cut yourself short with a quick trip to the museum alone. The city has been dramatically regenerating itself by implementing an ambitious urban plan comprising the development of new amenities, green spaces and infrastructure. In the process, the river (Ría Nervión), horribly polluted by industry, has been cleaned, and its waterfront is being transformed into a prime location for new cultural buildings and business centers. There are several truly innovative projects by leading, world-class architects.

There are no direct trains from San Sebastián, but buses (PESA) go frequently and take 1 hr. Train from Barcelona, 9 hr; from Madrid, 6 hr. The lack of fast, direct trains to the Basque region makes air travel very appealing: flights from Madrid or Barcelona take approximately 1 hr.

Sondika Airport

architect: Santiago CALATRAVA
terminal, 1990–2000
control tower, 1993–96

Using a V-shaped roof, similar to the inventive form he developed for the Satolas train station at the Lyon airport, Calatrava has created another spectacular design for the main terminal at Sondika. Called *La Gaviota* (*The Seagull*) because the buoyant, sweeping roof resembles a spread-winged bird about to take flight, it also gives evidence of the architect's strong inspiration from nature.

The dazzling aluminum skin of the roof hovers over glazed walls that bathe the interior with natural light while offering panoramic views of the landscape. The vast concourse includes commercial zones and restaurants with parking and other facilities located beneath and around the main structure.

Unlike generic control towers, *El Halcón* (*The Hawk*) takes the form of a cone topped by a glass-enclosed observation deck and positioned within a columnar base whose shape is cut away in front, yielding prominence to the cone and its invading volume. Constructed in concrete, the tower is clad in shiny aluminum.

Jeff Koons

Puppy, 1997
Located on the plaza in front of the Guggenheim Museum.

Perhaps your sophisticated soul groans at the thought of a 39-ft-tall (12 m) sculpture of a seated puppy. And it's not just a puppy, but one of those irresistibly cute breeds, a West Highland terrier. And it's not just the image of a cute puppy, but a puppy whose fuzzy, soft fur has been fashioned out of velvety

Jeff Koons, *Puppy*

rich pansies and other colorful flowers. No matter how low your level of kitsch tolerance, like everyone else you'll probably ooh and aah with wide-eyed awe at Jeff Koons's monumental *Puppy*.

Puppy first made an appearance in Germany at the time of *Documenta IX* in 1992 and has since been reincarnated in various cities, including a stint at Rockefeller Center, New York, in 2000. The injection of fantasy into urban territory has proved to be a popular success even among hard-nosed art critics. The image and form upset prevailing public art conventions, though they offer a Disneylandish revival of the 18th-century spirit of the sublime.

Technically, the sculpture is built for survival. Flowers, embedded in soil, are planted as tiny buds in a steel frame with an internal irrigation system. They grow into a deep, spongy carpet over a period of about six months and then are replaced. Colors and surface character change throughout the cycle.

Museo Guggenheim Bilbao

architect: Frank O. GEHRY, 1991–97
Abandoibarra Etorbidea 2, 48001
94-435-9080 f: 435-9010
www.guggenheim-bilbao.es
Tues–Sun, 10–8; closed Mon
admission: 800/400 ptas

With one fell swoop, this building made Bilbao a prime destination of tourists and art lovers from all over the world. Now every city, whether off the beaten track, economically depressed or world-class, wants to have a Gehry-Guggenheim trophy. Apart from all the hype, it's glorious to see architecture in the limelight, being praised by everyone from conservative politicians to the flower vendor on the corner. Amazingly, no matter what your expectations or expertise, you won't be disappointed. This building—it can rightfully be called an icon and national monument—is mind-boggling. It functions like a magnet,

drawing you in and keeping you in a state of awe, if not rapture. And yes, it can encumber artwork contained within because *it* is an extraordinary work of art, not a passive white cube or neutral backdrop like classic modernist buildings. More than presenting a new style, it intrinsically transforms architectural precepts, endowing space and structure with the same qualities of risk and tension that distinguish many contemporary avant-garde creations as well as the current era itself. At its core, it challenges the idea of the autonomous, standardized, sacrosanct object.

Whether you approach the museum from the city streets of the Abandoibarra district or from riverfront pathways, you get tantalizing glimpses of the shimmering surfaces and sensuously curving or oddly protruding forms well before seeing the building as such. But unlike the drama of seeing small parts which then coalesce into a unified, symmetrical whole (as with St. Peters in Rome), here the whole presents a diversity of dynamic, eccentric, interconnecting parts fanning out in various directions. Moreover, the image of the whole radically changes as you move around the building and see it from different perspectives. Be sure to save time to cross the river, from where you'll get some of the best views and can watch the ways in which light and reflections continuously play against the surfaces and forms. At times, the building appears like a huge ship bouncing about in a rough sea with violent waves.

Gehry chose to sheath the unconventional, fluid and sharp-angled volumes in "fish-scaled" titanium panels (special exhibition galleries), contrasting them with cubic forms clad in cream-colored limestone (collection galleries). Glass curtain-walls occur at many interstices, and a deep blue exterior denotes the office wing (street level).

Although built on a difficult, tight plot of hillside land, the museum gracefully and imaginatively occupies the entire space with peripheral plazas and access points on all sides. Shallow pools in front and back reiterate the river setting while further enhancing

F. Gehry, Guggenheim Museum Bilbao

reflections on and of the architecture.

A giant architectonic sign announcing the feature exhibition greets you on the street-level plaza, where there is also an inviting, long bench should you wish to sit and absorb the scene. But this is not the main entrance. Reversing the usual trope of a grand staircase ascending to the front doors of a museum, Gehry takes you down a widening flight of stairs to the river level. From here you can enter the reception lobby or walk along the river plaza, investigating the small terrace covered by a curving metal canopy atop a 92-foot (28 m) pillar and the eastward extension of the building that goes under a major city bridge (Puente de La Salve) and terminates in a two-pronged tower enveloped in stone except for the one side left open to expose the steel frame.

The architect's playfulness seeps into his wild designs even as he pays heed to such practical considerations as placing the restaurant-café, auditorium and gift-bookstore off to one side so they can function independently from the galleries.

After entering the lobby, you circle around to the soaring atrium, which once again bedazzles you with the visionary audacity of Frank Gehry's genius. High walls painted white or sheathed in stone interpose sculptural forms; suspended bridges and balconies cut across and into the space at various levels; window walls give views of the outdoor surrounds; and natural light streams in from the breathtaking height of a glazed roof. Off to a side in front of a towering wall, a pair of two-sided, red-blue LED sign columns, commissioned from Jenny Holzer, scroll aphoristic messages in Castilian, Basque and English.

From the atrium, various nonlinear, disjunctive paths lead around the building. There is no prescribed or logical order and it's easy to miss entire sections, so try to keep track of what you've seen with reference to the floorplans included in the free exhibition brochure, available at the admission desk. Fortunately, this is a visitor-friendly museum with good signage.

The building contains 19 galleries organized on three levels fanning out from the atrium. Suspended walkways link the spaces on the upper levels, and glass-enclosed elevators and stair turrets connect the levels. Half of the galleries are classically proportioned and rectangular in shape. These typically are used for displays of work from the Guggenheim's permanent collection. The other galleries, which have eccentric proportions and oddities like wall cutouts, irregular contours and curving or slanted walls, usually house non-collection exhibitions. For the most part, the spaces accommodate all sorts of art and art forms. Perhaps the biggest challenge is finding high-quality work of grandiose scale to suit the mammoth expanses in some of the spaces.

Regardless of their orientation, all galleries have natural light, though few have traditional windows and doors or predictable links to one another. If nothing else, you won't get bored walking about since each turn opens onto an unusual space, and the character of the whole keeps shifting as you move throughout the building.

The most extreme gallery, running parallel to the river on the bottom floor and called "the fish" or "the boat," is 433 feet (130 m) in length. Free of support columns, the space is instead spanned by a framework of white-painted steel arches and hanging trusses. Skylights enhance the ambience, and converging side walls, which curve slightly at the far end, eliminate the bland boxiness that characterizes such vast halls. Richard Serra's *Snake* (1996), another work commissioned for a particular space in the museum, customarily occupies the center of this gallery.

Although the Bilbao museum might easily have become a great building devoid of a notable collection and without sufficient resources to sustain an exciting exhibition

F. Gehry, Bilbao Guggenheim Museum

program, the partnership established between the city of Bilbao, the Basque Government and the Solomon R. Guggenheim Foundation prevented this from happening. According to the agreement, the two Basque partners paid for the museum's construction and cover the basic operating expenses while the American partner provides loans from its esteemed collection and contributes its expertise. Significantly, the Spanish government has no part in the project, which effectively asserts autonomous regional pride and the international stature of the Basque Country.

Thus far, the programming, which presents several exhibitions at once, has not only been a drawing card for Bilbao but has placed exemplary works of modern and contemporary art on public view in Spain. Surveys, thematic and one-person shows from the Guggenheim collections (i.e., holdings of the Solomon R. Guggenheim Museum, New York; Peggy Guggenheim Collection, Venice; Deutsche Guggenheim Berlin; and new purchases of the Guggenheim Museum Bilbao) may change four or five times a year. These are complemented by non-collection exhibitions on tour from New York or Germany, or curated specifically for Bilbao. A no-holds-barred approach at times aggrandizes the exhibitions with spicy installations, like the one Gaetano Pesce designed for *Andy Warhol* or the construction Frank Gehry developed for *The Art of the Motorcycle*. Conferences, lectures, roundtables, films and other events round out the museum's program.

Recent exhibitions: *Amazons of the Avant-Garde, Giorgio Armani, Art of the Motorcycle, Francesco Clemente, Degas to Picasso—The Painter, the Sculptor, and the Camera, The Panza Collection, Nam June Paik, David Salle, The Tower Wounded by Lightning, Andy Warhol.*

There's always a lot to see in this museum, so plan to spend a fair amount of time or consider making several visits. Even if you don't dine in the restaurant, run by Martín

Berasategui, the star of modern Basque cuisine, at least look inside at the industrial decor. You might also want to check out the shops, whose narrow, high-ceilinged layout of two spaces on different floors is highly unappealing. The book selection, consisting mainly of expensive, coffee-table books about big-name artists or Guggenheim catalogues, is also unfortunate.

Bilboko Arte Eder Museoa (Museo de Bellas Artes)

Plaza del Museo 2, 48011
94-439-60-60 f: 439-61-45
www.museobilbao.com
museobilbao@museobilbao.com
collection: Tues–Sat, 10–1:30 and 4–7:30; Sun, 10–2; closed Mon
temp. exhib: Tues–Sat, 10–8; Sun, 10–2; closed Mon
admission: 600/300 ptas; free on Wed
From the Guggenheim, turn right (west) on Alameda de Mazarredo; a few blocks ahead is Plaza del Museo.

Bilbao's Museum of Fine Arts encompasses the city's Museum of Modern Art with the former housed in a neoclassical building and the latter in a modern structure. The whole museum is closed for renovation and will open in October 2001.

Various gems enrich the old master collection of largely Spanish, Dutch and Flemish paintings, and in the modern period works by Bacon, Cassatt, Cezanne, Gauguin, Picasso, Delaunay, Léger, Gargallo, Bacon and Tàpies are the highlights. Though its rank as the city's major museum has been usurped by its splashy new neighbor, you'll often find well-curated, historical exhibitions on modern art as the special fare here.

Recent exhibitions: *Willi Baumeister, Jean Dubuffet, Julio González, Auguste Rodin and the Bronze Age, Spanish Still Life—Zurbarán to Picasso, The Surrealist Landscape.*

PAÍS VASCO

Metro station

architect: Norman FOSTER, 1988–95

From the Fine Arts Museum, walk south down Elcano for a few blocks and you'll come to Plaza Moyúa, the main, center-city intersection with streets radiating in all directions. This is a good place to see the new subway system.

Norman Foster, the venerable British architect, added a few more gems to his crown with his design for Bilbao's metro stations. The caterpillar-like entrance canopies of glass and ribbed steel instantly became signature images, so admired by the citizenry that they were dubbed "fosteritos." Not only are they practical, providing welcome protection from the all-too-familiar inclement weather of the area, but their airy, organic structure is a visual delight. During the day their transparency allows natural light to penetrate inside, and at night they glow in the dark. As Foster expressed it: "The form invites you to descend. It also tells you about

the dynamic of rising to the light."

The development of a metro system was a key element in the plan projecting Bilbao's rebirth and the economic upswing of the Basque region. It will eventually link the inner city with suburbs, outer-lying industrial zones and coastal villages. Even if you don't ride the metro during your stay in Bilbao, at least make a brief perusal of the station's interior so you can see how Foster continued the understated finesse of the entrances.

Escalators within the glazed entry enclosures lead down into a cavernous two-level area with a suspended ticketing zone above and platforms below. Spaciousness is a dominant impression since there are no support columns, and a single, grand arched structure contains the whole. Contrast between the cast concrete walls and shiny steel of the staircases, ticket barriers and trains notwithstanding, a carefully modulated harmony prevails.

A striking aspect of the Bilbao metro, along with the architecture, is its ultra-spotless,

Norman Foster, Metro station

192

graffiti-free, pristine condition. True, Foster did research to find a graffiti-proof concrete, fearing a barrage of pasted placards and sprayed messages linked to the separatist unrest in Basque Country. Civic pride has prevented this from occurring, though the presence of eight security cameras plus a guard on duty at all times in each station have also helped.

Sala Rekalde

📧 Alameda de Recalde 30, 48009
94-420-87-55 f: 420-87-54
salarekalde@bizkaia.net
Tues–Sat, 10–2 and 5–9; closed Mon
admission: free

This exhibition space was created by the Basque government in 1990 as a prelude to the construction and arrival of the Guggenheim Museum. It's a large, flexible space occupying the main floor of a downtown office building. Although structural columns and a low ceiling forestall displays of large works of art, during its early years Sala Rekalde presented an impressive program, including exhibitions of Eduardo Chillida, Sol LeWitt, Robert Rauschenberg, Rafael Ruiz, Julian Schnabel, Sean Scully, Cindy Sherman, Tony Smith, Antoni Tàpies, Francesc Torres, Andy Warhol.

Not surprisingly, the nature of the program has shifted since the opening of the Guggenheim. Big-name American and Spanish artists are no longer a predominant focus. Shows still feature innovative work from the contemporary period, but now the perspective is more European, and the schedule embraces emerging artists, architecture, design and thematic exhibitions. In addition to the main space, the big display window fronting the street contains installations by young Basque artists. Catalogues, which accompany each exhibition, are available at the reception desk.

Recent exhibitions: *Marisa González, Jésus M. Lazkano, Mechanization and Industrial*

Esthetics, Tony Oursler, Jean-Michel Othoniel, Javier Pagola, Fernando & Vicente Roscubas, 7 x 7 x 7, Dario Urzay, Vitra Museum Collection, Michael Wilford.

Galería Windsor Kulturgintza

🏛 Juan de Ajuriaguerra 14, 48009
tel/fax: 94-423-89-89
windsork@teleline.es
May–Sept: Mon–Fri, 11–2 and 5–9; closed Sat
Oct–Apr: Tues–Fri, 11–2 and 5–9; Sat, 12–2 and 6–9; closed Mon

Galería Windsor Kulturgintza has been around since 1971 but underwent a decisive transformation when it moved to its current location in 1989. Having originally concentrated on traditional figure painting, it converted into a gallery focused on contemporary currents of young and established artists, largely from Spain and the Basque region. The work shown here covers a wide diversity of styles and orientations. Not all exhibitions are scintillating, but the gallery offers a good cross-section of art not often seen outside the country.

Artists: Pablo Aizoiala, Alfonso Albacete, José Ramón Amondarain, José Ramón Anda, Ángel Bados, Joan Brossa, Luis Candaudap, Ricardo Cavada, Leandre Cristófol, Mikel Díez Älava, Javier Elorriaga, Pepe Espaliú, Jon Mikel Euba, Juan Luis Goneaga, Curro González, Alfonso Gortázar, Xabier Grau, Antón Lamazares, Jesús Mari Lazkano, Edu Lopez, Txemi Mediero, Chus Meléndez, Pablo Milicua, Juan Luis Moraza, Manu Muniategiandikoetxea, Carmen Olabarri, Leire Ormaetxe, Guillermo Paneque, Manolo Paz, Perejaume, Paco Polán, Alberto Rementería, Sonia Rueda, Francisco Ruiz de Infante, Dora Salazar, Daniel Tamayo, Juan Ugalde, Darío Urzay.

Zubizuri Pedestrian Bridge

🏛 architect: Santiago CALATRAVA, 1997

Located on the east side of the city just south of the Guggenheim Museum.

For his design of the Zubizuri (or Volantín) footbridge, Calatrava created a sweeping parabolic arch that seems to defy gravity by remaining upright despite a considerable lean to one side and the lack of customary pylons underneath. The image from all perspectives is utterly stunning and mind-boggling. A pipe forms the elongated curve of the arch above, and thin strands of cable fan out from it to a glass-plated deck below. The deck, in turn, curves gracefully around in the opposite direction from the arch and connects to the long access ramps that rest atop open, triangular structures of cast concrete—the supporting armatures for the bridge.

Calatrava's signature use of white paint defines the bridge's shape during the day. At night it's even more striking with the glass deck illuminated from below.

If the bridge in and of itself is not enough to woo you, consider crossing it to get to the right bank (east side) of the Nervión River, where you'll get the best views of the Guggenheim Museum.

Gernika (Guernica)

Suburban Eusko train from Bilbao (Atxuri station or Bolueta metro), 45 min.

Gernikako Arbola (Árbol de Gernika)

🔑 Casa de Juntas, garden
🗓 summer: daily, 10–2 and 4–7
winter: daily, 10–2 and 4–6
admission: free

From the train station, take Adolfo Urioste Kalea, a street that winds through the village past a garden plaza (on your left) and up a hill alongside the monumental U-shaped layout of Escuelas Publicas (also on the left). At the intersection, turn left onto Angel Allende Salazar Kalea; after you pass the Escuelas complex, turn right into the hillside garden that lies adjacent to Casa de Juntas, a neoclassical building where the council of Bizkaia meets.

The Tree of Gernika symbolizes the ancient roots of the Basque peoples and has long represented and embodied their freedom. The tree acquired additional significance by miraculously surviving a massive midday bombing by the Condor Legion, a unit of the German Air Force sent by Hitler to aid Franco's rebellion, on April 26, 1937, a crowded market day in this small village town. It was the first time air power was used against a civilian target. Close to 2,000 people, including many women and children, died, and the town center was virtually demolished. The bombing horrified the world and was memorialized for all time in Picasso's renowned painting, *Guernica*, which now hangs in the Reina Sofía Museum, Madrid.

The old oak tree that survived the bombing died recently, and its petrified trunk is now enshrined in a colonnaded gazebo in the garden of Casa de Juntas. A new tree generated from a shoot of the old one is planted alongside.

Henry Moore

🗿 *Large Figure in a Shelter,* 1985–86
🗓 Parque de los Pueblos de Europa
🕐 summer: daily, 10–9
winter: daily, 10–7
admission: free

Located in the far corner of the wooded park abutting the garden with the Tree of Gernika. If the park gates are open, you can walk its length, at the end of which you'll cross over a road on a Japanese-style footbridge and arrive at a grassy hillside containing the sculpture. If the gates aren't open, or should you prefer to walk along the street, return to Angel Allende Salazar Kalea, backtracking your steps past the Escuelas. This time

Henry Moore, *Large Figure in a Shelter*

continue beyond for another block; cross and turn left at the first street, Allende Salazar Etorbidea, and immediately enter the grass field on the corner.

Moore's bronze sculpture, selected as a peace memorial, sits atop a hill overlooking the town of Gernika. The work was one of the artist's last creations and is his largest. It relates to a series of helmet sculptures using the recurring image of an outer form protecting an inner form. In this version, an organically shaped figure, suggestive of a woman, stands upright in the middle of a thick-walled, man-made refuge such as one might need as a shield against modern weapons of war.

The sculpture was installed here in 1990. (The original cast of this work is part of the collection at the Perry Green estate in Hertfordshire, Moore's last residence, now property of the Henry Moore Foundation.)

Eduardo Chillida

Our Father's House, 1988
Parque de los Pueblos de Europa
summer: daily, 10–9
winter: daily, 10–7

Located alongside the Henry Moore sculpture.

To commemorate the 50th anniversary of the bombing of Gernika, the Basque artist Chillida was commissioned to create a sculpture for this site. His work features a grandiose concrete wall in the form of an apse with a curlicue-framed opening in its midst looking onto a nearby oak tree. A small but solid pillar made of steel, which in the artist's view represents freedom and tolerance, stands in the center of the symbolic house, in the heart of the ancestral home.

Kortézubi

Agustín Ibarrola

Painted Forest, 1980s
Bosque de Oma

Located in the Oma forest, 3 mi (5 km) northeast of Gernika and close to the Santimamiñe cave, famous for its prehistoric animal paintings. Eusko train from Bilbao (Atxuri station or Bolueta metro) to Gernika, 45 min, then short bus ride to the Santimamiñe cave. Follow the signs to *Bosque Animado*.

Some 500 pine trees adorned with brightly colored stylized figures and geometric forms make up the *Painted Forest* created by the Basque artist Ibarrola. The eye shapes, concentric circles, linear markings, abstract motifs and patterns appear as autonomous images on single trees, repetitive groupings, serial alignments or enlarged, composite designs spread across several trees. The work covers a considerable land expanse requiring more than an hour's trek to see completely.

GIJÓN

Edouard Chillida

Elogio del Horizonte, 1990
Parque de la Atalaya, Cerro de Santa Catalina

Should you be in the province of Asturias, or if you're a fan of Chillida's sculptures, consider visiting the industrial, seaport city of Gijón to see Eulogy to the Horizon.

Set on a crest overlooking the ocean, this monumental 500-ton sculpture of reinforced concrete stands almost 33 feet (10 m) high. Although quite solid in appearance, the image is mainly shaped by empty space. Two leglike structures curve around to frame an opening directed toward the horizon. They, like the C-ring up above, seem to have been cut from a cylinder that is now only suggestively present. The dialectic between solid and void, interior and exterior, is a theme running throughout the artist's work.

In explanation of the title, Chillida has stated: "Public works are open to the horizon and are in a public scale, the scale of man. Horizon is very important to me, it always has been. All men are equal and at the horizon we are all brothers, the horizon is a common homeland."

GALICIA

Galicia, or Galego, is another one of the Spanish provinces in the process of reasserting its native language. You will therefore find word and spelling changes in signs and written texts and spoken variants from Castilian. Consistency doesn't exist on any level. The language seems to have something in common with Portuguese, and this is not surprising since the region has a closer bond, in many respects, with its southern neighbor than with its own country. This is particularly true in the arts, where links to Porto are far stronger than to Madrid and other Spanish cities.

Santiago De Compostela

In addition to being a pilgrimage city with the most important Romanesque building in Spain (the cathedral, begun 1077), Santiago de Compostela is a lively, very friendly, university town with an active cultural dimension. Indeed, the city's modest population of 100,000 residents is augmented by 30,000 students, and the university's presence is evinced by such annual events as the jazz, folk music and film festivals. Having been named the European Cultural Capital for the year 2000, Santiago furthered its association with culture by announcing plans to construct a colossal, utopian, futuristic project, the City of Culture. This modern acropolis of two museums, auditorium, opera hall, library and archives will occupy the whole of Monte de la Gaias, a knoll facing the historic center of Santiago. An international competition for the design gleaned entries from preeminent architects with the award going to the American Peter EISENMAN (November 2000). His proposal creates an undulating topography in which the roofs of buildings rise and fall like a continuum of waves across the landscape. Time will tell if this megaproject becomes a new cultural-tourist Mecca like Gehry's Guggenheim in Bilbao, or if it turns into an oversize, expensive, weakly conceived boondoggle like the Millennium Dome in London.

Train from Madrid, 7 1/4 hr; from Bilbao, 11 1/4 hr.

Polisportivo y Parking de San Clemente

architect: Josef Paul KLEIHUES, 1992–94

Pazo de Raxoi

Located on the west and south sides of Praza do Obradoiro in front of the cathedral.

Most of the San Clemente project, designed by the German architect Josef Paul Kleihues, was discreetly positioned so as not to intrude on the grand plaza which fronts the cathedral or cut off views of the surrounding landscape. Grass and paved areas cover the underground parking garage, and a high stone wall blocks visibility of the gym, which lies just off to the side. The wall is actually the north facade of the gym, a modest, narrow building whose east and west walls are glazed and whose entrance and main level are below ground.

Markus Lüpertz

Untitled
Praza do Obradoiro

Located on a grass area on the south side of the plaza.

It's strange to find this fanciful image of a long-necked, big-busted woman with vases as one of the few contemporary works of public art in the city and the only one situated on the main cathedral square. Harking back to sculptures by Picasso, this painted bronze has diverse characteristics, both witty and grotesque, when viewed from the front, back or in profile. The work is by Markus Lüpertz, an artist associated with the figurative, expressionist revival in Germany in the 1970s.

Markus Lupertz, Untitled

Centro Galego de Arte Contemporaneo

architect: Álvaro SIZA, 1988–95
Rúa Valle Inclán, 15704
98-154-66-19 f: 54-66-05
Tues–Sun, 11–8; closed Mon
admission: free
www.cgac.org
cgac@xunta.es

If you wind your way eastward through the narrow streets and plazas behind the cathedral—still laid out according to the original 12th-century urban plan—you'll end at Rúa da Virxe da Cerca. Head to the left (north), and at a large intersection, Porta do Camiño, turn right onto Rúa de San Domingos, a short street that abuts Rúa Valle Inclán. The museum is to the left of this corner.

The building designed by Álvaro Siza, an award-winning Portuguese architect (Pritzker Prize, 1992), for the Galician Center for Contemporary Art (CGAC) was one of the first signs of the region's desire to establish itself as a world-class cultural center. Clad with austere, granite walls, the museum appears rigorously modern, though its stone facades bear witness to historic city buildings, like the 12th–17th-century Convent of Santo Domingo de Boneval alongside. "The facades are monumental because they have almost no windows. Because of their lack of detail, they can achieve a strength which is equal to that of the church or the convent." And like many of the structures Siza sought to emulate, his gives little evidence of the complexity lying behind the planar wall bordering the street. With an emphatic cubic form articulated in front, you aren't even aware that the building occupies a triangular lot and consists of two L-shaped wings converging in the entrance area (south end). Nor do you realize that the back lies at the base of a steep hillside, part of a neighboring park.

A cutout space containing the entrance ramp is the only open area on the facade, and it stands in sharp contrast to the otherwise solid volume of the building. Striking juxtapositions, as well as exaggerated perspectives, are the norm in the museum's interior. As is immediately apparent when you enter the lobby, Siza's love of purity, conspicuous in vast expanses of white, is inextricably wed to architectural idiosyncrasies, like the ultralong reception desk, slanted wall and extreme ceiling heights.

Because the museum was designed before it had a collection, curator or defined program, Siza sought to create flexible, varied spaces. He gave each gallery a distinctly different size, shape and character and devised a layout suggesting "a series of alternatives" rather than a set itinerary. Some of the spaces are large, spare rooms, ideal for displaying contemporary art. Others, however, have distracting eccentricities, like an inexplicable walkway suspended high up in the back of a gallery and angled walls that distort viewing or overwhelm the art. Siza's aversion to natural light is also unfortunate.

Temporary exhibitions are presented on the ground and upper floors, and the collection is in galleries on the lower level. Usually three special exhibitions—typically retrospectives or projects by emerging talents—run simultaneously. Many shows feature Galician artists since a major aim of the museum is to place them in the context of art from elsewhere. Although leading foreign and Spanish artists from outside the region are also a significant component of the program, the emphasis on hot, international stars that prevailed during CGAC's opening years no longer exists. Catalogues and informative, well-designed, free brochures, with texts in Galego, Castilian and English, accompany each exhibition.

Recent exhibitions: *Helena Almeida, Rafael Baixeras, Juan Navarro Baldeweg, Stephan Balkenhol, Jean-Marc Bustamante, Vari Caramés, Loris Cecchini, Sarah Dobai, Garage, José Antonio Hernández-Díez, Rebecca Horn, Marine Hugonnier, Francisco Leiro, Robert Mangold, Mondo-phrenetic TM, Florence Paradeis, Pamen Pereira, Georges Rousse, Elisa Sighicelli, Transfer, Peter Wüthrich.*

The museum's collection is quite small and mainly composed of work by Galician artists. It would pose severe limitations if it were not complemented by the ARCO Foundation Collection, which is on long-term loan to CGAC. Acquired through annual purchases from the ARCO International Art Fair in Madrid, selected by esteemed professionals in the art world, the collection includes an impressive group of objects by such figures as Carl Andre, Francesco Clemente, Hanne Darboven, Dan Flavin, Anish Kapoor, Jannis Kounellis, Guillermo Kuitca, Juan Muñoz, Gabriel Orozco, Sigmar Polke, Thomas Schütte, Richard Tuttle.

Álvaro Siza, Galego Center of Contemporary Art

Giuseppe Penone exhibition, 1999

Lectures and series, jointly sponsored by departments at the University of Santiago de Compostela, enrich the exhibition program. For example, in June–July 1999, Marina Abramovic gave a performance, and Jürgen Partenheimer lectured as part of an incredibly rich series entitled "Science, Technology and the Arts." More recently, conferences have focused on photography and architecture. Weeklong workshops with artists, concerts and other events further diversify and distinguish the museum's activity base.

In addition to its galleries, the museum contains an auditorium, publicly accessible library, café, small bookstore, which exclusively sells museum publications, and roof terrace intended for sculpture installations. (Only one work, by Dan Graham, is currently on the roof, and the space is generally not open to visitors.)

Parque de Santo Domingo de Bonaval

architects: Alvaro SIZA, Isabel AGUIRRE, 1990
Rúela da Carmoniña

The main entrance to the park is at the top, off the surrounding road, but you can also enter via steps at the bottom behind Centro Galego de Arte Contemporaneo.

This park, formerly belonging to the Convent of Santo Domingo de Bonaval, attracted the interest of Siza when he was designing CGAC. He embraced the abandoned land by integrating the zigzag paths of the adjacent slope into the angular rhythms of the museum's building and by working to transform the property into a public park

The land, which covers a large area, had been divided by the old convent into three sections: a terraced kitchen garden, an old oak grove and an octagonally shaped cemetery.

Not only was the vegetation returned to its past order, but the stone walls, ruins, paths, tombstones, streams and fountains were restored, as much as possible, to their original forms and locations. *The Door of Music* (1994), a steel sculpture by Eduardo CHILLIDA, was also added atop one of the old platforms in the terraced area just above the museum.

Auditorio de Galicia

🚋 Avenida do Burgo das Naciôns, 15704
98-157-38-55 f: 157-42-50
Tues–Sun, 12–8; closed Mon
www.audigal.es/exposic_n.html

Located on the periphery of the city at the entrance to the university's north campus.

Poetically landscaped with a lake and willow trees, this regional concert hall houses two auditoria and Galicia's Royal Philharmonic Orchestra and Music School. A large section of the building is also devoted to gallery space for art exhibitions. The program is quite varied, though it evinces a preponderant orientation toward abstract, mid-20th-century art. Some shows include objects of major historical value, and occasionally exhibitions feature adventurous work from the contemporary era. It's worth checking the current schedule in the local newspapers. Recent exhibitions: *American Abstract Expressionism, Eduardo Chillida, Manolo Millares, Reimundo Patiño, Esteban Vicente.*

A Coruña

This seaport town (called La Coruña in Castilian) twists and turns around a landscape of hills, inlets, cliffs and beaches. Train from Santiago de Compostela, 1 hr.

Domus: La Casa del Hombre

🏛 architect: Arata ISOZAKI, 1993–95
Santa Teresa 1, 15002
98-121-70-00 f: 122-89-34
www.casaciencias.org
domus@casasciencias.org
winter: daily, 10–7
summer: daily, 11–9
admission: 300/100 ptas
bus: 5 from the train station to the end of the route.

The museum is at the north end of the city, situated on a plot bordered by Paseo Marítimo, Calle de Ángel Rebollo and Calla Santa Teresa.

Among recent efforts to upgrade and modernize A Coruña were the creation of a waterfront esplanade (1997) and the construction of Domus, a new component of the city's conglomerate science museum. Apart from being an innovative center with interactive displays focused on the body, Human House is one of the most outstanding buildings of late-20th-century architecture.

Set atop a high rock promontory overlooking the sea, the design by Arata Isozaki has two very different facades. The side facing the sea is a monumental, nearly windowless curved wall covered in shingles of metallic-gray slate. It has the semblance of a billowing sail or ocean wave. And from an oblique perspective, it appears implausibly weightless, standing upright with no visible means of support. In contrast, the back is a zigzag arrangement of geometric volumes clad in granite. The image here can be likened to a Japanese folding screen or the jagged stone cliffs of Galicia. A Coruña couldn't have asked for a more striking landmark.

Araka Isozaki, Domus

A grand stone staircase leads from the esplanade to the entrance, an unexpectedly dark, inhospitable area that makes the interior seem all the more extraordinary. It's an eye-popping, continuous expanse of open space organized as a sequence of exhibitions on three levels connected by a series of ramps crisscrossing the length of the hall. As on the exterior, the giant wall has a dominant presence, though here it is fully exposed as raw concrete panels and structural ribs extending from floor to ceiling.

In addition to the exhibits dealing with such topics as identity, genetics, reproduction, birth, the senses, DNA, muscular movement, human organs, the heart and circulatory system, Domus presents related films in a large-screen IMAX theater. Temporary exhibitions, like a series of photographs by Sebastião Salgado showing life in a Latin American neighborhood, inject art and culture into the science domain.

If you walk all around the exterior of the building after your visit, you'll discover a number of terraces at the north end. Outfitted with stone benches and facing the sea, they are superb places for picnicking. A restaurant is planned for the glass-fronted area extending onto one of the terraces. Occupying a prime position on another patio is one of the bulbous-bodied bronze sculptures by Fernando BOTERO, this one in the image of a nude Roman warrior (*Soldado Romano*).

Museo Arte Contemporáneo Unión Fenosa

Avenida de Arteixo 171, 15008
tel/fax: 98-124-83-66
Tues–Sat, 10–2 and 5–8; Sun, 10–2; closed Mon
admission: free
bus: 11, exit Ronda de Outeiro, intersection with Avenida de Arteixo.

The Fenosa center, located in an industrial area of A Coruña, is a short walk ahead.

Fenosa, the regional electric company, created this space to show the art collection developed by its foundation. The art museum (MACUF) shares the building with Museo Eléctrico Unión Fenosa.

With all good intentions, Fenosa has supported the local community by concentrating exclusively on contemporary Galician art. Unfortunately, the results have yielded a very provincial collection of bland, retrograde and derivative art, mainly abstract painting and collage compositions. The exhibition space, though an enormous box building of double-floor height with a balcony running around the main hall, also has an amateurish appearance due to overcrowded displays and tacky room dividers. This is not a place where you're likely to get a rich panorama of avant-garde art, but you may discover a few, previously unknown individuals whose work merits attention.

Along with the permanent collection, the museum presents special exhibitions. These aren't limited to Galician artists and offer a good opportunity to see a select body of work by a recognized talent from the Spanish mainstream of contemporary art. Recent exhibitions: *Eduardo Chillida*, *Luis Gordillo*.

Pontevedra

Train from Santiago de Compostela, 1 hr. Both sites of contemporary art interest are slightly east and across the river from the town center. Though you can walk there on a direct route from the train station, it's far better to take a slight detour through the heart of Pontevedra, a medieval village with lots of charm and character.

Sala de Exposiciones, Pazo da Cultura

architect: Manuel de las CASAS, 1993–98
Rúa Alexandre Bóveda, 36005
98-683-30-61 f: 687-40-70
www.pazodacultura.org
coordinacion@pazodacultura.org
Tues–Fri, 5–9; Sat, 11–2 and 5–9; Sun, 11–2; closed Mon
admission: free
Located on the north bank of the Lérez River in a cylindrical building facing the new cable

Manuel de las Casas, Cultural Center

bridge. (With its leaning concrete pylon, twisting cables and asymmetrical design, the bridge may look like a creation of Santiago Calatrava, but it's only a clone.) The entrance to this building is from a vast terrace reached either by the steps at the end of the wall along the riverfront road (Ingeniero Rafael) or by the staircase a short distance down Alexandre Bóveda Street.

The unusual circular structure, clad in stone with a flared skirt of windows at the bottom and two wings in the rear, houses Pontevedra's Culture Center. It comprises a concert hall, smaller auditoria, conference rooms and a large exhibition space in its own domain and is attached to a very long, almost windowless building that serves as a separate but related Convention Center. The entire complex, all the constituent parts and the character of everything is big. And though the architecture initially seems intriguing, based on an exterior view of the cylindrical form, it quickly loses its flair as the design shows itself to be mundane, cold and uninviting.

If you follow the Culture Center's entrance lobby to the left and descend a short staircase, you'll come to the exhibition space. Having opened in the spring of 1999 with one of the best shows of contemporary art presented anywhere in the past decade, the program got off to an exciting start. *Veronica's Revenge: Contemporary Perspectives on Photography*, spanned the gamut from Man Ray to Claude Cahun, Robert Frank, Joseph Beuys, Hamish Fulton, Sigmar Polke, Cindy Sherman, Robert Gober, Nan Goldin, Rosemarie Trockel, Kiki Smith, Sarah Lucas, Matthew Barney and on and on. Each work was a gem, and ideas spawned by the exhibition about image authenticity were highly engaging. (The accompanying book is an excellent resource on contemporary art.)

Following its glorious beginning, the program has become more conservative with such exhibitions as *Architectures*, *Galician Life in the 1950s (Prints from the Caixa Ourensa Collection)*, *Mexican Sculpture from the Second Half of the 20th Century*, *Transversals (New Views of Galician Photography)*. Who knows what to expect in the future, but it's worth checking the local listings just in case there's a Veronica reprise!

Illa das Esculturas

Illa da Xunqueira do Lérez

From Pazo da Cultura walk north along the river road, Rúa Areses, and you will soon cross a narrow stream of water and be on Xunqueira Island. Continue on the path veering right, in the direction of the pedestrian bridge.

If you're not a pilgrim heading for Santiago de Compostela and need a reason for visiting the remote Atlantic coast area of Spain, this is it. True, it's only a tiny island (17.3 acres; 70,000 sq m) on the edge of the Lérez River, a stone's throw from an urban setting, so accessible you don't need a boat or bathing suit. And there's no denying that the ground can be swampy and that the vegetation is mainly wild rushes and eucalyptus trees, not lush flora and exotic fauna. Nevertheless, if you want to spend a marvelous hour, day or weekend just relaxing outdoors in the quiet company of twelve, masterfully situated, endlessly stimulating artworks, you should put the Island of Sculptures (also known as Xunqueira Island) at the top of your must-see list.

You probably have never heard of this place because it didn't run an advertising campaign when it opened in the summer of 1999. It's not a tourist attraction (yet), but don't be surprised to find local residents strolling, jogging and picnicking there because it's long been a favorite spot—a patch of raw, unmanipulated, "unimproved" nature with no buildings, just indigenous plants and animals.

When two art curator–historians (A. Antón Castro and Rosa Olivares) developed the project, they asked a select group of artists—a mix of leading international sculptors and

Giovanni Anselmo, *Shortened Sky*   Enriqaue Velasco, *Road of Rushes*

local talents—to create works related to nature, to the history or cultural tenor of the setting and to human sensibility at the end of the 20th century. Respect for the natural setting on the island was an overriding factor, and the only stipulation was that the artists use stone (granite), a material present in all cultures and an element particularly identified with Galicia.

Unlike most other sculpture parks, which are developed over time, Pontevedra's island was planned as a self-contained project with all the objects commissioned at once. Most of the works are located off the gravel path that runs along the eastern edge of the island. A helpful map, stanchioned at the beginning of the path, identifies the sculptures and locations.

Giovanni ANSELMO, *Cielo acortado* (*Shortened Sky*), 1999. The placement of this sculpture—a square column of black granite about four feet (1.2 m) tall—adjacent to the intersection of the main path and the walkway going across the island from the pedestrian bridge reinforces its appearance as a directional sign. But the text (*Cielo acortado*), written on the polished top of the post, is more an impossible concept regarding distance than a useful measurement. By providing a reflection of the sky on the shiny stone surface, Anselmo attempts to shorten the distance between land and sky, thus approaching infinity. At the same time, he manifests the absurdity of such a quest by presenting it within the context of a minimalist, precisely configured, utterly physical object.

Enrique VELASCO, *Camino de juncos* (*Road of Rushes*), 1999. The artist has positioned two elevated stone paths on the riverbank so they don't interfere with indwelling animals or the water flowing past. Set at right angles to one other without converging, one is covered with grass and the other has a tree growing in a squared-off section at its end. Velasco thus aims to show the assimilation of stone and nature as well as the potential for a symbiotic relationship between man-made roadways and the natural environment.

Ulrich RÜCKRIEM, Untitled, 1999. (Located in the middle of the next intersection where a second path cuts across the island.) As is his custom, Rückriem created this sculpture

Robert Morris, *Pontevedra's Labyrinth* (ground plan)

matter-space relationships embedded therein. The direct source for his island sculpture, however, was the oldest labyrinth in Western Europe (A.D. 3000), found in a petroglyph in Mogor (Marín), a fishing village just south of Pontevedra. Duplicating the winding circular paths of the ancient rock carving, Morris created a walk-in object with walls 6 1/2 feet (2 m) high, fabricated from granite lined on the top edges with black slate. The young eucalyptus trees planted around the work are the only points of reference (apart from the sky) within the labyrinth and a telling counterpoint to the stone.

from granite blocks with their raw quarry cuts exposed around the edges. Here the form is a tall pillar, over 16 feet (5 m) high and 3 feet (1 m) square. It stands at a crossroad not marking anything in particular but serving as a point of conspicuous verticality and fixity in contrast to the horizontality and continuous movement of the adjacent river.

Robert MORRIS, Pontevedra's Labyrinth, 1999–2000. (Located on the inland area to the left of the crossroad marked by the Rückriem.) In the late 1960s Morris began making art on the land using natural materials. His prodigious output over the subsequent decades also reveals a repeated interest in the form of the labyrinth and the subject-object,

Richard LONG, *Pontevedra Line*, 1999. (Located on the opposite side of the crossroad from the Morris.) Using white granite stones, Long has created one of his famous lines extending like a path through the landscape. "The path is a place. It is also a line, a road that takes us from one place to another." On a primal, spiritual level, Long views a path as the traces left by an individual and then followed by others thereafter. Here, the artist derived the line, which is over 121 feet (37 m) long, from an actual path formed by people walking through the wild grasses.

José Pedro CROFT, Untitled, 1999. (Located on the riverbank just beyond the second crossroad.) In reverse of the usual practice of cutting down trees to clear space for a

José Pedro Croft, Untitiled   Francisco Leiro, *Resting Zone*   Dan Graham, *Pyramid*

Ian Hamilton Finlay, *Petrarch*   Ulrich Rükriem, Untitled   Richard Long, *Pontevedra Line*

building, Croft has shaped a house around existing trees. Constructed of stone with no windows or doors, the solid, geometric form offers a striking contrast to the living, growing trees. And yet, the house's human scale and accommodation of the trees suggest a harmonious relationship with nature.

Jenny HOLZER, Untitled, 1999. Eight granite benches placed along the length of the main path are by the American artist known for using poetic aphorisms as the substantive element of her work. Here each bench has 12 different phrases inscribed on its seat. Among them are "You must live in harmony with nature," "It's essential to reconcile the heart with the head," "To look backwards is the first sign of getting old and deteriorating," "Moderation kills the spirit." Holzer thus provides functional furniture for the island even as she stimulates thinking about ideas beyond the commonplace and practical.

Anne and Patrick POIRIER, *Una Folie o Pequeño paraíso para Pontevedra* (*A Folly or Little Paradise for Pontevedra*), 1999. (Take the third path across the island and go over the footbridge to a forested area on the other side.) As you walk down a lovely riverside path, bordered by stones and native plants and flowers, you pass under four wire-cage arches. Each has a plaque on the ground beneath it. Engraved on these are the words "Esquecemento," "Rescendo," "Soidade," "Soños" (Oblivion, Scents, Solitude, Dreams). At the end of the path, the Poiriers have built a small shrinelike structure, also made of wire cages. The plaque at the entrance reads "Hortus Conclusus" ("Enclosed Garden") and inside three stone chairs face a granite sculpture set on the ground. It depicts an oversize brain. Characteristically, the Poiriers create installations in which elements from the past engage in a dialogue with the present. Here, they cleverly develop an experiential folly, replete with real sensory stimuli and historically loaded props, to provoke contemplation of a particular landscape and the classic modes civilizations have devised to embellish and venerate nature (and themselves).

Dan GRAHAM, *Pyramid*, 1988–99. (Located on the riverbank alongside the main path.) Although well known for his geometric objects and installations made of transparent and double-sided glass, mirrors or aluminum panels, Graham conformed with the request to use granite for the Pontevedra project and created a volumetric sculpture. Nevertheless, his pyramid, with its cutout segments that play with issues of solid and void, triangular plane and pyramidal form, still conveys

Anne & Patrick Poirier, *A Folly* or *Little Paradise for Pontevedra*

the artist's preoccupation with spaces and surfaces that reveal, conceal, reflect, block, enclose and open.

Fernando CASÁS, *Los 36 justos* (*The Just 36*), 1999. Interspersed among the trees in the forested area near the end of the island are 36 stumps made of black granite. The impression of trees having been destroyed by a forest fire or foolishly chopped down for commercial use is unmistakable. Indeed, Casás sought to criticize society's disrespect of nature. His choice of 36 trees makes reference to a Hebrew legend contending that there are 36 just, wise men and women who keep watch over the world, but neither they nor others know who they are. With the legend in mind, the truncated trees become a vivid metaphor of stalwart righteousness.

Francisco LEIRO, *Saavedra. Zone de descanso* (*Resting Zone*), 1999. Floating on the river off the end of the island is Leiro's sculpture: a raft configured as a private room, albeit in full view of the general public. A couch and set of shelves containing two chunks of cheese are the only objects in the room, yet each is intensely present, confronting one another like protagonists in a murder mystery or couples in a romantic comedy. Absurdity and irony reign, especially since Leiro has situated his mundane, domestic setting out of easy access and in a decidedly pastoral stretch of nature.

Ian Hamilton FINLAY, *Petrarca* (*Petrarch*), 1999. Three green slate medallions set high on the trunks of eucalyptus trees in the northwest sector near the end of the island constitute Finlay's contribution to the Island of Sculptures. The name "Petrarch" and Roman numerals referring to one of his love sonnets are inscribed on each plaque. Whereas Petrarch was a 14th-century Italian humanist, poet and nature lover, Finlay is a concrete poet, gardener and artist who explores the complex relationship between nature and culture. His artwork often entails the placement of words in an outdoor setting to manifest the power of language.

EXTREMADURA

Although not very well known and relatively distant from modern culture, the region of Extremadura ("the land beyond the River Douro") has some notable sites related to contemporary art and architecture. Since transportation to and within this remote area lying on the border of Portugal is limited, plan extra time for travel from place to place.

Mérida

If you can't get to Rome or Athens and want to see splendors of the ancient world, Mérida is the place to visit. The well-preserved treasures dating from 25 B.C. include an amphitheater, theater, arena, forum, temple, aqueduct, bridges, hippodrome, houses and much more. Train from Madrid, 4 hr.

Museo Nacional de Arte Romano

architect: Rafael MONEO, 1980–86
Calle de José Ramón Mélida, 06800
92-431-16-90 f: 430-20-06
Oct–May: Mon–Sat, 10–2 and 4–6; Sun, 10–2
June–Sept: Mon–Sat, 10–2 and 5–7; Sun, 10–2
admission: 400/200 ptas; free Sat afternoon, Sun

Located across the street from the Roman theater and amphitheater.

Rafael Moneo's seamless integration of an excavation site, mosaics, frescoes and other historic artifacts into the architecture of Mérida's National Museum of Roman Art galvanized worldwide attention and elevated his name to the top echelon of his profession. The building is a captivating design, though hardly a conspicuous object. Moreover, the museum exemplifies curatorial excellence in its modes of installation and communication about everyday life in Roman Mérida.

An archaeological dig uncovered ruins of

Rafael Moneo, National Museum of Roman Art

houses, tombs and streets in Augusta Emérita, the ancient capital of Lusitania, and Moneo preserved these findings in a crypt, accessible for public viewing and scholarly study. Artifacts from this and other excavations (sculptures, paintings, architectural fragments, coins, pottery, jewelry, glassware, etc.) are displayed along a central nave, divided by 10 arched walls, or within intimate side spaces on the ground floor and two upper levels. All the walls, inside and out, are clad in beige-toned bricks, following ancient Roman conventions. Light, streaming in from overhead windows, and a multifaceted circulation system enliven and diversify the simple, handsome layout. Indeed, the open interconnectedness of the spaces enables tantalizing glimpses from one section into another as well as diverse perspectives of the works. Individual objects are given due attention and groupings clarify important relationships. But it's Moneo's architecture that expressly creates an ambience in which past and present intertwine, demonstrating continuity and consistency.

Puente de Lusitania

architect: Santiago CALATRAVA, 1988–91

Commissioned to create a new bridge across the Guadiana River so that the 2,000-year-old Roman bridge could be spared contemporary road traffic, Calatrava designed a showcase of modern engineering. Lusitania Bridge has a midspan, white steel arch with a wide path for pedestrians and bicycles running down the center and dual automobile roadways on the outer sides. As always, Calatrava's bridge is a creative statement in simple elegance.

Biblioteca Pública del Estado

architect: Luis ARRANZ, 1993–97
Avenida de la Libertad, 06800
Mon–Fri, 9:30–1:30 and 5–8
Located adjacent to Calatrava's bridge on the left bank of the river.

Like the Calatrava bridge, this building, situated on the border of ancient Mérida, conveys a vivid image of Mérida as a forward-looking, modern city. Embracing some of the eccentricities of postmodern design, the architect Luis Arranz spread the functional areas of this public library around an angular, four-story-high atrium, formed at the confluence of three interlocking cubes. From the front facade, the impression is mainly of a big box with smooth grid surfaces of gray granite. Even the recessed window planes and triangular inset at the entrance are relatively sedate, especially when compared with the rest of the building, where jutting glazed walls, which expose structural steel beams painted bright yellow, tall columns and voids prominently interrupt the volumetric form. A wedge-shaped structure housing an auditorium adds further pizzazz to the architecture. Rising from the ground, its diagonal edge serves as a staircase leading to a terrace with superb views of the river and city.

Luis Arranz, Public State Library

Malpartida de Cáceres

Malpartida is a small village where traditional white houses line winding streets, except around the fringe, where row houses denote the infiltration of suburbia. Train to Cáceres from Mérida, 1 hr; from Badajoz, 1 3/4 hr. Bus from Cáceras to Malpartida, 15 min. Check ahead for connections and return schedules. Taking intercity buses is often a better option than trains in Extremadura.

Museo Wolf Vostell

Centra de los Barruecos (P.O. Box 20), 10910

92-727-64-92 f: 727-64-91
www.museovostell.com
mvm@ctv.es

spring: Tues–Sun, 10–1:30 and 5–7:30; closed Mon

summer: Tues–Sun, 10:30–1:30 and 6–9; closed Mon

fall–winter: Tues–Sun, 10–1:30 and 4–6:30; closed Mon

admission: 200/100 ptas; free Wed

Located 1 3/4 mi (3 km) from the town of Malpartida. Taxis are usually available, though it's an easy walk along a country road with no hills and no turns to get you lost. You pass through fields of wildflowers, grazing sheep, bulls lounging by the roadside, fantastical rock formations that outdo those created by Yves Tanguy and nothing but the sounds of crickets and birds to interrupt your thoughts. After such tranquility, it's a real shock to see a long lineup of tour buses at the museum entrance.

If you're not up on the cultist movements of the 20th century or artists not favored by American museums, you may well not have heard of Wolf Vostell. And if you know the name, you may wonder why this German artist has a museum in the hinterlands of Spain. Before dismissing this as a vanity museum by a marginal figure, consider that a visit here will undoubtedly be a truly enjoyable, unusual experience. In the process, you'll see some extraordinary antecedents to the performance, assemblage, installation, conceptual, text-based, video, multimedia and social commentary art that predominated in the 1980s and 1990s.

Although Vostell was familiar with Malpartida because his wife was from the region, it wasn't until he saw Los Barruecos (the granite boulders) that he realized how perfect the landscape was for a museum focused on Fluxus, the movement in which he was a leading member. The stark scenery with the marvelous rocks and a reservoir lake is the backdrop for an 18th-century complex of stone-and-brick buildings originally used as a wool processing and clothing factory. In 1998, when restoration work on the main structures was finished, the museum came alive. (The official founding was in 1976; Vostell died in April 2000.)

Like Dada and Surrealism before it, Fluxus was an interdisciplinary movement involving an international group of artists. Ideas and images drew freely from music, literature, theater, the visual arts and above all, everyday life. Boundaries didn't exist, and a postwar (1950s) sense of freedom, exuberance, rebellion and irony fueled the creative process.

When you tour the first building, where a major selection of Vostell's large-scale installations, performance videos and paintings are on display, you'll see vivid evidence of a Fluxus expression of flamboyant chaos, brutality and biting humor. The key materials used are old television sets, supersize American cars of the 1950s, concrete, tools, junk and sound tracks.

The right side of the second building exhibits a modest selection of conceptual art by Spanish and Portuguese artists of post-Fluxus generations (e.g., Helena Almeida, Rafael Canogar, Equipo Crónica, Esther Ferrer, Julião Parmenter, etc.). To the left and occupying the majority of the building is the Gino Di Maggio Donation, a superb collection of Fluxus art, including works by Arman, Joseph Beuys, George Brecht, John Cage, Dick Higgens, Allan Kaprow, George Maciunas, Charlotte Moorman, Yoko Ono,

Wolf Vostell, *Automobile Fever*, 1973

Nam June Paik, Daniel Spoerri, Ben Vautier, La Monte Young, etc. Occasionally, the museum presents a special retrospective of a Fluxus artist.

Be sure to walk all around the buildings so you don't miss any of the eccentric sculptures installed outdoors. A favorite is *Pilato*, a 50-foot-high (15.2 m) tower of old cars, pianos and a Mig-21 fuselage anchored in cement. You'll also find a bookstore, café, picnic terrace and exhibition on the history of the site, its factory and wool making.

Badajoz

Train from Merida, 1 hr; from Cáceres, 1 3/4 hr.

Museo Extremeño e Iberoamericano de Arte Contemporáneo

architect: José Antonio GALEA, 1995
Calle de Museo 2, 06003
92-426-03-84 f: 426-06-40
www.meiac.org
meiac@extremanet.com
winter: Tues–Sat, 10:30–1:30 and 5–8; Sun, 10:30–1:30; closed Mon
summer: Tues–Sat, 10:30–1:30 and 6–9; Sun, 10:30–1:30; closed Mon
admission: free

Located one block up from Plaza de la Constitución and just east of Avenida Fernando Calzadilla.

The enclosing brick and stone walls and

highly structured geometric design of the formal gardens and postmodern buildings are a bit off-putting, but don't let this inhibit you from visiting the Museum of Contemporary Art from Extremadura and IberoAmerica (MEIAC). Interestingly, a prison previously occupied the site and contributed the old panoptic, now set atop the dome, in the new building.

Shaped as a cylinder, the museum contains four floors arranged like balconies around a center atrium. With their low ceilings and narrow width, these exhibition spaces are suitable for photography and small objects, but quite restrictive to the scale and character of much contemporary art. In contrast, the underground level is a large, flexible, raw space bearing an industrial aesthetic with exposed pipes, concrete support columns and pitched-roof skylights. Since the architecture often determines the placement of a particular exhibition, the permanent collection and temporary exhibitions have no set location within the building.

Despite these anomalies, the museum has carved out a laudable territory for itself. Rather than try to be all-inclusive or follow an unsophisticated provincial mandate, the MEIAC has a two-pronged focus: art from the Extremadura region (1920s to the present) and Iberoamerican contemporary art—work by Spanish, Portuguese and Latin American artists. Because it is a young museum, only open since 1995, you wouldn't expect it to have much of a collection. It may not be sizeable, but MEIAC's holdings are well-chosen examples of vanguard trends and talented individuals. They include: Helena Almeida, Francis Alÿs, José Bedia, Luis Buñuel, Pedro Cabrita Reis, Saint Clair Cemin, Juan Dávila, Pepe Espaliú, Alfredo Jaar, Guillermo Kuitca, Eva Lootz, Jorge Molder, Leonel Moura, Juan Muñoz, Manuel Ocampo, Gabriel Orozco, Jaume Plensa, Liliana Porter, Miguel Rio Branca, Julião Sarmento, Andres Serrano, W. Eugene Smith, Ray Smith, Susana Solano, Juan Uslé.

Susana Solano, *Gelato,* 1986

The temporary exhibition program is less exciting than the collection, though at least one show a year is a truly notable retrospective of an Iberoamerican artist from the contemporary era. Recent exhibitions: *Helena Almeida, Juan Barjola, Luis Buñuel—Las Hurdes, José Manuel Ciria, Photographs of Extremadura.*

The square brick building behind the museum contains an auditorium, library, café and offices.

SEVILLA

Old-world beauty is the main attraction here, and it's hard not to be impressed by the Moorish architecture, especially the interlacing patterns of the plasterwork and the fine geometric designs of ceramic-tile mosaics. Add to this the charm of window grilles, courtyard patios and lush gardens, and you have a city rich in visual pleasure and proud of historic traditions.

Unfortunately, Sevilla does little to champion or nourish current art activity. (This is a big sports town, not a culture haven.) The fine arts museum hardly acknowledges modernism in either the 19th or 20th century; the contemporary art center struggles to stay alive; the main art school adheres to a strict classical training; and conservatism abounds in most every realm related to the arts. If it weren't for a handful of forward-thinking galleries that present vanguard work by recognized and young artists, it would be easy to omit Sevilla when considering the art scene in present-day Spain.

Though Sevilla marks each street with tile letters on the walls of corner buildings, it's not easy to navigate your way around the center city. The old urban plan, which is still operative, is made up of narrow streets that twist, turn and intersect in a seemingly illogical manner. One wrong move and you're lost in a labyrinth. Asking directions is of little help, so just plan extra time to get from place to place. Most sites within the center city are within walking distance of one another, and walking is far preferable to driving through the tangle of one-way streets and nonstop traffic. Walking also imbues you with the fun-loving, upbeat character of the people and city.

Sevilla is one of the few cities currently served by AVE, Spain's speed train. This makes it feasible to zip down for a day or weekend if your time is limited. Train from Madrid, 2 1/2 hr.

San Pablo Airport

architect: Rafael MONEO, 1987–91

Moneo was strongly guided by symbolism in his design of Sevilla's new airport. Aiming to have the architecture convey the idea of being in transit between an earthbound building and the sky, he defined the main concourse with curving vaults. He then painted them deep blue to ensure their image as "a threshold to the sky." In other respects, the building is fairly traditional, following Moneo's clear, direct, reductive style.

Estación de Santa Justa

architects: Antonio CRUZ, Antonio ORTIZ, 1988–92
Avenida de Kansas City

If you cringe at the sight of a staircase and circuitous corridors when you get off a train with heavy luggage, this is your dream station. Moving ramps go directly from the platforms to the lobby, and a refreshing elegance greets you when you look up at the tall, narrow vaults roofing the tracks. Though the vast expanse of the boxlike brick lobby reverts to the overwhelming, functionally impaired space that has become synonymous with mass-transportation architecture, its spare design with long, vertical lines and cutout forms has redeeming value.

Galeria Juana de Aizpuru

Calle Zaragoza 26, 41001
tel/fax: 95-422-85-01
Tues–Sat, 10:30–2 and 5–9; closed Mon

Located south of Plaza Nueva in the Centro district, just after Calle Madrid becomes Calle Zaragoza.

This classy gallery with white stone floors and three light-filled stories around a central atrium is also a showcase for top-notch contemporary art. No matter what the exhibition, you'll see work that is testing new waters. Spanish and foreign artists, young and established talents are featured, and the range of mediums and styles included is far-reaching. The gallery had a long history of supporting innovative art both in Sevilla and Madrid, where it has a second space. Because it doesn't rest on past laurels, you're as likely to see unfamiliar names as big stars, and the objects aren't retreads!

Artists: Rafael Agredano, Ana Laura Aláez, Pilar Albarracín, Art & Language, Juan Navarro Baldeweg, Miroslaw Balka, Pedro Cabrita Reis, Miguel Ángel Campano, Nuria Carrasco, Rui Chafes, Eduardo Chillida, Luis Claramunt, Jordi Colomer, José Pedro Croft, Jiri Dokoupil, Carmela García, Dora García, Alberto García-Alix, Ferrán García-Sevilla, Pierre Gonnord, Federico Guzmán, Georg Herrold, Juan Hidalgo, Mike Kelley, Martin Kippenberger, Joseph Kosuth, Aitor Lara, José María Larrondo, Sol LeWitt, Rogelio Lopez Cuenca, Ingeborg Lüscher, Sigfrido Martin Begue, Albert Oehlen, Markus Oehlen, Andres Serrano, Xesús Vazquez, William Wegman, Franz West.

Ana Laura Alaez, *Two-Headed,* 1996

Galería Pepe Cobo

Plaza Cristo de Burgos 5–6, 41003
95-450-07-39 f: 450-03-47
www.pepecobo.com
pepe.cobo@pepecobo.com
Mon–Fri, 5–8; closed Sat

Located northeast of Plaza Nueva. For the most direct route, go north on Calle Tetuan, which turns into Calle Velázquez; turn right (east) onto Calle Campana and continue straight ahead despite repeated changes in the street name (Calle Martíín Villa, Calle Laraña, Plaza de la Encarnación, Calle Imagen) to Plaza San Pedro. Plaza Cristo de Burgos (a rectangular strip of green bordered by a street) abuts this intersection to the right, and the gallery is immediately on the left but back from the street behind gates, at the rear of a driveway and courtyard.

Pepe Cobo began in Sevilla (1984) with a gallery called Máquina Española (Spanish Machine). He then opened a branch in Madrid (1988) and kept both galleries going until 1994. During the years 1990–93, he also joined John Weber and Brooke Alexander from New York in launching a glitzy space near the Reina Sofía Museum with a star-studded exhibition program. In 1999, he inaugurated the current gallery in Sevilla.

Don't be deceived by the two modest rooms comprising the exhibition space. And don't be surprised if a show includes only a few works. Typically, each is a choice object and the artists are recognized talents or intriguing upstarts. The gallery favors work with a conceptual, rather than a formalist character, though exhibitions present a broad spectrum of current tendencies. Indeed, the program is enhanced by special showings of leading international artists like Barbara Ess, Jorge Molder, Bruce Nauman, Gina Pane, Sigmar Polke, Thomas Ruff, Kiki Smith, Rosemarie Trockel.

Artists: Joan Brossa, Pepe Espaliú, Cristina Iglesias, Marcel Mariën, Juan Muñoz, MP & MP Rosado Garcés, Julião Sarmento, Augustina von Nagel.

MP and MP Rosado Garcés, *Palm Tree,* 2000

Rayas

Almirante Apodaca 1–3, 41003
daily: 12 p.m.–1 a.m.

Just around the corner from Galería Pepe Cobo is one of the best ice cream and chocolate shops in Spain. The two tiny shops with a few sidewalk tables are likely to be crowded and noisy, but if you have a sweet tooth or enjoy comestible creativity, Rayas is not to be missed. The sumptuous swirls and rich color tones in the endless lineup of ice cream flavors may bring to mind lush gobs of impasto paint in an expressionist painting, but here the visual merges with the gustatory. And for those who are more interested in pragmatic mergers between technology and commerce, check out the automatic ordering and payment machines!

Galería Rafael Ortiz

Calle Mármoles 12, 41004
95-421-48-74 f: 422-64-02
www.galeriaortiz.com

galortiz@arquired.es
Mon, 6–9; Tues–Fri, 11–1:30 and 6–9; Sat, 11–1:30

Located in the maze of the Santa Cruz district. From Raza walk down Plaza Cristo de Burgos; at the end turn left onto Calle Descalzos; turn right when this short block hits Plaza San Ildefonso; continue ahead on Calle Cabezadel; two short blocks ahead, at the intersection, take the second left onto Calle Muñoz y Pavón; walk one block to the next small plaza. The gallery is on the corner between Calle Mármoles and Calle Federico Rubio.

Galería Rafael Ortiz has been around since 1984 and is housed in nicely renovated, picturesque rooms on the ground floor of an old dwelling. Specializing in contemporary Spanish art, the gallery mainly shows paintings and collages. Styles range from minimalist to realist, expressionist, surrealist, figurative and geometric abstraction. Though some artists shown here inventively play with the medium or imagery, many follow more traditional strains deriving from modernism.

Artists: Eugenio Ampudia, Juan Asencio, José María Baez, Jaime Burguillos, Patricia Cabrera, Carmen Calvo, Gerardo Delgado, Terea Duclós, Dorothea von Elbe, Equipo 57, Carlos Forns Bada, Isabel Garay, J. García Pfretzschner, María José Gómez Redondo, Luis Gordillo, Ciuco Gutierrez, Juan Francisco Isidro, Carmen Laffón, Luis Mayo, Pedro Mora, Antonio Murado, Ángel Padrón, Guillermo Pérez Villalta, Paco Reina, Manuel Rufo, Joaquín Saenz, Antonio Sosa, Antonio Socias, Ignacio Tovar, Zush.

Galería Cavecanem

Calle San José 10, 41004
tel/fax: 95-456-42-71
www.galeria-cavecanem.com
ojoalperro@teleline.es
Tues–Fri, 11–2 and 6–9; Sat, 11–2; closed Mon

Follow Calle Muñoz y Pavón as it swerves east at the intersection with Calle Mármoles and turn right onto Calle San José at the next little plaza. The gallery is not far ahead on the right.

The gallery occupies one of the compact, old houses in the Santa Cruz barrio and uses every inch of space for exhibiting art. Be sure to poke around the various rooms so you're sure to see everything on display. With its focus on young artists and new forms of expression, Cavecanem is a vitalizing presence in the city and region. It's a good place to see feisty work by emerging figures in the Spanish art scene.

Artists: Javier Alkain, Tete Álvarez, José Ramón Amondarain, Layla d'Angelo, Nono Bandera, Mira Bernabeu, Fernando Bernejo, Gilles Berquet, Jesus Cánovas, Luis Manuel Fernández, Manuel Flores, Angustias García & Isaías Griñolo, Alberto García-Alix, Alsono Gil, Dionisio González, Pep Guerrero, Ciuco Gutiérrez, Joaquín Ivars, Oscar Marin, Teresa Moro, Manu Muniategiandikoetxea, Joan Hernández Pijuan, Mar G. Ranedo, Antonio D. Resurrección, Pepa Rubio, Mireia Santís, Adriana Torres, Javier Velasco.

Mira Bernabeu, *Bedroom*, 2000

Librería Vitruvio

Plaza de la Contratación 5, 41004
tel/fax: 95-422-63-98
Mon–Fri, 10–2 and 5–8; Sat, 10:30–2

Continue down Calle San José, which becomes Santa María La Blanca; turn right into a wide plaza that becomes Calle Ximenez de Enciso, Pie Vila Andreu, Calle Rodrigo Caro and Plaza del Triunfo. At this point, you'll be in front of Reales Alcázarez (left) and across from the cathedral (right). If you zigzag off to the far left, you'll arrive at Plaza de la Contratación.

Despite its location in the middle of Sevilla's tourist hub, this bookstore is tucked away in a quiet spot out of sight and earshot of the traffic and crowds. The ambience inside is more like a library than a commercial shop, and the selection includes monographs on major contemporary architects as well as thematic texts. Most are in Spanish.

Eduardo Chillida

Monumento a la Tolerancia, 1992
Muelle de la Sal

Located on a quay of the Guadalquivir River, adjacent to Puente de Isabel II (also known as Puente Triana) and down the street from the city's bullring.

Chillida titled this yellow granite sculpture, centered on a semicircular wall with curving appendages reaching out to embrace a larger area, *Monument to Tolerance*. It's an impressive work despite its out-of-the-way, almost hidden-from-view location next to a parking lot, well below street level and above the walking path bordering the river. True, it can be seen by boats on the river, but considering the paucity of public art in Sevilla, it's a shame that it wasn't placed in a more prominent setting.

Isla de la Cartuja

This large stretch of land between two branches of the Guadalquivir River was developed as the fairgrounds for Expo '92. Garden and park zones were created, and 86 pavilions or new buildings were constructed, including innovative designs by Tadao Ando, Nicholas Grimshaw and Santiago Calatrava. But unlike Barcelona and Lisbon, which used a big event to permanently rehabilitate and transform their cities, most of Expo '92 was conceived as temporary. If you walk around the area today you'll find abandoned, derelict buildings, overgrown weeds, potholed streets and trash. Only a few isolated buildings and an amusement park remain as functioning sites, though a back section of the island has been developed as a science and technology park.

Edificio de Torretriana

architect: Francisco Javier SÁENZ DE OÍZA, 1988–95
Calle Jerónimo de Aguilar, Isla de la Cartuja

Located on the southern end of the island.

This enormous cylindrical building housing various departments of the Andalusian government was designed by one of Spain's most revered modern architects (the teacher of Moneo) who died in 2000. Looking like a 20th-century fortress clad in a golden-toned marble with encircling bands of a darker tone, it unabashedly manifests a formal order and geometric structure. Tiny square windows articulate a surface pattern on the facade, which is boldly interrupted by large ocular cutouts positioned at four equidistant points on the circumference. These demarcate the orthogonal organization on the interior, though nothing suggests that a central square building surrounded by a patio garden lies within the circular frame.

Centro Andaluz de Arte Contemporáneo

Monasterio Santa María de las Cuevas (Conjunto Monumental de la Cartuja)
Avenida Américo Vespucio 2, Isla de la Cartuja, 41071
95-448-06-11 f: 448-06-20
Apr–Sept: Tues–Sat, 10–9; Sun, 10–3; closed Mon
Oct–Mar: Tues–Sat, 10–8; Sun, 10–3; closed Mon
admission: 300 ptas; free Tues for E.U. citizens
bus: C1, C2

The Andalusian Center of Contemporary Art (CAAC) occupies one section of the Monumental Carthusian Complex, the former Monastery of Santa Maria of the Caves. From the 15th century until 1836, monks lived and worked in the several churches, numerous chapels, residential and study areas, patios, gardens and orchards, which together form the spacious conglomerate. It acquired additional significance because Christopher Columbus lived there for a time and was buried in the crypt for 27 years until his remains were moved to the cathedral. After the monastery closed, an Englishman purchased the property (1839) and turned it into a ceramics factory. The tall chimneys you see off to the side bear witness to the kilns that operated on the premises until 1982, when the factory closed. Four years later, the government began restoring the structure, soon escalating its schedule because the historic monastery was designated a primary exhibition pavilion for Expo '92.

The main area of the newly restored

buildings, replete with all the tiles, frescoes, sculptures, furniture and chapels outfitted for the monastery and church, became the home of CAAC in 1998. While several of the diversely proportioned spaces are well suited to contemporary art, it's quite bizarre and very distracting to find sacred iconography and a religious setting juxtaposed with the themes and images of recent creations.

Since opening, CAAC has presented a potpourri of exhibitions and activities but is still struggling to establish itself as a notable institution. It inherited a collection from Sevilla's now defunct Museum of Contemporary Art, which largely comprises Spanish graphic art from the 1960s and 1970s. Added to this are objects from the last decades of the century, including some works by foreign artists (Ross Bleckner, Louise Bourgeois, Jiri Georg Dokoupil, Rebecca Horn, Joseph Kosuth, Ana Mendieta, Andres Schulze, Andrés Serrano, Ray Smith, Bill Viola). The center intends for its collection galleries (open since May 2000) to focus on Andalusian art (e.g., Rafael Agredano, Chemo Cobo, Pepe Espaliú, Luis Gordillo, Federico Guzmán) with important examples of international and national art incorporated for contextualization. Perhaps when its holdings expand this will become a viable reality.

Recent exhibitions: *Tete Álvarez*, *Nacho Criado*, *Double Trouble—Tom Patchett Collection*, *Dionisio González*, *Federico Guzmán*, *Industrial Design in Spain*, *Pedro Mora*, *The Origin, Present and Future of Basic Figurative Art*, *Shadowless Architecture*, *Maura Sheehan*.

Puente Alamillo

architect: Santiago CALATRAVA, 1987–92

Located at the northern end of the center city.

Though not constructing great buildings or enhancing the city with outstanding public artwork, Sevilla added eight new bridges over the Guadalquivir River for Expo '92. Among them is a bridge that challenged gravitational and structural precepts even as it yielded a design with extraordinary elegance and pizzazz. Indeed, Alamillo Bridge by the renowned architect-engineer-artist Santiago Calatrava instantly went into history books and became one of Sevilla's landmark monuments.

The asymmetrical form and sharply tilted tower are clear evidence of Calatrava's attitude that bridges are not just functional, highway engineering projects. More like sculpture, this bridge has a presence as an engaging image. Though there was no specific association intended, critics have come to see it as a harp form, and locals have warmly dubbed it "the suspenders."

Even without knowing much about physics, one can tell that the solitary, leaning pylon with cables extending across the river but without any back anchoring is a wondrous feat. The way Calatrava achieved this was to counterbalance the weight of the concrete and steel pylon with that of the deck and cables.

If you've never crossed a bridge on foot, try this one! A wide pedestrian path positioned on the spine of the deck is set apart from the traffic lanes cantilevered out on the sides but set at a lower level. If you really want a special experience, take your walk across at night, when the aura of the bridge, embodying Calatrava's "poetics of movement," is especially strong due to the sublime lighting (which he also designed).

Santiago Calatrava, Alamillo Bridge

Subject Index

museums

A Coruña
Domus: La Casa del Hombre, 201–02
Museo Arte Contemporáneo Unión
Fenosa, 202–04
Badajoz
Museo Extremeño e Iberoamericano
de Arte Contemporáneo, 212–13
Barcelona
Fundació Antoni Tàpies, 109–10
Fundació Joan Miró, 163–66
Museu d'Art Contemporani, 83–87
Museu d'Art Modern, 105
Museu Nacional d'Art de Catalunya,
169
Museu Picasso, 98–99
Bilbao
Bilboko Arte Eder Museoa, 191
Museo Guggenheim Bilbao, 188–91
Cuenca
Museo de Arte Abstracto Español, 57
Figueres
Teatre-Museu Dalí, 179–80
Girona
Museu del Cinema, 178
Hernani
Museo Chillida-Leku, 186
Madrid
Fundación Colección Thyssen-Bor-
nemisza, 28–29
Museo de Escultura al Aire Libre, 48
Museo del Prado, 25–26
Museo Nacional Centro de Arte Reina
Sofía, 20–23
Malpartida de Cáceres
Museo Wolf Vostell, 211–12
Mérida
Museo Nacional de Arte Romano,
209–10
Port Lligat—Cadaqués
Casa-Museu Salvador Dalí, 182
Púbol
Casa-Museu Castell Gala Dalí, 183
Salamanca
Museo Art Nouveau y Art Decó, 58
Santiago de Compostela
Centro Galego de Arte Contemporaneo,
198–200
Segovia
Museo de Arte Contemporáneo Esteban
Vicente, 55
Sevilla
Centro Andaluz de Arte Contemporáneo,
218–19
Valencia
Institut Valencià d'Art Modern, Centre
Julio González, 63–64
Valladolid
Museo de Arte Contemporáneo Español
de Valladolid, 55

art centers, exhibition spaces

Barcelona
BD Ediciones de Diseño, 115
CaixaForum, 171–73
La Capella de l'Antic Hospital de la
Santa Creu, 91
Casa Milà, 113–14
Centre Cívic Pati Llimona, 95
Centre Cultural Caixa Catalunya, La
Pedrera, 114
Centre Cultural de la Fundació "la
Caixa," 117
Centre d'Art Santa Mònica, 92
Centre de Cultura Contemporània de
Barcelona, 87–89
Espai Fotogràfic Can Basté, 126
FAD, 87
Hangar, 154
Metronòm, 101–02
Palau de la Virreina, 91–92
Sala Montcada de la Fundació "la
Caixa," 99
Sala Picasso, 96
Vinçon, 114–15
Bilbao
Sala Rekalde, 193
Castelló
Espai d'Art Contemporani de Castelló,
75–77

Girona
  Espais—Centre d'Art Contemporani,
    177
  Sales Municipals d'Exposición, 177–78
L'Hospitalet de Llobregat
  Centre Cultural Tecla Sala, 174–75
Lleida
  Sala El Roser, 177
Madrid
  Círculo des Bellas Artes, 31
  Fundación Banco de Bilbao y Vizcaya,
    51
  Fundación Caja Madrid, 30
  Fundación COAM, 38
  Fundación Cultural Mapfre Vida, 51
  Fundación Juan March, 48
  Fundación "la Caixa," 45
  Fundación Telefónica, 31–32
  Museo Colecciones ICO, 29–30
  Palacio de Cristal, 27
  Palacio de Velázquez, 26
  PhotoGalería—La Fábrica, 25
  Sala del Canal de Isabel II, 50
Pontevedra
  Sala de Exposiciones, 203–04
Salamanca
  Palacio de Abrantes, 56
  Sala de Exposiciones, 56
San Sebastián
  Arteleku, 186
  Koldo Mitxelena Kulturunea, 184–85
Santiago de Compostela
  Auditorio de Galicia, 201
Valencia
  Almudí, 68
  Centre del Carme, 64—65
  La Gallera, 66
  Sala Parpalló, 66

film centers

Madrid
  Cine Doré, 25
  Círculo des Bellas Artes, 31
Valencia
  Filmoteca de la Generalitat Valenciana,
    66
  L'Hemisfèric, 73

Barcelona
  CaixaForum, 171
  Centre Cultural de la Fundació "la
    Caixa," 117
  Centre de Cultura Contemporània de
    Barcelona, 87–89
  Filmoteca, 112
Girona
  Museu del Cinema, 178
San Sebastián
  Film Festival, 182

art galleries

Barcelona
  Alejandro Sales, 115–16
  Antonio de Barnola, 95–96
  Berini, 101
  Carles Taché, 107–08
  Cotthem, 89
  Estrany—de la Mota, 111–12
  Ferran Cano, 89
  Joan Prats, 109
  La Xina Art, 90
  Maeght, 99–100
  Metropolitana de Barcelona, 117
  Senda, 107
  Senda—Espai 292, 107
  Toni Tàpies—Edicions T, 108–09
Bilbao
  Windsor Kulturgintza, 193
Madrid
  Antonio Machón, 37
  Arnés & Röpke, 36
  Buades, 31
  Elba Benítez, 41–42
  Elvira González, 40
  Estiarte, 49–50
  Espacio Mínimo, 24
  Fucarés, 36–37
  Heinrich Ehrhardt, 42
  Helga de Alvear, 23
  Javier López, 33
  Juana de Aizpuru, 37–38
  La Caja Negra, 40
  Marlborough, 34
  María Martín, 42
  Marta Cervera, 39–40

Max Estrella, 38–39
Metta, 35–36
My Name's Lolita Art, 24–25
Oliva Arauna, 44
Salvador Díaz, 23
Soledad Lorenzo, 34–35
San Sebastián
    DV, 184
Sevilla
    Juana de Aizpuru, 214–15
    Cavecanem, 217
    Pepe Cobo, 215
    Rafael Ortiz, 216–17
Valencia
    Luis Adelantado, 70–71
    Espai Lucas, 67
    Tomás March, 69–70
    My Name's Lolita Art, 67–68
    Ray Gun, 72
    Visor, 67

architecture

Aguirre, Isabel
    Santiago de Compostela: Parque de
    Santo Domingo de Bonaval,
    202–03
Amadó, Roser & Lluís Domènech Girbau
    Barcelona: Arxiu de la Corona
    d'Aragó, 141; Eurocity 1, 138;
    Fundació Antoni Tàpies, 109–11
Arranz, Luis
    Mérida: Biblioteca Pública del Estado,
    210
Arriola, Andreu & Carme Fiol
    Barcelona: Plaça del Virrei Amat, 126
Aulenti, Gae with Enric Steegman
    Barcelona: Museu Nacional d'Art de
    Catalunya, 169
Bach, Jaume & Gabriel Mora
    Barcelona: Central Telefónica, 138
Baldeweg, Juan Navarro
    Madrid: Biblioteca Pedro Salinas,
    54–55
Bellosillo, Javier
    Madrid: Tesauro Video Production, 53

Bofill, Ricardo
    Barcelona: Airport Terminal, 81; INEFC,
    168; Teatre Nacional de Catalunya,
    145–46
    Calpe: Anfiteatro, 61–63; La Muralla
    Roja, 60–61; Zanadu, 59–60
    Sant Just Desvern: La Fábrica—Taller
    de Arquitectura, 177; Walden 7,
    175–76
    Valencia: Jardí del Túria, 62–63
Bohigas, Oriol
    Barcelona: city plan, 81; Parc la Creu-
    eta del Colle, 122; Port Olímpica,
    136
Buxadé, Carles
    Barcelona: Anella Olímpica, 166–67;
    Estadi Olímpic, 166
Calatrava, Santiago
    Barcelona: Bac de Roda Bridge,
    149–50; Torre de Telefónica, 168
    Bilbao: Sondika Airport, 187; Zubizuri
    Pedestrian Bridge, 194
    Mérida: Puente de Lusitania, 210
    Sevilla: Puente Alamillo, 219–20
    Valencia: Cuitat de les Artes y les Ciències,
    72–75; L'Hemisféric, 73; Museu de
    les Ciències Príncipe Felipe, 73–74;
    Palau de les Artes, 75; Pont de
    Calatrava, 71–72; Pont de Monto-
    livet, 76
Candela, Félix
    Valencia: L'Oceanogràfic, 74–75
Casas, Manuel de las
    Pontevedra: Pazo da Cultura, 203–04
Clotet, Lluís and Ignasio Paricio
    Girona: Banc d'Espanya, 178
Cobb, Henry
    Barcelona: World Trade Center,
    127–28
Correa, Federico
    Barcelona: Anella Olímpica, 166–67;
    Estadi Olímpic, 166
Cruz, Antonio and Ortiz, Antonio
    Sevilla: Estación de Santa Justa, 214

Domènech i Montaner, Lluís
  Barcelona: Casa Thomas, 115; Fundació Antoni Tàpies, 109–10; Palau de la Música Catalana, 97–98
Foster, Norman
  Barcelona: Torre de Collserola, 120
  Bilbao: Metro stations, 192–93
  Valencia: Palau de Congressos, 74–75
Freixa, Jaume
  Barcelona: Fundació Joan Miró, 163–66
Galea, José Antonio
  Badajoz: Museo Extremeño e Iberoamericano de Arte Contemporáneo, 212–13
Gaudí, Antoni
  Barcelona: Casa Batlló, 111; Casa Milà, 113–14; Palau Güell, 91–92; Parc Güell, 120-22; Sagrada Família, 117–18
Gehry, Frank O.
  Barcelona: Peix, 135–36
  Bilbao: Museo Guggenheim Bilbao, 188–91
Graham, Bruce
  Barcelona: Hotel Arts, 136
Gregotti, Vittorio
  Barcelona: Estadi Olímpic, 166
Hollein, Hans
  Madrid: Banco Santander, 46–47
Isozaki, Arata
  A Coruña: Domus, 201–02
  Barcelona: CaixaForum, 171–72; Palau Sant Jordi, 167
Johnson, Philip and John Burgee
  Madrid: Puerta de Europa, 52
Kleihues, Josef Paul
  Santiago de Compostela: Polisportivo y Parking de San Clemente, 197
Lacasa, Luis
  Barcelona: Spanish Pavilion—Paris World's Fair (1937), 124–25
Luna, Roberto
  Barcelona: CaixaForum, 171–72
Mackay, David
  Barcelona: Parc la Creueta del Colle, 122; Port Olímpica, 136

Margarit, Joan
  Barcelona: Anella Olímpica, 166–67; Estadi Olímpic, 166
Martorell, Josep
  Barcelona: Parc la Creueta del Colle, 122; Port Olímpica, 136
Meier, Richard
  Barcelona: Museu d'Art Contemporani, 83–87
Mies van der Rohe, Ludwig
  Barcelona: German Pavilion at the International Exhibition, 170–71
Milà, Alfonso
  Barcelona: Anella Olímpica, 166–67; Estadi Olímpic, 166
Miralles, Enric
  Barcelona: Plaça dels Països Catalans, 157–58
Miralles, Enric and Carme Pinós
  Barcelona: Camp de Tir amb Arc, 122–123; Pergolas, 139
Moneo, Rafael
  Barcelona: Auditori de Barcelona, 143–44
  Madrid: Bankinter, 49; Estación de Atocha, 18–20; Fundación Colección Thyssen-Bornemisza, 28–29; Galería Metta, 35–36; Museo del Prado, 25
  Mérida: Museo Nacional de Arte Romano, 209–10
  Murcia: Ayuntamiento, 58
  San Sebastián: Palacio de Congresos y Auditorio Kursaal, 183–84
  Sevilla: San Pablo Airport, 214
Nouvel, Jean
  Madrid: Museo Nacional Centro de Arte Reina Sofía, 20
Peña, Luis & Francesc Ruis
  Barcelona: Parc de l'Espanya Industrial, 160–61
Piñón, Helio & Albert Viaplana
  Barcelona: Centre d'Art Santa Mònica, 92; Centre de Cultura Contemporània, 87–89; Eurocity 2, 3, 4, 139; Moll d'Espanya, 128; Plaça dels Països Catalans, 157–59; Plaça Joan Peiró, 159–60

L'Hospitalet de Llobregat: Centre Cultural Tecla Sala, 174–75
Puigdomènech, Albert
Barcelona: Port Olímpica, 136
Puig i Cadafalch, Josep
Barcelona: Casaramona, 171
Ritchie, Ian
Madrid: Museo Nacional Centro de Arte Reina Sofía, 20–21
Sáenz de Oiza, Francisco Javier
Madrid: Banco de Bilbao y Vizcaya, 51; Torres Blancas, 52–53
Sevilla: Edificio de Torretriana, 218
Sert, Josep Lluís
Barcelona: Fundació Joan Miró, 163–66; Spanish Pavilion—Paris World's Fair (1937), 124–25
Siza, Alvaro
Barcelona: Servicio Meteorológica, 136–37
Santiago de Compostela: Centro Galego de Arte Contemporaneo, 198–200; Parque de Santo Domingo de Bonaval, 200–01
Sola, Bernardo de and Pedro Barragán
Barcelona: Plaça de la Palmera, 152–53
Solà-Morales, Ignasi de
Barcelona: Gran Teatro de Liceu, 91
Solà-Morales, Manuel de
Barcelona: Moll de Bosch i Alsina, 129
Starck, Philippe
Madrid: Teatriz, 44
Tarrasó, Olga
Barcelona: Plaça de General Moragues, 150–51
Tusquets, Òscar & Carles Díaz
Barcelona: Palau de la Música Catalana, 97–98

public art

Anselmo, Giovanni
Pontevedra: Illa das Esculturas, 205
Arriola, Andreu and Carme Fiol
Barcelona: Plaça del Virrei Amat, 126
Baumgarten, Lothar
Barcelona: Plaça de Pau Vila, 131
Botero, Fernando
A Coruña: Domus, 202
Barcelona: Plaça de Blanquerna, 92
Madrid: Plaza de San Juan de la Cruz, 50
Brossa, Joan
Barcelona: Espai Escènic Joan Brossa, 103; Jardins de Marià Cañardo, 125–26; Plaça Nova, 96
Calatrava, Santiago
Barcelona: Avinguda de l'Estadi, 168
Caro, Anthony
Barcelona: Parc de l'Espanya Industrial, 159
Carr, Tom
Barcelona: Carrer de Rosa Sensat, 140
Casás, Fernando
Pontevedra: Illa das Esculturas
Castillo, Jorge
Barcelona: Plaça de Sants, 160–61
Chillida, Eduardo
Barcelona: Parc la Creueta del Colle, 122; Plaça del Rei, 95; Plaça dels Àngels, 84
Gernika: Parque de los Pueblos de Europa, 195
Gijón: Parque de la Atalaya, 196
San Sebastián: Paseo Peine del Viento, 185–86
Santiago de Compostela: Parque de Santo Domingo de Bonaval, 202–03
Sevilla: Muelle de la Sal, 217–18
Clavé, Antoni
Barcelona: Parc de la Ciutadella, 104
Cristòfol, Leandre
Barcelona: Plaça de George Orwell, 94
Croft, José Pedro
Pontevedra: Illa das Esculturas, 206–07
Finlay, Ian Hamilton
Barcelona: Carretera del Carmel, 121
Pontevedra: Illa das Esculturas, 207–08
Fontsere, Josep and Antoni Gaudí
Barcelona: Parc de la Ciutadella, 104–05
Gaudí, Antoni
Barcelona: Parc Güell, 120–21

Gehry, Frank O.
  Barcelona: Passeig Marítim, 135–36
Graham, Dan
  Pontevedra: Illa das Esculturas, 206–07
Holzer, Jenny
  Pontevedra: Illa das Esculturas, 207
Horn, Rebecca
  Barcelona: Platja de San Sebastia,
    132–33
Hunt, Bryan
  Barcelona: Parc del Clot, 147–49
Ibarrola, Agustín
  Kortézubi: Bosque de Oma, 196
Kelly, Ellsworth
  Barcelona: Parc la Creueta del Colle,
    122; Plaça de General Moragues,
    150–51
Koons, Jeff
  Bilbao: Museo Guggenheim Bilbao,
    187–88
Kounellis, Jannis
  Barcelona: Carrer de l'Admiral Cervera,
    133
Leiro, Francisco
  Pontevedra: Illa das Esculturas, 206,
    208
Lichtenstein, Roy
  Barcelona: Passeig de Colom, 129
Llena, Antoni
  Barcelona: Parc de les Cascades,
    137–38
Long, Richard
  Pontevedra: Illa das Esculturas, 206–07
Lüpertz, Markus
  Santiago de Compostela: Praza do
    Obradoiro, 197–98
Merz, Mario
  Barcelona: Moll de la Barceloneta, 131
Miralles, Enric & Carme Pinós
  Barcelona: Pergolas, 139
Miró, Joan
  Barcelona: Airport Terminal, 81; Parc
    Joan Miró, 156; Plaça de la Boque-
    ria, 91
  Madrid: Palacio de Congresos y Exposi-
    ciones, 51
Miyawaki, Aiko
  Barcelona: Avinguda de l'Estadi, 168

Moore, Henry
  Gernika: Parque de los Pueblos de
    Europa, 194–95
Morris, Robert
  Pontevedra: Illa das Esculturas, 206
Muñoz, Juan
  Barcelona: Plaça del Mar, 131–32
Nagel, Andres
  Barcelona: Parc de l'Espanya Industrial,
    158–59
Nemo (François Scali, Alain Domingo)
  Barcelona: Plaça de les Glòries Cat-
    alanes, 146–47
Oldenburg, Claes and Coosje van Bruggen
  Barcelona: Avinguda del Cardenal
    Vidal i Barraquer, 124
Oreiza, Jorge
  Barcelona: Plaça dels Àngels, 84–85
Palazuelo, Pablo
  Barcelona: Auditori, 144; Parc de
    l'Espanya Industrial, 159
Pepper, Beverly
  Barcelona: Parc Estació del Nord,
    142–43
Piñón, Helio & Albert Viaplana
  Barcelona: Moll d'Espanya, 128; Plaça
    Joan Peiró, 159–60
Piñón, Helio & Albert Viaplana with Enric
  Miralles
  Barcelona: Plaça dels Països Catalans,
    157–58; Moll d'Espanya, 128
Plensa, Jaume
  Barcelona: Passeig del Born, 100
Poirier, Anne & Patrick
  Pontevedra: Illa das Esculturas, 207–08
Ricard, André
  Barcelona: Avinguda de l'Estadi, 166
Roselló, Antoni
  Barcelona: Passeig Marítim, 137
Rückriem, Ulrich
  Barcelona: Pla del Palau, 130–31
  Pontevedra: Illa das Esculturas, 205–07
Serra, Richard
  Barcelona: Plaça de la Palmera,
    152–53
Solà-Morales, Manuel de
  Barcelona: Moll de Bosch i Alsina, 129
Solano, Susana

Barcelona: Avinguda de Martí i Codo-
lar, 123
Tàpies, Antoni
Barcelona: Fundació Antoni Tàpies,
109–10; Passeig de Picasso,
102–03
Torres, Francesc
Barcelona: Carrer de Guipúscoa,
151–52
Torres Monsó, Francesc
Barcelona: Rambla de Prim, 152
Turrell, James
Barcelona: Carrer del Comerç, 103
Ulloa, Luis
Barcelona: Avinguda del Bogatell, 140
Velasco, Enrique
Pontevedra: Illa das Esculturas, 205
Venet, Bernar
Barcelona: Placeta de Comerç, 104
Weiner, Lawrence
Barcelona: Avinguda de Mistral,
155–56

Centre Cultural de la Fundació "la
Caixa," 117
Centre d'Art Santa Mònica, 92
Fundació Antoni Tàpies, 110
Fundació Joan Miró, 163–66
Galería Maeght, 99–100
Interlibro, 116
Llibreria Cooperativa d'Arquitectes
Jordi Capell, 97
Llibreria Laie—CCCB, 88
Metronòm, 101–02
Museu d'Art Contemporani, 83
Museu Picasso, 98–99
Bilbao
Museo Guggenheim Bilbao, 188–91
Madrid
Casa del Libro, 30
Fundación Colección Thyssen-Bor-
nemisza, 29
Librería Gaudí, 40
Museo del Prado, 25–26
Museo Nacional Centro de Arte Reina
Sofía, 22–23
Malpartida de Cáceres
Museo Wolf Vostell, 211–212
San Sebastián
Arteleku, 186
Santiago de Compostela
Centro Galego de Arte Contempora-
neo, 200
Sevilla
Librería Vitruvio, 217
Valencia
Institut Valencià d'Art Modern, Centre
Julio González, 63

sculpture parks

Barcelona: Parc Estació del Nord, 142–43;
Parc de la Ciutadella, 104–05; Parc
de l'Espanya Industrial, 158–59;
Parc Güell, 120–21; Parc la Creu-
eta del Colle, 122; Vall d'Hebron,
124–28
Gernika: Parque de los Pueblos de Europa,
194–95
Hernani: Museo Chillida-Leku, 186
Kortézubi: Bosque de Omu, 195
Madrid: Museo de Escultura al Aire Libre,
48–49
Pontevedra: Illa das Esculturas, 204–08
Santiago de Compostela: Parque de Santo
Domingo de Bonaval, 200–01
Valencia: Jardí del Túria, 64–65

arts bookstores

Barcelona
Cafeteria Llibreria Laie, 98
CaixaForum, 171–73
Casa Milà, 113–14

index

Page numbers in **bold** refer to illustrations.

a

A Coruña, 201–03
AAVC (Catalonia Association of Visual Artists), 154
Abad, Antoni, 12, 44, 112
Abandoibarra, 188
Acción Paralela, 14
Aguirre, Isabel, 200–01
Agut, Pep, 12, 14, 23, 86, 112
Airport Terminal (Barcelona), 81
Alàez, Ana Laura, 12, 21, **22**, 38, 66, 70, **215**
Almeida, Helena, **112**, 199, 211, 213
Almudí, 68
Amadó, Roser, 138, 141
Amondarain, José Ramón, 12, 94, 184, 193, 217
Ando, Tadao, 218
Anella Olímpica, 166–67
Anfiteatro, **61**–62
Anselmo, Giovanni, **205**
Antiga Caserna de Sant Agustí, 103
Antoní Tàpies Foundation. See Fundació Antoní Tàpies
ARCO, 11-12, 37, 39, 199
ARCO Foundation Collection, 199
Arquitectura Viva, 14
Arranz, Luis, 210
Arriola, Andreu, 126, 142-43
Art Nouveau, 91, 105, 111, 113
Arte Povera, 57, 133
Arteleku, 186
ArteMadrid, 17
articket (Barcelona), 80
Artigas, Joan Gardy, 156
artists (introduction), 10
Arxiu de la Corona d'Aragó, 141
Asturias, 197
Atocha. See Estación de Atocha
Auditori de Barcelona, 143-44, **144**
Auditori de Galicia, 201
Auditorio Kursaal, **183**–84
Augusta Emérita, 209
Aulenti, Gae, 169
AVE, 14, 214

b

Bac de Roda Bridge, 149–50, **150**
Bach, Jaume, 138
Badajoz, 11, 212–13
Badiola, Txomin, 12, 35, **76**, 102
Baldeweg, Juan Navarro, 37, **54**, 65, 71, 107, 199, 215
Ballester, José Manuel, 12, 25, 50, **70**, 94–95
Banc d'Espanya, 178
Banco Santander, 46–**47**
Bankinter, 49
Barceló, Miquel, 29, 35, 48, 55, 86
Barcelona, 78–173
Barcelona Metròpolis Mediterrània, 80
Barcelona Museum of Contemporary Art. See Museu d'Art Contemporani
Barcelona Pavilion. See German Pavilion
Barceloneta. See La Barceloneta
Barragán, Pedro, 153
Barri Gòtic, 81, 92–105, 107
Barri Xinès, 81–83
Barruecos (Los), 211
Basque Country. See País Vasco
Baumgarten, Lothar, 131
BD Ediciones de Diseño, 115
Bellosillo,Javier, **53**
Benidorm, 59
Beragsategui, Martín, 191
Berenguer, Francesc, 121
Bernabeu, Mira, 12, 67–**68**, **217**
Biblioteca Pedro Salinas, **54**
Biblioteca Pública del Estado, 210
Bienal de Valencia, 13
Bilbao, 12, 182, 187–94
Bilbo. See Bilbao
Bilboko Arte Eder Museoa, 191
Blaufuks, Daniel, 42
Bofill, Ricardo, 12, 59–63, **60**, **61**, 81, **145–46**, 168, **175**–76
Bohigas, Oriol, 79, 91, 122, 136
Boqueria (La)
Born, 94, 100
Bosch, Hieronymus, 25
Bosque Animado, 196
Botero, Fernando, **50**–51, 92, 202

Brossa, Joan, 55, **96**, 103, 109, **125**–26, 193, 215
Broto, José Manuel, 29, 35, 50, 64, 86
Buchanan, Peter, 84
Burgee, John, 12, **52**
Buxadé, Carles, 166–67

C

Cáceres, 211
Cadaqués, 181
Cafeteria Llibreria Laie, 98
CaixaForum, 11, 171–73, **172**
Calatrava, Santiago, 12, 71–74, **72**, **73**, 149–50, **150**, **168**, 187, 194, 210, 219, **220**
Calder, Alexander, 124, 164–65
Calpe, 59–62
Camp de Tir amb Arc, 122–23
Candela, Félix, 74–75
Canogar, Daniel, 12, 23, 112, 177
Carneiro, Alberto, 42
Caro, Anthony, **159**
Carr, Tom, 92, 140
Casa Batlló, 111
Casa de Juntas, 194
Casa de la Caritat, 84, 88
Casa del Libro, 30
Casa Lis, 56
Casa Martí, 97
Casa Milà, 113–14
Casa Museu Castell Gala Dalí, 181
Casa Museu Gaudí, 121
Casa Museu Salvador Dalí, 181
Casa Thomas, 115
Casaramona, 171
Casas, Fernando, 208
Casas, Manuel de las, **203**–04
Casas, Ramón, 97, 105
Castelló, 11, 75–**77**
Castelló de la Plana. See Castelló
Castilian, 59, 81, 177, 182, 197
Castillo, Jorge, 160, **161**
Castro, A. Antón, 204
Catalan, 59, 80–81, 94, 105, 121, 130–31, 155–56
Catalunya, 59, 155
Cecchini, Loris, **39**, 199
Central Telefónica, 138

Centre Cívic Pati Llimona, 95
Centre Cultural Caixa Catalunya, La Pedrera, 80, 114
Centre Cultural de la Fundació "la Caixa," 117
Centre Cultural La Beneficència, 66
Centre Cultural Tecla Sala, 174–75
Centre d'Art Santa Monica, 92
Centre de Cultura Contemporània de Barcelona (CCCB), 80, 87–89, **88**
Centre del Carme, 63–65
Centre Julio González, **63**
Centro Andaluz de Arte Contemporáneo (CAAC), 218–19
Centro Galego de Arte Contemporaneo (CGAC), 11, 39, 198–200
Cervera, Carmen, 28
Chillida, Eduardo, 11, 22, 29, 30, 37, 40, 48, 55, 84, 95–96, **122**, **185**–86, 193, 195, 196, 201, 203, 215, 217–18
Chueca, 32
Cine Doré, 25
Cine Estudio, 31
Círculo des Bellas Artes, 31
Ciutat de les Artes y les Ciècies, 72–75
Ciutat Vella, 81–105,132
Civera, Victoria, 12, 35
Civil War, 11, 118, 124–25, 171, 179, 194
Claramunt, Luis, 12, 38
Clavé, Antoni, 104
Clotet, Lluís, 178
Cobb, Henry,127–28
Cobo, Chema, 12, 37, 219
Colección Arte Contemporáneo, 55
Col-legi Oficial d'Arquitectes de Catalunya (COAM), 96–97
Colomer, Jordi, 12, 14, 38, 86, **108**
Congost, Carles, 12, 21, **71**
Contemporary Art Space, Castelló. See Espai d'Art Contemporani de Castelló
Convent of Santo Domingode Boneval, 198, 200
Correa, Federico, 166–67
Costa Blanca, 59
Cragg, Tony, **46**, 64, 112
Craig–Martin, Michael, **65**
Cristòfol, Leandre, 94, 193
Croft, José Pedro, 107, **206**–07

Cruz, Antonio, 12, 214
Cuenca, 56–57
current exhibitions and events, 14, 17, 80

d

Dada, 64, 211
Dalí, Gala, 181
Dalí, Salvador, 11, 22, 105, 115, 178–81,
   178, 180
Dau al Set, 86–87
Dean, Tacita, 87, **99**
Deutsch Guggenheim Berlin, 191
Díaz, Carles, 97–98
Documenta IX, 188
Domènech Girbau, Lluís, 138, 141
Domènech i Montaner, Lluís, 96–98, 110, 115
Domingo, Alain, 146
Domus, 201, **202**
Donastia. See San Sebastián
Durán, Pep, 12

e

Edificio de Torretriana, 218
Eisenman, Peter, 12, 197
Eixample, 106–15
El Carme, 65
El Casón del Buen Retiro, 20
El Diario Vasco, 182, 184
El Greco, 25, 29
El Halcón, 187
El Quatre Gats, 63, 97
El Rastro, 54
El Raval, 81–92
Espai d'Art Contemporani de Castelló, 11,
   75–77
Espai Escènic Joan Brosso, 103
Espai Fotogràfic Can Basté, 126
Espai Gaudí, 114
Espai Lucas, 67
Espai 13, 164–65
Espais, Centre d'Art Contemporani, 177
Espaliú, Pepe, 12, 14, 86, 193, 213, 217,
   219
Estación de Atocha, 18–20, **19**
Estación de Santa Justa, 214
Estadi Olímpic, 166
ETA, 182
Eurocity 1, 138

Eurocity 2, 3, 4, 139
European Cultural Capital, 197
Euskadi. See País Vasco
Euskera, 182
Exit, 14
Expo '92 (Sevilla), 218–19
Extremadura, 209–13

f

FAD, 87
fairs & festivals, 13, 80
Figueres, 178–80
filmoteca, 31
Filmoteca (Barcelona), 112
Filmoteca de la Generalitat Valenciana, 66
Finlay, Ian Hamilton, 121, 164, **207**, 209
Fiol, Carme, 126, 142–43
Fluxus, 211
Fontcuberta, Joan, 12, 94, 117
Fontsere, Josep, 105
Foster, Norman, 12, **74**–75, 120, **192**–93
"fosteritos," 192
FotoPres, 173
foundations, 13
Fragateiro, Fernanda, 42
Franco, Francisco, 11–13, 20, 125
Freixa, Jaume, 163–66
Freixes, Daniel, 147–48
Fundació "la Caixa" (FLC), 14, 117, 171–73
Fundació Antoni Tàpies, 11, 80, 109–11
Fundació Caixa Catalunya, 113–14
Fundació Joan Miró, 11, 80, 96, 109, 121,
   163–66
Fundación Banco de Bilbao y Vizcaya, 51
Fundación Caja Madrid, 30
Fundación COAM, 38
Fundación Colección Thyssen-Bornemisza,
   17, 28–29, 114
Fundación Cultural Mapfre Vida, 51
Fundación "la Caixa," 45
Fundación Juan March, 48, 57
Fundación Santander Central Hispano,
   46–47
Fundación Telefónica, 30–31

g

Galea, José Antonio, 212–13
Galicia, 11, 197–208

Galego Center of Contemporary Art. *See* Centro Galego de Arte Contemporaneo
Galería Alejandro Sales, 115–16
Galería Antonio de Barnola, 94–95
Galería Antonio Machón, 37
Galería Arnés & Röpke, 36
Galería Berini, 101
Galería Buades, 31
Galería Carles Taché, 107–08
Galería Cavecanem, 219
Galería Cotthem, 89
Galería Elba Benítez, 41–42
Galería Elvira González, 40
Galería Espacio Mínimo, 24
Galería Estiarte, 49–50
Galería Estrany–de la Mota, 111–12
Galería DV, 184
Galería Ferrán Cano, 89
Galería Fúcares, 36–37
Galería Heinrich Ehrhardt, 42
Galería Helga de Alvear, 23–24
Galería Javier López, 33
Galería Joan Prats, 109
Galería Juana de Aizpuru, 37–38, 214–16
Galería Luis Adelantado, 70–71
Galería Maeght, 99–100
Galería María Martín 42
Galería Marlborough, 34
Galería Marta Cervera, 39–40
Galería Max Estrella, 38–39
Galería Metropolitana de Barcelona, 117
Galería Metta, 35–36
Galería My Names Lolita Art, 24–25, 67–68
Galería Oliva Arauna, 44
Galería Pepe Cobo, 215–16
Galería Rafael Ortiz, 216–17
Galería Ray Gun, 70
Galería Salvador Díaz, 23
Galería Senda, 107
Galería Senda–Espai 292, 107
Galería Soledad Lorenzo, 34–35
Galería Toni Tàpies–Edicions T, 108–09
Galería Theo, 36
Galería Tómas March, 69–70
Galería Visor, 67
Galería Windsor Kulturgintza, 193
Ganchegui, Luis Peña, 185–86
García, Carmela, 12, 21, **38**

García, Dora, 12, 38
García-Alix, Alberto, 12, 38, 217
Gargallo, Pablo, 105
Gaudí, Antoni, 11, 29, 91–92, 105, 111, 113–14, 115, 117–18, **120**–121, 135, 142, 175
Gehry, Frank O., **cover**, 11–12, 72, 134–36, **135**, 187, 188–91, **189**, **190**, 197
German Pavilion, International Exhibition, **170**–71
Gernika, 194–95
Gernikako Arbola (Árbol de Gernika), 194
Gerona. *See* Girona
Gibraltar, 59
Gijón, 196
Gino Di Maggio Donation, 211
Girona, 177–78
Gluckman, Richard, 34
Gómez, Susy, 12, 35, 50, 65, **108**
González, Julio, 55, **63**–64, 105
Gordillo, Luis, **37**, 86, 203, 217, 219
Goya, Francisco, 25, 114, 164
Gràcia, 106–07, 115–18
Graham, Bruce, 136
Graham, Dan, 110, 200, **206**, 207-08
Gran Teatre del Liceu, 91
Gregotti, Vittorio, 166–67
Grimshaw, Nicholas, 218
Gris, Juan, 11, 21, 29, 30
Guadalquivir River, 218–19
Güell, Eusebi, 91, 121
Guernica. *See* Gernika
Guernica, 20, 22, 124
Guggenheim Museum Bilbao. *See* Museo Guggenheim Bilbao
Guía de Exposiciones, 14
Guía del Ocio, 17, 80
Guipúzcoa (Gipuzkoa), 182
Guzmán, Federico, 12, 38, 69, 110, 215, 219

h

Halley, Peter, **33**, 64
Hammer, Jonathan, **36**
Hangar, 154
hanging houses (Cuenca), **57**
Hemingway, Ernest, 31
Hernández-Díez, José Antonio, **41**, 42, 112, 199

Hernani, 186
holidays, 15, 17
Hollein, Hans, 12, 46–**47**
Holzer, Jenny, 189, 207
Horn, Rebecca, 132, **133**, 199, 219
Horror and Fantasy Film Festival, 182
Hotel Arts, 136
Hotel Barceló Sants, 80
Hunt, Bryan, 147, **148**

i

Ibarrola, Agustín, 196
Ifach, 59, 61
Iglesias, Cristina, 42, 55, 64, 173, 215
Illa das Esculturas, 204–08
IMAX, 73, 128, 202
INEFC, 168
informel, 64
Institut Valencià d'Art Modern (IVAM), 11, 63–65
International Design Festival of Barcelona, 80
International Exhibition, Barcelona (1929), 170
International Festival of Avant-Garde Music and Multimedia Art. *See* Sònar
International Festival of Photography, 13, 25
International Film Festival (San Sebastián), 182
International Institute for Historic Studies, 125
Iruña (Pamplona), 182
Isla de la Cartuja, 218–19
Isozaki, Arata, 11, 12, 94, **167**, 171, **172**, 201, **202**
IVAM. *See* Institut Valencià d'Art Modern

j

Jardí d'Aclimatació, 167
Jardí del Túria, 62–63
Jaume Figueras Archive and Library, 125
Joan Miró Museum (Foundation). *See* Fundació Joan Miró
Johnson, Philip, 12, **52**
Justicia, 32–42

k

Kandinsky, Wassily, 157
Kcho, **27**
Kelly, Ellsworth, 22, 122, 150, **151**
KIO Towers, **52**
Kleihues, Josef Paul, 12, 197
Kolbe, Georg, 171
Koldo Mitxelena Kulturunea, 184–85
Koons, Jeff, **187**–88
Kortézubi, 196
Kounellis, Jannis, 22, 50, 108, **133**, 173, 199
Kursaal. *See* Auditorio Kursaal

l

L'Aquàrium, 132
La Barceloneta, 130–34
"la Caixa." *See* Fundació "la Caixa"
La Caja Negra, 40
La Capella de l'Antic Hospital de la Santa Creu, 90
La Casa del Hombre. *See* Domus
La Coruña. *See* A Coruña
La Fábrica, 176
La Gaviota, 187
La Gallera, 66
La Manzanera, 59
La Muralla Roja, **60**–61
La Pedrera, 113–14
La Primavera Fotogràfica, 80
La Ribera, 83,94–107
La Sagrada Família. *See* Sagrada Família
La Xerea, 71
Lacasa, Luis, 126
Lapiz, 14
Las Meniñas, 25, 98
Le Corbusier, 53, 61, 96, 114, 125
Leiro, Francisco, 34, 65, **206**, 208
Lérida. *See* Lleida
L'Hemisféric, **72**–73
L'Hospitalet de Llobregat, 176
Librería Gaudí, 41
Librería Vitruvio, 219
Lichtenstein, Roy, 66, **131**
Lleida, 128
Llena, Antoni, 137–38, **138**
Llibreria Cooperativa d'Arquitectes Jordi Capell, 97
Llibreria Laie–CCCB, 88

L'Oceanogràfic, 74–75
Long, Richard, 206, **207**
Lüpertz, Markus, 197, **198**

m

MACBA. *See* Museu d'Art Contemporani
Mackay, David, 122, 136
Madrid, 16–54
Maeght Foundation, 163
magazines, 14, 80, 182
Maldonado, José, 14, 24, 66, 111, 173
Malevich, Kasimir, 152
Mallol, Tomàs, 178
Malpartida de Cáceres, 11, 211–12
Manglano-Ovalle, Iñigo, 12, 35
maps: Atocha–Parc Retiro, 18; Barcelona
    districts, 78; Barcelona metro, 78; Barri
    Gòtic & La Ribera, 93; Eixample &
    Gràcia, 106; El Raval, 82; Justicia, 32;
    Madrid districts, 17; Madrid metro, 16;
    Montjuïc, Parc Güell—Parc la Creueta
    del Coll—Vall d'Hebron, 119; Plaça
    de les Glòries Catalanes, 141; Port
    Vell—La Barceloneta, 127; Puerta del
    Sol, 28; Salamanca, 43; Sant Martí,
    149; Sants, 155; Spain, 7; Vila Olímpica,
    134
Maremagnum, 128
Margarit, Joan, 166–67
Marsá, Mont, **101**–02
Martín, Josep María, 94–**95**
Martorell, Josep, 122, 136
Matador, 25
Matta, Roberto, 29
Meier, Richard, 11, 12, **83**–88, **84**
Mérida, 209–10
Merz, Mario, 22, 108, 131, 173
metro: Barcelona, 78; Bilbao, **192**; Madrid,
    16
Metonòm, 11, 101–02
Mies van der Rohe, Ludwig, 19, **170**–71;
    Foundation, 170
Milà, Alfonso, 166–67
Miralles, Enric, 12, 122–23, **139**, 157–58,
    158
Miró, Joan, 11, 22, 25, 29, 40, 48, 51,
    81, 91, 100, 109, 124, 156–57, **157**,
    163–66, **164**

Mistral, Frédéric, 155–56
Miyawaki, Aiko, 168
Modernisme, 80, 106, 111, 115
modernista, 41, 91, 97, 105, 109, 114
Mogor (Marín), 206
Moll de Bosch i Alsona, 129
Moll d'Espanya, **128**
Moll de Gregal, 136
Moneo, Rafael, 12, 18–20, **19**, 26, 28–29,
    35, 38, 47, 49, **58**, 115, 143–44, **144**,
    183–84, **209**–10, 214
Monte de la Gaias, 197
Montjuïc, 162–73
Moore, Henry, 194–95, **195**
Mora, Gabriel, 138
Mora, Pedro, 12, 35, 107, 217, 219
Morris, Robert, **208**
Mullican, Matt, 110, **111**
Muñoz, Juan, 29, 64, 86, 131–32, **132**, 199,
    215
Muntadas, Antonio, 31, 178
Murcia, 58; city hall, **58**
Museo Art Nouveau y Art Decó, 56
Museo Arte Contemporáneo Unión Fenosa,
    202–03
Museo Chillida-Leku, 186
Museo Colecciones ICO, 29
Museo de Arte Abstracto Español, **57**
Museo de Arte Contemporáneo Español de
    Vallodolid, 55
Museo de Arte Contemporáneo Esteban
    Vicente, 55
Museo de Bellas Artes, Bilbao, 191
Museo de Escultura al Aire Libre, 48, **49**
Museo del Prado, 17, 20, 25–26, 28, 144
Museo Español de Arte Contemporáneo, 20
Museo Extremeño e Iberoamericano de Arte
    Contemporáneo (MEIAC), 11, 212–13
Museo Guggenheim Bilbao, **cover**, 11, 72,
    188–91, **189**, **190**, 197
Museo Nacional Centro de Arte Reina Sofía,
    11, 17, 18, 20–23, **21**, 26, 70, 194,
    215
Museo Nacional de Arte Romano, **209**–10
Museo Picasso, 11, 98–99
Museo Reina Sofía. *See* Museo National
    Centro de Arte Reina Sofía
Museo Wolf Vostell, 11, 211–12

Museu d'Art Contemporani (MACBA), 11, 80, 83–87, **83**, **84**, 88, 111
Museu d'Art Modern, 105
Museu de les Ciències Príncipe Felipe, **73**–74
Museu del Cinema, 178
Museu Nacional d'Art de Catalunya (MNAC), 80, 105, 169
museum ticket, 17, 80

n

Nagel, Andres, 158–59
Navarro, Miguel, **35**
Nemo, 146–47, **147**
New Art Barcelona, 13, 80
Nonell, Isidro, 51, 97, 105
Nouvel, Jean, 12, 20
Nuñez, Marina, 12, **69**–70, 76

o

Oe, Kenzaburo, 168
Olaf, Erwin, **24**
Oldenburg, Claes, 64, **124**, 165
Olivares, Rosa, 204
Olympic Games, 11, 12, 79, 120, 123, 125, 130, 135–36, 162, 166–68
Olympic Ring. See Anella Olímpica
Olympic Stadium. See Estadí Olímpic
Olympic Village. See Vila Olímpica
1 + 1, 102
Ortiz, Antonio, 12, 214
Oteiza, Jorge, 22, 29, 57, 84–85

p

País Vasco, 182–96
Palacín, Mabel, 12, 24, 70, **116**
Palacio de Abrantes, 56
Palacio de Cristal, 27
Palacio de Congresos y Auditorio Kursaal, **183**–84
Palacio de Congresos y Exposiciones (Madrid), 51
Palacio de Exposiciones, 26
Palacio de Velázquez, 26
Palau de Congressos (Valencia), **74**
Palau de la Mùsica Catalana, **97**–98
Palau de la Virreina, 80, 90–91
Palau de les Artes, 74

Palau de Mar, 130
Palau Güell, 91–92
Palau Nacional de Montjuïc, 105, 169
Palau Sant Jordi, **167**, 172
Palazuelo, Pablo, 35, 48, 57, 59, 144, 159
Palma de Mallorca, 89
Pamplona, 182
Parc de la Ciutadella, 81, 104–05
Parc de l'Espanya Industrial, 158–59
Parc del Clot, 147–48
Parc Güell, **120**–21
Parc la Creueta del Coll, **122**
Parc Joan Miró, 156–57
Paricio, Ignasi, 178
Parque de los Pueblos de Europa, 195
Parque de Santo Domingo de Bonaval, 200–01
Parque Ferial Juan Carlos, 13
Paseo del Arte, 17
Pazo de Cultura, **203**–04
Peggy Guggenheim Collection, 191
Pei Cobb Freed, 127–28
peineta, 72
Peña, Luis, 158–59
Penone, Guiseppe, **200**
Penyal de Ifach, 59, 61
Pepper, Beverly, **142-143**
Pere Romeu, 97
Perejaume, 86, 109, 193
Pérez, Javier, 12, 23
Pericas, Enric, 142–43
Pesce, Gaetano, 191
PHE, 13, 25
PhotoEspaña, 13, 25
PhotoGalería, 25
Photographic Forum, 126
Picasso Museum. See Museu Picasso
Picasso, Pablo, 20, 22, 29, 30, 40, 50, 55, 63, 105, 107, 194
Pinós, Carme, 12, 122–23, **139**
Piñón, Helio, 87–**88**, 92, **128**, **139**, 159–60, **160**, 174
Plaça de la Palmera, 152–53
Plaça de les Glòries Catalanes, 141–48
Plaça del Virrei Amat, 126
Plaça dels Països Catalans, 157–58, **158**
Plaça Joan Peiró, 159–60, **160**
Plensa, Jaume, **26**, 29, **100**, 108

Poblenou, 81
Poirier, Anne & Patrick, 207, **208**
Polisportivo y Parking San Clemente, 197
Pont de Calatrava, 62, 71–72
Pont de Montolivet, 75
Pontevedra, 203–08
Port Lligat, 181
Port Olímpica, 136
Port Vell, 127–29, 133
Portugal, 112, 136, 209, 213
practicalities, 14
Prado Museum. *See* Museo del Prado
Pritzker Prize, 18, 25, 46, 136, 198
public art, 79–80
Púbol, 181
Puente Alamillo, 219, **220**
Puente de La Salve, 189
Puente de Lusitania, 210
Puerta de Europa, **52**
Puerta del Sol, 28–31
Puig i Cadafalch,Josep, 171
Puigdomènech, Albert, 136

r

Rambla del Mar, 128
ramblas, 81
Rayas, 216
Reina Sofía Museum. *See* Museo Nacional
     Centro de Arte Reina Sofía
Retiro Park, 18, 26
Ría Nervión, 187
Ricard, André, 166
Rio Lérez, 204
Ritchie, Ian, 20
Rivero, Elena del, 40
Rosado Garcés, MP and MP, 12, **216**
Roselló, Antoni, 139
Rubens, Peter Paul, 25
Rückriem, Ulrich, 42, **132**–33, 207–08, **209**
Ruis, Francesc, 158–59
Ruiz de Infante, Francisco, 12, 42, 193
Rusiñol, Santiago, 97, 105

s

Sáenz de Oiza, Francisco Javier, 51, 52–**53**,
     218
Sagrada Família, 117–18
Sala de Exposiciones (Pontevedra), 203–04

Sala de Exposiciones (Salamanca), 56
Sala del Canal de Isabel II, 50
Sala El Roser, 177
Sala Montcada de la Fundació "la Caixa," 99
Sala Parpalló, 66
Sala Picasso, 96
Sala Rekalde, 193
Salamanca, 56
Salamanca (Madrid), 43–50
Sales Municipals d'Exposición (Girona),
     177–78
Salgado, Sebastião, 202
San Pablo Airport, 214
San Sebastián, 182–86
Sánchez, Alberto, 21, 124
Sánchez Castillo, Fernando, 12, 39
Sander, Karin, **23**–24
Sant Just Desvern, 175–76
Sant Martí, 149–54
Santiago de Compostela, 11, 197–201
Sants, 155–61
Scali, François, 146–47
Schütte, Thomas, 164, **165**, 199
Segovia, 55
Sempere, Eusebio, 48, 57
Serra, Richard, 152–53, **153**, 165, 190
Sert, Josep Lluís, 11, 124, 163–66, **164**
Servicio Meteorológica, 136, **137**
Sevilla, 37, 214–20
Seville. *See* Sevilla
Sicilia, José María, 30, 35, 50, 55, 70, 86, 109
Sinaga, Fernando, 39
site icons, 15
Siza, Álvaro, 11, 12, 115, 136, **137**, 198–00,
     199
Skidmore, Owings & Merrill, 136
Sociedad General de Autores y Editores, 41
Sola, Bernando de, 153
Solà-Morales, Ignasi de, 91
Solà-Morales, Manuel de, 129
Solano, Susana, 29, 40, 44, 86, 87, 107,
     123, **213**
Solomon R. Guggenheim Foundation, 191
Sònar, 80
Sondika Airport, 187
Spanish Pavilion, Paris World's Fair of 1937,
     124
Starck, Philippe, 12, 44–45

Steegman, Enric, 169
Streuli, Beat, **86**
Subirachs, Josep, 118
Surrealism, 105, 179, 211

t

Tanguy, Yves, 22, 211
Tàpies, Antoni, 21, 22, 29, 30, 35, 38, 55, 57,
    76, **85**–86, 100, **102**–03, 109–11, **110**
Tarrasó, Olga, 150
Teatre–Museu Dalí, 178–80
Teatre Nacional de Catalunya, **145–46**
Teatriz, 44–45
Tesauro Video Production, **53**
Thyssen-Bournemisza Museum. See
    Fundación Colección Thyssen-
    Bournemisza
Torre de Collserola, 120
Torre de Telefónica, **168**
Torres, Francesc, 31, 42, 102, 109, **151–52**,
    174–75, 193
Torres Blancas, **52**–53
Torres Mapfre, 136
Torres Monsó, Francesc, 152
Tous, Rafael, 102
transportation, 14
trencadís, 121
Turrell, James, **103**
Tusquets, Óscar, **97**–98 , 115

u

Ulloa, Luis, **140**
Umberg, Günter, 40
urban planning, 81, 94, 97, 127–28, 134,
    142, 155
Urumea River, 183
Uslé, Juan, 35, 64, 86, 213

v

Valencia, 59–77
Valencia (city), 11, 13, 62–75
Vall d'Hebron, 122–25
Valladolid, 55
Valldosera, Eulàlia, 12, 24, 67, 110
Vallhonrat, Valentin, 12, 42, 56, 67
van Bruggen, Coosje, **126**
Velasco, Enrique, **205**
Velázquez, Diego, 25

Velòdrom, 125
Venet, Bernard, **104**
Viaplana, Albert, 87–89, **88**, 92, **128**, 139,
    157–60, **158**, **160**, 174
Vicente, Esteban, 55, 201
Vidal, Carlos, 12, 39, **107**
Vila Olímpica, 134–40
Villahermosa Palace, 28
Villar, Francesc de Paula del, 117
Vinçon, 44, 114–15
Viscaya (Bizkaia), 182
Volantín Bridge, 194
Vostell, Wolf, 211, **212**

W

Walden 7, **175**–76
Weiner, Lawrence, 27, 155–56, **156**
World Trade Center, 127–28

X

Xanadu, 59–**60**
Xunqueira Island, 204

y

Ydáñez, Santiago, **70**, 71

z

Zabalaga, 186
Zehar, 184, 186
Zóbel, Fernando, 57
Zhang Huan, **89**
Zubizuri Pedestrian Bridge, 194
Zush, 21, 86, 87, **109**

photo credits

p. 23	courtesy Galería Helga de Alvear, Madrid
p. 24	courtesy Galería Espacio Mínimo, Madrid
p. 33	courtesy Galería Javier López, Madrid
p. 35	courtesy Galería Soledad Lorenzo
p. 36	courtesy Galería Fúcares
p. 37	courtesy Museu d'Art Contemporani, Barcelona
p. 38	courtesy Galería Juana de Aizpuru
p. 39	courtesy Galería Max Estrella, Madrid
p. 42	courtesy Galería Elba Benítez, Madrid
p. 46	courtesy Fundació "la Caixa"
p. 47	Gonzolo Echenique, courtesy Banco Santander
p. 63, 65	courtesy Institut Valencià d'Art Modern, Centre Julio González
p. 68	courtesy Galería Visor, Valencia
p. 69	courtesy Galería Tómas March, Valencia
p. 70 (top)	courtesy Galería Ray Gun, Valencia
p. 70 (bot.), 71	courtesy Galería Luis Adelantado, Valencia
p. 76, 77	courtesy Espai d'Art Contemporani de Castelló
p. 86	courtesy MACBA
p. 89	courtesy Galería Cotthem, Barcelona
p. 90	courtesy Institut de Cultura de Barcelona
p. 95	courtesy Galería Antonio de Barnola, Barcelona
p. 99	courtesy Fundació "la Caixa"
p. 101	courtesy Metrònom, Barcelona
p. 107	courtesy Galería Senda, Barcelona
p. 108	courtesy MACBA, Barcelona
p. 108	courtesy Galería Soledad Lorenzo
p. 109	courtesy MACBA, Barcelona
p. 111	courtesy Fundació Antoni Tàpies, Barcelona
p. 112	courtesy Galería Estrany–de la Mota, Barcelona
p. 116	courtesy Galería Tomas March, Valencia
p. 148	courtesy Bryan Hunt
p. 151, 152	courtesy Francesc Torres and Galería Elba Benítez, Madrid
p. 156	courtesy Lawrence Weiner and Moved Pictures, New York
p. 174	courtesy Centre Cultural Tecla Sala, L'Hospitalet de Llobregat
p. 184	courtesy Galería DV, San Sebastián
p. 200	courtesy Centro Galego de Arte Contemporánea, Santiago de Compostela
p. 212	courtesy Museo Wolf Vostell, Malpartida de Cáceres
p. 215	courtesy Galería Juana de Aizpuru, Sevilla
p. 216	courtesy Galería Pepe Cobo, Sevilla
p. 217	courtesy Galeríía Visor

All other illustrations courtesy of the author.

we appreciate your help

If you found errors regarding information about a site we discussed or know about sites we missed, please tell us.
art•SITES, 894 Waller Street, San Francisco, CA 94177 USA
fax: 415-701-0633, website: www.art-sites.com, email: info@art-sites.com

art-SITES™

ORDER FORM

Check your local bookstore or order directly from us.

NAME _____

STREET _____

CITY _____ STATE ____ ZIP _____

COUNTRY _____ TEL(___) _____

PLEASE SEND (show quantity of each title)

_____ BRITAIN & IRELAND @ $19.95		$_____
_____ FRANCE @ $19.95		$_____
_____ PARIS @ $19.95		$_____
_____ SPAIN @ $19.95		$_____
_____ SAN FRANCISCO @ $19.95		$_____

sales tax ($1.70 per book) for CA residents $_____

shipping

   in US, $4 for the first book, $1.00 for each additional book $_____

   international airmail ($7 per book) $_____

TOTAL $_____

PAYMENT

○ Check or money order (payable to **art-SITES** in US dollars drawn on a US bank. Send to: **art-SITES,** 894 Waller Street, San Francisco, CA 94117 USA

○ MasterCard   ○ Visa

CARD NUMBER _____ EXP DATE _____

EXACT NAME ON CARD _____

SIGNATURE _____

ORDER BY

telephone: 415-437-2456 fax: 415-701-0633 Internet: www.art-sites.com

also available

art-SITES FRANCE

art-SITES PARIS

art-SITES SAN FRANCISCO

art-SITES SPAIN